REMINISCENT REFLECTIONS

of a

Youthful Octogenarian

by

George Henry Gerberding, D. D., L L. D.

AUGSBURG PUBLISHING HOUSE
MINNEAPOLIS, MINN.
1928

CHAPTER I

EARLY CHILDHOOD

I WAS born in Pittsburgh, Pennsylvania, August twenty-first, 1847. It was a good place in which to be born. The then small town, with its crooked, narrow cobblestone streets, was already pulsing with energy and seemed to have a premonition of what it was to become.

It was a stirring time in which to be born. The spirit of revolution was ripe in Europe. There was a panting after freedom and a crying for individual rights. In our own land the Mexican War was on. Lincoln was serving his first term in Congress. Anti-slavery agitation was flaring up in spots and was spreading all over the land.

Pittsburgh was a stronghold of Scotch Presbyterianism. Its "Western Seminary" was active and ambitious across the river. Some of its greatest men occupied Pittsburgh pulpits.

Methodism, ever ambitious, active and aggressive, was there. "Brimstone Corner" was only a few yards from the First English Lutheran Church of which the zealous young W. A. Passavant had just taken charge. "New Measurism" and wild revivalism were troubling the Lutheran and German Reformed Churches. Dr. Nevin had sent out his epochal tract on "The Anxious Bench." A good place and time in which to be born.

My father had come from Germany as a boy. He

3

was an accomplished musician, played first violin for a time in the old Drury Theater on Fifth Avenue, Pittsburgh, and then traveled for a while with a circus band. He was an earnest young man, and this life did not suit him. He readily fell in with a little group of pious Germans, some of whom were Lutherans and some were Baptists. He assisted their colporteurs, and with their aid came into possession of some choice literature. He acquired some of the finest devotional books which the Lutheran Church has produced. He also got possession of "Gerlock's Auswahle," or selections from Luther's works, and D'Aubigne's History of The Reformation. Thru the influence of the pious Germans and the reading of the books which he so judiciously selected, and especially thru the gracious influence of the young woman who became his wife, he gradually came to a true conversion. He gave up his profession of music, learned the trade of cigar-maker, and afterwards set up a little cigar store. My father was a reader and a thinker. He was a zealous Lutheran. He loved to argue with all who disagreed. He was a theorist, a dreamer. He was no manager. He was not a business man. He did not love labor. Hard, steady work was always obnoxious to him. Naturally, therefore, we were very poor. My childhood was one of poverty, privation and hardship. I had little of the joys that childhood ought to have.

My mother, born in Pittsburgh, of Swiss parentage, whose maiden name was Josephine Lustenberger, died before I was four years old. My personal recollections of her are faint. I recall her dying bed, the sad funeral, the weeping of my elder sister, who would not be comforted for days after the burial. I recall that I was told that one of my mother's last prayers

4

was that her only son might become a minister. From my father and from others, who knew my mother well, especially from the sainted Father Berkemeier, the wonderful Emigrant Missionary, I learned that she was a sweet saint of God, who lived in intimate fellowship with her Savior, lived the prayer life and taught her little children to pray. The slight memory I have of her, my childhood dreams about her, my vivid belief that on two distinct occasions in different places in the twilight I saw her in the form of a beautiful tall maiden dressed in white, all these have been a benediction to me all my life. Truly the memory of the just is blessed. I have often felt that next to the dear Savior Himself no one can be so precious a heritage as a saintly, praying, Christian mother.

I might add that my mother was brought up a Methodist. If I mistake not she was a member of the famous church called "Brimstone Corner." After she married my father she became a Lutheran and joined Pastor Berkemeier's German Lutheran Church. I sometimes wonder whether my mother's erstwhile earnest Methodism has had anything to do with my admiration of and love for Wesley and Whitefield, their eminent, consecrated followers, the heroic early circuit riders of whom the world was not worthy? I am sure, however, that this has not hurt my Lutheran orthodoxy. Indeed, I often wish that many of our cold, intellectual preachers might have some of the burning love, the consuming zeal for souls that these old time true Methodists had. Such experimental heart power and love for souls does not injure sound orthodoxy.

My mother did not like the close, stuffy little rooms above the cigar store on loud Liberty Street, and

5

longed for a home in the country. My father, who was never afraid to contract a debt, borrowed the money, bought a little hilly, stony, sterile soil farm four miles north of Pittsburgh. While the little house was in the building my mother died. In a few months, father, with his four little children, moved out to the farm.

We now became poorer than ever. I should not like to tell how poor we were. As soon as, if not before, I was strong enough I had to clean out the cow stables every day, haul out the manure, plow and mow and dig and market our scanty crops. I truly did come up from the dung-hill. Afterwards I drove a milk wagon, rose up at three every summer morning and delivered the milk for our customers' breakfasts. Later on I drove an ice-wagon. Then a brick-wagon. Many a time I stood shivering in the stalls of the public market selling produce. How glad I used to be to run into a coffee house, get a cup of strong coffee and three greasy doughnuts—all for six cents. Have never enjoyed breakfasts more!

Yes, poverty is hard, especially hard for childhood and early youth. This period of life ought to be filled with sunshine and joy. I believe that the good Lord wants it so. On the other hand, poverty has its uses and can teach helpful lessons. It taught me that there are many things that are generally counted among the necessaries of life that one can really do without. In after life I came across a saying of the old, out-door naturalist and philosopher, Henry Thoreau, which has stuck to me thru life: Here it is. It may do you good as it has often helped and braced me: "A man is rich in proportion to the things that he can do without." How many things we can do without if we will or must. To this day I have done without an automobile. Had I done like hundreds of others I probably could not be sitting in my own cheerful home as I write down these octogenarian reflections.

Poverty teaches one to do the uncongenial, the unwelcome, the hard tasks and duties. It disciplines one in the daily grind of toil: An invaluable life lesson. Many never learn it. They get nowhere.

Poverty teaches one of the value of a dollar. In poverty one learns the art of making a little go far. It reminds me of a minister's wife. On a small salary she had three husky boys to feed, clothe and school. When starting for a down town store she would often say: "Well, I'm going shopping to see how far I can throw a five dollar bill." Many a time have I been thankful that early in life I learned to throw a dollar much farther than many others could.

Yes, poverty is a hard school, but it can teach most helpful life lessons. Jeremiah was right when he said: "It is good for a man if he learn to bear the yoke in his youth." This inspired saying I tried for many years to rub into the consciousness of my theological students. As a rule they did not take to it kindly. I had to prove its truth by experience that was often bitter and hard to be borne. When rightly taken, poverty is one of those disciplinary chastenings which, for the present, do not seem to be joyous but grievous; nevertheless, afterward they yield the peaceable fruit of righteousness to them that are exercised thereby. This is not true of poverty that is brought on by one's own fault. It is true of all chastenings that come directly or indirectly from God.

7

Chapter II

SCHOOL DAYS, COMPANIONS
AND TEACHERS

I WAS not brought up in a Lutheran community. The neighbors were Catholics, Methodists, Presbyterians, and some German Rationalists and freethinkers. There were in and about Pittsburgh about half a dozen of German free churches that called themselves *Evangelisch*. They belonged to a *Protestantenverein* that had its headquarters in Cincinnati. They were rationalistic thruout, and cast a baleful blight over hundreds of homes and into thousands of hearts. Many of my schoolmates belonged to such homes. I instinctively noticed that these were rough and coarse as compared with the Methodists and Presbyterians. I felt myself drawn to the boys of these churches.

Our English Lutheran Church in Pittsburgh was four miles distant. Sunday mornings I went with my schoolmates to the Methodist Sunday School and Church. Sunday afternoons I attended a union Sunday School whose leaders were Presbyterians. It was a joy to me to go from my home, which was none too attractive, to these Sunday Schools. There I met warm-hearted Christian people who took an interest in me.

In the Methodist Sunday School I was put into a class of small boys of my size. We had a young lady teacher. She used to come before the class like a sunbeam. She had a kind word for every boy. As a poor, motherless boy I was hungry for love. The little attentions and kind words of this bright young woman impressed my child heart. I thought her very beautiful. I do not recall that I carried home many lessons from her. Her personality and manner impressed me.

In the Union Sunday School I also had lady teachers: Two of them taught by turns. Both were Presbyterians. Not so young, attractive and gushing as my Methodist teacher. They were more intelligent and more serious. Both of them were real teachers. They knew their lessons. They lived together. I learned afterwards that every evening, after supper, they gave an hour to the study of next Sunday's lesson. From these good women I carried home something every Sunday. Some truths that they taught me are with me today. And so in these impressive years I was influenced by Reformed Churches. I felt myself especially drawn towards the Methodists, who were not like the Methodists of our day, but had that old-time warmth and consecration.

My father, who was a member of the German Lutheran Congregation, noticed how his children were drifting away from his church. He knew his church, was deeply interested in her history, knew and loved her teachings. As I have said above, he would rather sit and read D'Aubigne or Luther than work his farm. He wanted his children to be in the church which he knew and loved. I recall how, on a certain occasion, I spoke of my admiration for the Methodist Church. I have never forgotten his innocent and ready reply, which was something like this: "Yes,

9

there is good in all the Evangelical Churches. God has dealt with them as with individuals. To one church He gave one talent, to another three, and to another five, and that is the Lutheran Church." Tho he loved and lived in his German Bible and other books, when he saw that his children were not German, he, for the sake of his children, united with the First English Lutheran Church of Pittsburgh. I have often thought that if my father had not taken this step I probably would not be a Lutheran today.

In that old First Church which had been served and brought into prominence by the wonderful, youthful Passavant, and then by the scholarly young Dr. C. P. Krauth, I was instructed and confirmed by Dr. Reuben Hill.

Dr. Hill was a consecrated and warmhearted worker in his Master's vineyard. His catechetical instruction was not formal, perfunctory, cold and schoolmasterly, as the manner of too many catechists is. It was warm, hearty, personal, simple and sympathetic. It gave me my first understanding of Lutheran teaching. It applied the doctrine to the heart and life. I can never forget some of the touching, tender, loving prayers that Pastor Hill offered up before and for his catechumens.

I must go back to my school days in the little one-room country school-house. I had a most wonderful teacher. He had a formative influence on my young life. I have often, mentally, classed him with Goldsmith's "Village Schoolmaster." William B. Dummet had a crowded school. His pupils comprised all ages from the six year olds to the young men and women of eighteen and twenty. Dummet was an eloquent reader and speaker. He was concerned to teach his pupils to read well. He wanted us to interpret by our inflection and emphasis. He was a reasoner. He loved mental arithmetic. His delight was to take his advanced pupils thru Stoddard's Mental Arithmetic. Without paper, slate or blackboard he had each one to analyze orally those intricate and difficult algebraic problems. It was a valuable drill in logic and clear thinking.

He had other original ways of making his pupils think. Before he closed the schoolday he would often give the whole school a question to think about and answer next day; for example: What is paper good for? What is a sheep, a horse, a dog, a cow good for? Sometimes it would be a question in American History, in Elementary Science, in Nature Study, in Economics, as: Why do we pay taxes? His resourcefulness seemed to be without limit. At evening roll call, all except the lower classes were expected to answer the given question. After all the guessing and blundering and would-be-smart answers he would give a concise, informing and clear answer. And so, as with Goldsmith's Village Schoolmaster:

And still we thought and still the wonder grew,
That one small head could carry all he knew.

Most of us carried our dinners. Mine was meager compared to others. When the weather was too inclement to play out of doors, Mr. Dummet would direct all to quietly eat in their seats, and when all had eaten he would spend half an hour telling us classic stories, e. g. *Sinbad The Sailor, The Forty Thieves, Aladdin's Lamp, Swift's Lilliputians and Giants.* His own comments and explanations were also classic. I often wished that more noon hours might be stormy.

11

Mr. Dummet had few rules. Two were outstanding: There was to be no cursing or swearing. There was to be no fighting. One evening after school there was a big, bitter fistfight at the coal bank by two full-grown boys. Our teacher knew about it when school opened next morning. As was his custom, a chapter in the Bible was read responsively, and the Lord's Prayer was repeated in unison. Then Mr. Dummet took off his coat, and we knew that something was coming. The traditional pin drop might have been heard distinctly. Then came one of the most eloquent impromptu short speeches I have ever heard. The teacher spoke of his two rules and of his reasons for them. He spoke of the uselessness, the ugliness, the horridness of swearing. Then of the coarseness, the brutishness, the utter lack of manliness of two grown ups beating each other up. And these two he had loved as among his best boys: He closed quietly, got out his big birchen rod, which he used very rarely, called the two principal culprits forward, ordered them to hold out their hands and gave each hand a sharp blow. It was a tense moment. The teacher was pale as he sat down. Then came an impressive and unexpected sequel. From a back seat stepped out a big boy, walked forward, held out his open hand and said:

"Here, Mr. Dummet, I was in that fight too."

Tears were in the teacher's eyes as he gave that boy a light tap. Tears are in my eyes as I write it. Then came another brief talk on true manliness, on the true hero who cannot even act a lie; much less tell it.

That morning in the little, unkempt country schoolhouse will never be forgotten. Its influence has been a moral tonic to me all my days. It lingers still. The hero, Alfred Lindsey, afterward began to study for the Methodist ministry. When the Civil War broke out he was among the first to enlist. He was soon promoted for bravery, made captain of his company, and fell in one of the early battles of the war. He neither lived nor died in vain.

As I look back over my boyhood years, I often have a feeling of sadness and regret. I could not have the affection and kindly attentions that I saw others enjoy. My young heart was often hungry for love and for home comforts. I could not be dressed and groomed as neatly and comfortably as my companions were. I felt all this keenly. Yet God was good to me. In the neighboring Sunday Schools and churches which I attended I made many friends and received much kindly attention. God had also blest me with a cheerful and hopeful disposition. It didn't take much to make me happy. I had a sense of humor. I loved fun. I craved companions and found great pleasure in being among them. I had my chum age and was happy with successive chums. With them I planned wonderful plans and builded the most alluring air castles. How carefully, cautiously, and confidentially all was considered and arranged. It was good to live in hero-land and to bask in fairyland. I had my gang age. My gangs were not always the best. Their influence was not always ennobling. I passed thru the stage of aversion to girls and was quite uncomfortable when I had to sit or even stand next to one in class. And yet I can recall how kind some of them were, how they helped me in my lessons, whispered answers into my ears, and sometimes even refused to go above me when they had beat me in spelling or in answering. My aversion, however, did not last long. By and by I learned to like girl company and frequently preferred it to that of boys.

After being a widower for about four years, my father married again. This new wife was much younger than he. She undertook a great responsibility when she came to mother four untrained children. She was industrious and energetic. She tried her best to make the household what it ought to be. But means and equipment were lacking. She had to work against heavy odds. Her painful efforts were not appreciated. She was a good stepmother. In spite of her strenuous efforts, the heavily mortgaged farm was afterwards sold under the hammer. She bore eight more children to my father. All of them received a good common school education. One of them afterwards entered the ministry. He is the Rev. P. J. Gerberding of Chicago.

I look back to my youthful mingling with the Methodists, Presbyterians and United Presbyterians. I had found among them so many truly good people, such exemplary Christians, God's own beloved sons and daughters, that I could not but admire them and their Christianity. I was often perplexed as to the relative worth of their churches as compared with my own. I had to learn to distinguish between the people in a given church and the doctrines held and taught by that church. My sanguine temperament made me inclined to jump at conclusions and to take extreme positions. Had it not been for the influence of the good Reformed Christians I might have and probably would have become an extreme Lutheran. It would have been in harmony with my temperament and disposition for me to become a polemical preacher. I might have become a one-sided, heartless zealot. Like some other Lutheran preachers I might have acquired the baleful habit of railing against the sects and their false teachers and doctrines. I therefore count it among the merciful providences of my dear heavenly Father that I learned by a delightful experience what the preface to the Formula of Concord teaches, viz.:

"We have no doubt whatever that even in those churches which have hitherto not agreed with us in all things many godly and by no means wicked men are found."

Many Lutheran preachers either never learned this or have completely forgotten it. They have not learned from Paul to preach the truth in love. They hurt instead of helping the cause.

I was afterwards helped in this matter by my sainted professor, the Rev. Dr. Wm. J. Mann. He was the most helpful and inspiring professor I ever had. From the Philadelphia Seminary I carried away more from Dr. Mann than from any other teacher.

In one of his classes in Ethics I once asked, in substance, this question: "Doctor, if the Lutheran Church is so much better than others, how does it come that we find so many superior Christians in the Reformed Churches around us?" As always, the doctor was ready with his answer: "That's easy, my good friend; you might live on the juiciest beefsteak and be a lean dyspeptic. Your neighbor might have nothing but soup-bone and thin soup, and he might be healthier than you. Does that prove that thin soup is better than beefsteak? Ach, no. But he assimilates his soup-bone soup better than you do your beefsteak. That's all!"

That answer helped me more than all the symbolics, or comparison of doctrines that I had ever had. The soup-bone is not so nourishing, but its eaters are strong and healthy because they make use of all they can get out of it. The juicy steak is better, but its eaters do not always assimilate and use its nourishing qualities. They grow weak and lean. Not the meat's fault, but their own. To us Lutherans more has been given. Of us more will be required.

This has been an anticipation, but it helps to clear up many a youthful perplexity as it did mine. Dr. Mann helped me for life.

Now I go back to the days of my youth.

Chapter III

WAR DAYS AND ACADEMY EXPERIENCES

WHILE I was still in Mr. Dummet's school the Civil War broke out. The early days were tense with excitement. How eager I was to go frequently into the city. Pittsburgh was wild with war fever. The streets, stores, and homes were bright with flags, banners and bunting. Recruiting stations with their stirring martial music were scattered over the city as well as over Birmingham and Allegheny. Bands of boys in blue were marching up and down the busy streets. How their smart, new uniforms, their manly mien, their stately stepping, their flags and banners and above all, their fife and drum corps did stir my sentimental boy heart and fire my imagination.

I was by nature and by temperament an ardent American and an enthusiastic patriot. Mr. Dummet kindled and kept the home fires burning. He selected for us and had us read patriotic poems and orations. One hour a week we had to "speak pieces." These were all patriotic selections. We sang war songs, and Mr. Dummet told us war stories. He kept us informed on the battles, the defeats and the victories. On stormy winter mornings he would often say: "I wonder how the boys on the Potomac are today?" A number of the big boys from our school had enlisted and gone. I wanted to go, but I was too little and puny. I did once sneak away from home to enlist, but the recruiting sergeant found me underweight and undersize. He treated me kindly and told me to go home and get fat and big and then come back. So I had to keep on in my dull, tiresome toil on the uninviting and unprofitable little home farm. How I devoured the war news and stories. I learned all the war songs, knew them by heart, and sang them at my work. During the early dark days when McClellan, with his splendid Army of The Potomac, was so inactive and the South was winning victory after victory, fear took hold of the cities of the North. Forts were constructed on the hill-tops on the north and south sides of Pittsburgh. The trenches and breast works are still visible. The labor was all voluntary. I wanted to do something for my country. The recruiting officer had refused to enlist me, so, on a Fourth of July, when crowds of men were busy throwing up the earth-works at the forts, I secured a tin bucket and tin cup and went and offered myself to the toilers as a water-carrier. All day long I carried my heavy pail full up to the steep hill and was happy in my heavy toil. That Fourth stands out in my memory above all other Fourths of my youthful years.

Once, during the war, it was my great privilege to see Abraham Lincoln. I do not know the date, but the great President, whose life and character have always been an inspiration to me, came to Pittsburgh. In Pittsburgh he knew that he was always welcome. There was scarcely one disloyal man in the city. As Lincoln rode in an open carriage in a great parade along Grant street, I got a clear view of him standing up in his carriage. With his "stove pipe" hat in his hand he was constantly bowing to the enthusiastic crowds, who were wildly cheering, singing, clapping, and waving flags, hats and coats on his right and

18

left. I see him yet. His tall, quaint figure and his pale, sad face are still before me. It was an event in my young life.

I finished my school with Mr. Dummet. My father still wanted me to be a minister. For two winters he managed to send me to two academies in Pittsburgh. My course was much broken up. I had to lose many days to work at home or to drive the milk wagon. On school days I used to get up several hours before daylight, light my tin perforated lantern, go to the barn, clean out the stables, feed the cattle, snatch a hasty breakfast, gather up my books and run a mile and a half to catch a school train for the city. After my evening chores I studied for several hours every night. I had no time for night loafing or dissipating.

Bogle's Academy was the first select school I attended. Here I came in contact with a new regime and a new set of schoolmates. Our principal, Mr. Bogle, was a serious, stern Puritan. His teaching was matter of fact, routine and dry. It was informing but not inspiring. He lacked magnetism. Still we learned much from him. We had to.

He had several maiden lady assistants. One of these, a Miss Harriss, was vivacious and sparkling. She took a personal interest in her pupils. She tried to awaken in us an ambition to want to make something of ourselves and to be somebody. She left an impress on me.

A friend of Mr. Bogle offered a prize of a pair of skates to the student who would memorize and speak, without being prompted, the Declaration of Independence. Miss Harriss, who seemed to realize my environing handicaps, took a sympathetic interest in me. She came to me and said that I could and she wanted me to win the skates. Because of he. encouragement I did. How proud I was of those skates. When I left that school Miss Harriss spoke to me very kindly. Said she wanted to keep track of me and expected me to make something of myself. She expected to hear about me. Those kind and encouraging words did me a world of good. A word in season, how good it is. Why are we so stingy with such helpful words? Specially to boys and girls. Miss Harriss died a few years later.

My next school was different. Gourley's Academy was in brighter quarters on Fifth Avenue, Pittsburgh. Professor Gourley, afterwards mayor of Pittsburgh, was a personality. He was bright, attractive and magnetic. After Mr. Dummet he was the most brilliant character with whom I had come in contact as a teacher. His teaching was inspirational. He stirred ambitions. He waked up the dull and drowsy. He made us hungry to know more. He deepened in me a desire to make my life count for good. I am glad that I had the privilege to sit at Professor Gourley's feet.

He had several assistants, but they neither made nor left an impress. Gourley's school had a more varied class of students than Bogle's. At neither school did I find a single Lutheran student.

I now recall a number of celebrities that came out of this school. Several of the boys became politicians and statesmen. Some made good in law, others as teachers, a few as preachers, and one became an editor. There I met a quiet, modest young girl who became a teacher, and later on the mother of my children. Gourley's school was worth while.

CHAPTER IV

THIEL HALL. DOCTOR PASSAVANT*

THE time had now come when I was ready for college. Poor as my father was, he wanted me to get a college education. There was no first class English Lutheran college west of the Allegheny Mountains. Father could not possibly afford to send me to an Eastern college.

That wonderful philanthropist and educator, the Rev. Doctor Passavant of Pittsburgh, had started several academies in smaller near-by towns. None of them had attained to a college grade. He saw and felt that there was a pressing need for a school that could take the academy graduates farther. A Lutheran junior college was the present and pressing need.

Dr. Passavant had found a pious German layman in Petroleum Center named Louis Thiel, who had invested his life's savings in oil lands. He had promised the Lord that if He would prosper this venture he would give back to Him at least one-tenth of his profits. The Lord did prosper him, and he kept his promise.

Dr. Passavant prayed and counseled with Mr. Thiel. He showed Mr. Thiel the need of a high-grade academy. The term, junior college, was not then in vogue. But it was a junior college that he wanted. In the spring

---

*For more detailed information on things contained in this chapter, see *Life and Letters of Passavant,* P. 501 ff.

of 1865 Mr. Thiel put into the hands of Doctor Passavant $5,505.00 to invest at his discretion.

In a quiet sylvan villa, then called Phillipsburg, on the south bank of the Ohio River, twenty-five miles below Pittsburgh, Dr. Passavant found a site. The little, well shaded and improved tract had on it several buildings. The place had been used as a water-cure health resort. With a few alterations this place fitted finely for its purpose and became the attractive home of Thiel Hall.

With his keen gift of discovering and using the brightest and best young men, Dr. Passavant had found the young Henry E. Jacobs, who has since become the Nestor of American Lutheran theologians. With Professor Jacobs as principal and Professor Feitzahus as assistant, the new school was opened. During its short life it became an American-Lutheran Rugby.

After much inquiry and consultation with my pastor, the Rev. Dr. Samuel Laird, it was decided that I should go to Thiel Hall. My heart beat high at the prospect. The fondest dream of my youth was coming true. I was to live in a college! During the college year at least I was to be free from the obnoxious drudgery of the poorly equipped and unprofitable farm. No more getting up in the dark to clean out cow stables or drive the milk wagon. No more running out barefoot over the hoar-frost to chase up the cows in the pasture and to jump up and down in the place where they had lain to warm my red, cold feet. No more spending days hauling the manure out over the hill-sides, spreading it and plowing it under, somehow, rightly or wrongly. I had a feeling that I was made for and ought to be at something higher. I loved and devoured newspapers. My father had taught me German so that I could read and understand it with ease. He kept a German weekly. How eagerly I would sneak it away and devour it. It gave me a weekly glimpse into the great, throbbing, busy world. Magazines were not as corrupt and corrupting as so many of them are today. When I could now and then borrow one it was a feast for me. A college story would open a vista into fairyland. There were a few German juvenile books in the house. These I read and re-read, but I had a feeling that they did not describe life as it is in America. A rich man named Brewer, a friend and helper of Dr. Passavant, invested thousands of dollars in carefully selected books for Sunday School libraries. To every new mission Sunday School he offered a library of a hundred or more books. The Union Sunday School that I attended had one of these Brewer Libraries. I believe I read about all of the books in them. Some were too softly sentimental. Many were high-toned, instructive and stimulating. Among them were real character builders. These made lasting impressions on my hungry, young mind and heart. They influenced me for life. They set before me high ideals. They deepened my desire to know more and to amount to something in life. Oh, if I could live among books and with people like those described in the best of Brewer's Sunday School books!

And now I was going to college! I was going to spend my days and nights under the care and guidance of noble Christian teachers. I was going to have college boys for companions; refined, cultured, high-toned boys. How I would learn from them! How I would imitate them! How I would emulate them! And there would be a college library. I would live among and in books. College, O college, college life was to be mine. I was going. It seemed too good to be true!

But it came true. My small, cheap, light little new trunk was packed. My wardrobe was scant and cheap. My pocket had a few loose dollars. But I was going to college. No well-groomed, slick, pampered boy with fat purse ever started to college more happy than I.

In less than two hours the train carried me to Rochester, Pa. There I got out. I shouldered my trunk and carried it to the ferry landing. On the other side of the Ohio I shouldered it again and carried it quite a distance up a hill and landed at the "upper house" of Thiel Hall. I was assigned a room with a Pittsburgh boy, in the "lower house." Could it be true? I was in college!

I soon fell into the routine of college life. Somehow or other it seemed natural to me. I liked it all. We had enough study and work to keep us busy. But we were not overworked. We had time for recreation. The high bluffs along the beautiful Ohio afforded the finest and most varied scenery. The quiet valley running south of the town, the wooded hillsides, the variety of trees and flowers and mosses, the birds and squirrels and chipmunks and cottontail rabbits, all invited to walks and talks and confidences, When the weather was fine we had them. The clear waters of the Ohio invited rowing, bathing and swimming. I could not swim. I tried hard to learn. I did sometimes venture out beyond my depth. I recall one such occasion where the stream was rapid. It carried me out, and I got frightened and went down. I came up again, and in terror I went down again. Will Passavant came to my rescue, caught me by the hair as I came up again and towed me to land. That was one hair-pulling to which I did not object. He saved my life. I never learned to swim. The former health resort had left behind a bowling alley, which we used on inclement days. On fine evenings, after supper, a group of us would often carry our chairs out on the side of the lower house fronting the grass-grown street. There, into the twilight we would tell stories, discuss and argue the questions of church and state or settle them all. Then to our rooms for two hours of real study. Then our prayers and to bed. We had a few tacit understandings. There was to be no indecent talk and no profanity. The very atmosphere of our school made us feel that such things would be unbecoming and would violate our self-respect. If an uncouth, coarse, rough boy came to our school he had to either reform or he would soon leave. We played corner-ball, shinny, pitched horse-shoes, ran races, had wrestling matches and were real, roistering, red blooded boys.

I came to like the young Professor Jacobs more and more. While not as magnetic or scintillating before his classes as some other teachers, he was always instructive and interesting. His kindly, quiet, patient ways compelled attention and respect. His study with its array of bulky, hog skin tomes, was always open to us for questions or short interviews. I recall how I was still unsettled and more or less disturbed by the momentous question as to whether I ought to be a minister. One evening I timidly knocked at the study door, went in and opened my heart to Dr. Jacobs. He encouraged me to tell him all my difficulties and doubts and then gave such kindly and clear instruction and encouragement that I soon made the great decision.

I had the inner call. It had germinated in early

childhood, when it was impressed on me that it had been my mother's wish and last prayer that her only boy should become a minister. As I grew up I had some occasional experiences in business. I liked it. I thought I should like to be a business man. But the inner call was with me. My pastor, Dr. Hill, while visiting our home inquired for me and was told that I was working in the field. Mr. Hill came out to where I was, said he wanted to talk to me, and we sat down on a grassy bank together. He talked kindly to me of my sainted mother and of her desire that I should be a minister and expressed his own ardent desire to the same end.

This conversation with my good pastor deepened in me the consciousness of the inner call. My above named, good Reformed Sunday School teachers also spoke to me of the ministry, Mr. Dummet had mentioned it more than once. My father seemed to take it for granted. I was undecided if not unwilling. That evening visit to Dr. Jacobs' study made me willing. It would have been better still if he had knelt and prayed with me. I, too, have often omitted this where I should have done it. As it was, I was henceforth satisfied that God wanted me in the holy office. I was resolved to follow the inner call. Dr. Jacobs helped me. Thru his valuable writings he has helped me ever since. I owe much to him.*

Of the general character and conduct of old Thiel Hall, under the youthful President Jacobs, I wrote, among other things, twenty years ago, in *Life and Letters of Passavant*, the following reminiscences:

"Of the life and character of that school the writer

---

*For a full discussion of the Inner Call see *The Lutheran Pastor*, the chapter on *The Inner Call*.

of this can speak from experience. Never can we forget the blessed days we spent there. At no school that we ever attended did we find so good a spirit, so homelike an atmosphere and such affection among the students as there.

"Professor Jacobs preached on Sunday evenings in the German Church of the village and organized a little English Lutheran Church. The membership consisted mainly of the students, the professors and the Downing family, who had charge of the buildings and the boarding. Students were elected as elders and deacons; students, with the assistance of the Misses Wagner, made up the choir. Students gathered, superintended and taught the Sunday School. (It was my privilege to have in my Sunday School class little Agnes Schade, who has since become one of our most efficient missionaries in Rahjamundry, India.) The unconfirmed students were catechized by Dr. Jacobs, and when the time came for confirmation it was left to each one to decide whether he desired to take this step or not. Among those who applied for confirmation in the autumn of 1869 was Wm. A. Passavant, Jr. Dr. Passavant came down from Baden on Sunday afternoon, led the devotions at our supper table and preached the confirmation and communion sermon. How he prayed for the students as we knelt in that dining room that Sunday evening. The memory of that prayer after thirty-five years (now fifty-five years) still touches the heart and moistens the eye. And then that sermon! We can see the silver-crowned saint in that wine-glass pulpit now. The text was: "He brought me into the banqueting house and His banner over me was love." We know that sermon today. How tender and touching were the applications to those about to be con-

27

firmed, and the appeals to all of us to give our hearts wholly to the dear Savior and our lives to His service in the ministry. More than half of the boys who heard that sermon became ministers. Of that little family congregation we recall these familiar ministerial names: H. Peters, J. A. Zahn, D. L. and T. B. Roth, J. C. Kunzmann, W. A. Passavant, G. C. Berkemeier, J. W. Myers, H. L. McMurray, F. C. E. Lemcke and G. W. Critchelow.

"The boys always looked forward to the visits and chapel talks of Dr. Passavant. His generous nature could not help but win our youthful hearts. Here is an incident: We were at the supper table at whose head sat Dr. Passavant. We had little link sausages that evening. The rule had been that each student should get one. The housefather of that evening put two on each plate, and when the platter was empty called out: 'Sister D., you must bring more sausages; these boys have a good appetite.' We voted him a good man.

"Nor have we ever forgotten the Communion seasons of that little student church. When Pastor Jacobs announced a Communion he earnestly impressed it on our minds and hearts that no one ought to come to the altar with any spite or bitterness in his heart against a fellow student; that if any of us had quarreled we ought to be reconciled before we came. Those preparatory services we never can forget. In my after ministry I tried to model my preparatory services after those that Dr. Jacobs, our pastor, had with us in Thiel Hall. Quite vividly I recall how the boys who had quarreled came together, made up, shook hands and were reconciled." So much from *Life and Letters of Passavant.*

One Thiel Hall student experience that may seem trifling was rich for us boys. It was our rare privilege to witness, watch and discuss the courtship of our president and the bright and attractive Miss Laura Downing. That was indeed a unique courtship! It was stately. It was dignified. It was impressive! There never had been a courtship like it. There has been none since. I feel safe in saying that none of us students ever imitated it. But what a match it made! Generations following will reap the blessings.

In my long life I have come in contact with and observed many of our church schools and colleges. I do not hesitate to say that in none of these have I found a spirit and a life so beautiful, so impressive, so inspiring, so truly Evangelical and so happy as in old Thiel Hall. It was a model Christian school. The spirit of Passavant and Jacobs pervaded its walls and its boys. Oh, that we might pray down and instil a like scriptural and consecrated spirit into all our church schools and colleges! Is not this one of our deepest needs? Would not such a consummation bring life from the dead into our parsonages, our pulpits, and thru them into our homes and churches? Would it not be the revival that our dear Church needs? Would it not make us the power that we ought to be in America? O God, come and visit this vine that Thou hast planted.

Chapter V

IN MUHLENBERG COLLEGE

A S noted above, Thiel Hall was of junior college grade. There were only three of us who finished the classical course and were ready for junior class in college. The three were D. Luther Roth, J. A. J. Zahn and myself. Thiel Hall was now moved to Greenville, Pa., and became Thiel College.

As it would have required a considerably enlarged faculty to carry us three thru and graduate us, arrangements were made that Muhlenberg College would receive us into its Junior Class and graduate us to the credit of Thiel.

And so in the autumn of 1871 we three were off for Allentown, Pa. As was usual with me, I could not go with my two classmates but went about a month later. In all my common school, academy and Thiel years, I had to miss school much, because I had to help out on the farm. I missed the beginning and ending of practically every year. Out of the four college years I missed forty-three weeks, so I really had three weeks less than three years in college. While I was graduated with my class, I could not take any of the class honors.

At Allentown I was introduced into a new world. Eastern Pennsylvania was different. The land, the people, the traditions, the manners and customs were all different. Allentown was in the heart of the Pennsylvania German Section. They had a dialect that was all their own. It was amusing to us to see the children scrap and fight in what was called "Pennsylvania Dutch." Later on, during Allentown fair week, it amused us still more to see and hear the country swains courting their sweethearts in the same lingo. I recall one of these lovers, whose girl could not see for the crowd, taking her around her skirts and holding her high above the crowd. He enabled her to see. Meantime both were munching peanuts.

As a class the Pennsylvania Germans belong to a clear-headed, energetic, sturdy stock. There is an element of solidity, of safety and of sincerity about them that made them reliable in their character and in their religion. As a class they are above shallow emotionalism, above religious pretense and cant both in their personal and in their church life. These good characteristics may and often do become a peculiar danger. They make these people apt to become cold and formal in their church life. They need constant self-examination, heart searching, watching and praying against externalism and cold intellectualism.

The students that we found in Muhlenberg College were practically all of this stock. The great majority were from the country and the small towns. While these had the peculiar characteristics that belong to their people, we found among them noble characters, fine students, men with an ambition and an outlook. These I learned to admire and love.

At Muhlenberg I got my first experience of real college life. Here was a student body, counting the preps, of nearly two hundred. Here were class organizations and class badges. Here were two rival literary societies. Here were some incipient old time athletics. How tame compared to the college athletics of today!

Here were several small college fraternities. I had been warned against uniting with a fraternity. I watched them and their influence. They did not seem good to me. They seemed to breed and promote a clannish, sectional spirit and an artificial bond of friendship. It seemed to me that it was far more natural and free for me to select as my personal friends those whom I found to be congenial spirits, with mutual interests, hopes and ambitions. True, some of these were fraternity boys. They were special friends not because of fraternity bonds, but in spite of them, because we had found each other to be kindred spirits. I needed no fraternity. In later life I also noticed that fraternities are natural stepping stones to the secret orders whose religion and principles are so dangerous to an earnest Christian life.*

To get back to college and college life, our faculty was a most interesting group of professors. The president was the venerable and beloved Dr. F. A. Muhlenberg, a great grandson of Henry Melchior Muhlenberg. He was highly esteemed and beloved by his students. As a teacher he was clear and painstaking. He wanted the students to understand and know. He had little patience with shirkers. Tho of a mild Johannine temperament, he could also be a son of thunder. During my two years under him two of my classmates were expelled from college for conduct unworthy of a student in a Christian college.

The chapel talks, the lectures on Luther's Small Catechism were deeply impressive and edifying. They helped me in my Christian life. His earnest, childlike prayers for his students cannot be forgotten. I count

---

*See *The Lutheran Pastor*, pp. 237 ff.

it a privilege that I could sit at the feet of Dr. Muhlenberg for two years.

Dr. T. L. Seip was our professor of Latin language and literature. He was secretary of the faculty. He was a scholar and a gentleman of the old school. Dignified, reserved, exact and exacting, he commanded respect and attention. There was no fooling in his classes. He instilled an interest in Roman History, in Roman character, in Roman literature, law and government that are with me still. We honored the stately Dr. Seip.

Matthias H. Richards, D. D., professor of English language and literature, was also an outstanding teacher. He also was a great grandson of Patriarch Muhlenberg. As a teacher he was the most entertaining of all. He knew his subject. He was full of it. His discussions, observations and remarks were brilliant and ofttimes startling. He scintillated wit and wisdom. Sometimes his sarcasm was biting. He certainly did show up and hold up to scorn all pretense, sham and shallowness. For the beautiful, the good, the true, the ennobling, the uplifting and helpful in literature, he had true appreciation and admiration. He was a keen critic, a just judge, a teacher who wanted his students to learn to distinguish the real from the pretended, the true from the fraudulent, the helpful from the hurtful, the noble from the ignoble, the good from the bad. If any of his students did not learn how to judge, discriminate and sift out the wheat from the chaff in literature it certainly was not our teacher's fault. It was a rare privilege to sit in his class. His stinging reproofs, too, were helpful to all who really needed help. We can never forget Professor Matthias Henry Richards.

Doctor Davis Garber was our teacher in Mathematics, Astronomy, Physics and Geology. This wide and varied course was entirely too much for one man. And in those early days the equipment for laboratory work and demonstrations was all too meager. But Professor Garber did the best he could. Doubtless we did not always do the best we could and did not carry away from the over-worked professor all we might have gotten there. Our professor was always a kindly Christian gentleman who wanted to help his students.

Our professor in Chemistry and Botany was T. C. Yeager, M. D. He was a temporary helper in distress. He had too many irons in the fire. He was physician, druggist, politician, and in the year of my graduation, mayor of Allentown. He was brilliant as a speaker and lecturer. He was often absent from his classes. When present he gave us some entertaining and flowery lectures. I recall one on Sleep and another on The Chicago Fire, which he had witnessed. We did not become either botanists or chemists—at least I did not.

Our professor of German Language and Literature was the Rev. Geo. F. Miller. He knew the German language. He was master of its rich literature. Many of the great masterpieces he knew by heart. He was eloquent in reciting them. He was no drill-master in teaching language. He was no disciplinarian. A number of the boys took advantage of his easy good nature. His classes were often places for fun and rough-housing. We did not learn much German. It was our own fault. Fortunately for me I had learned German from my father and can use the language intelligently.

We come back to life in the school. The present great and gorgeous equipment of Muhlenberg College was not even a dream in those days. We were housed in the old building of the Allentown Collegiate Institute and Military Academy in the southeastern part of the city, with a fine, spacious grove between the long, five-story building and the street. Beside the student rooms there was a bright, cheerful, commodious room that was used as a chapel, another as a library and reading room with two finely furnished rooms for the literary societies. The student rooms were large and light. Each room was intended for two and had two curtained off, separate alcoves, each with a single cotbed. In those days the importance of abundant fresh air in sleeping rooms was not recognized as it is today. Those shut-in alcoves with no circulation of fresh air were not healthful. The students would have been fresher, brighter and more ready for good mental work if they had slept in modern rooms flooded with God's pure and invigorating out-door air. This the builders and directors did not then know. But we survived.

When I arrived I had very little money, and poor assurance of a future supply. I could not afford to board with the other students. Fortunately for me my roommate, Mr. Zahn from Thiel Hall, was about as poor as I was. We arranged to board ourselves. Dr. Muhlenberg kindly gave us permission to put in a small cookstove. (The rooms were all heated with stoves, and the boys had to carry up their own coal and empty their own ashes.) We found another impecunious fellow who wanted to enter our self-boarding club. He was accepted into the firm. From a common purse we purchased the few, absolutely necessary kitchen utensils. We agreed on a division of labor. One was to be purchaser, one cook, and one dishwasher. We rotated week about. We arranged with a wholesale house to buy in quantities at wholesale rates. We laid in a barrel of crackers, a ham, a side of bacon, a can of coffee, a peck of beans, several bushels of potatoes and other necessaries. Our bread and milk were carried in daily. We had our table prayers at every meal and read a Scripture passage at supper. The romance of it was fun for us. True, we had occasional disagreements and scraps and sometimes a calamity. Here is an instance: I prided myself on being able to make good ham-bone bean soup. It requires several hours' boiling. I had put it on the stove at ten o'clock, and buried myself in my next lesson. At eleven we had a recitation. I forgot that beans soak up lots of water. After recitation we heard a commotion on our floor. Boys were running up and down the hall yelling. Windows were thrown open, smoke was pouring out of our transom into the hall, and our room was permeated with suffocating scent and smoke of burnt beans! We had no soup that day. It didn't happen again. We grew fat on our self-boarding. After we had paid for our small kitchen outfit we figured out that our eating cost us from eighty cents to a dollar a week apiece.

During our two college years I helped in a Sunday School at Hanover, and for a time also in Clapboard Stetele. At the latter place we had a great Christmas celebration. College students had charge of the school. College students made the Christmas treat addresses. The schoolhouse was crowded to capacity. How we did spread ourselves and make the welkin ring with our eloquence. The countryside listened with rapt attention. I hope we did some good and made some lasting impressions for The Holy Child, God's Christmas gift to us.

Our college church was St. John's English Lutheran,

a short walk from the school. The Rev. Dr. Fahs was the pastor. He was an earnest and able preacher. We college boys were wonderful critics. We knew exactly where the sermon was weak and where and how it should have been improved! Such is the wonderful self confidence of youth.

The great attraction of St. John's was the music. Professor Herman had gathered and trained a wonderful chorus choir. He had enlisted much of the best talent in the city. What a choir, what voices, what a harmony and blending of tones! The choir laid itself out on the great classical masterpieces every Sunday night. Selections from the great oratorios, the Hallelujah Chorus, Mozart's Twelfth Mass and other heavenly selections crowded the church on Sunday evenings. We were filled, we were thrilled, we were entranced, we were lifted up spell-bound into a higher, a heavenly world.

I fear that the sermon counted for little. Was forgotten, left no lasting impression. It is a serious question. Were we really worshipping when we were lifted out of ourselves by those Sunday evening feasts of festive music? Was it worship or was it subjective enjoyment? If so, is that the best, the ideal service in God's House? Can there be too much of a good thing like that at church? Is that what we ought to go to church for? Is that what we ought to carry away from the service? Well, there is not much danger of having too many volunteer chorus choirs like the one Professor Herman had.

This reflection reminds me how, some years ago, I preached in the church in which I had been confirmed in Pittsburgh. The high-priced, paid quartet choir rendered some sublime selections. I was entranced. I almost forgot where I was. Then I asked myself: Are you worshipping? I had to confess to myself: No, I am not worshipping. I am admiring and enjoying those wonderful singers.

Our two college years sped by all too rapidly. The class of '73 was a famous class. It numbered nineteen, the largest class up to that time. Eleven of the nineteen went to the Philadelphia Seminary and became ministers of the Gospel. Four of these became authors of books. The most scholarly of the group, was Doctor John Nicum, who went Home some years ago. One went to Congress, others became lawyers, doctors and educators. It was good to be a member of the class of seventy-three.

As I look back upon those two college years I recall one more incident that made an impression on me: Doctor Passavant and Doctor Muhlenberg had been college-mates in Washington and Jefferson College, Washington County, Pa. A warm friendship had sprung up between the two students. This friendship had ripened into a closer intimacy in the after college years. On one of Doctor Passavant's many trips to the East, Dr. Muhlenberg had invited him to visit himself and Muhlenberg College. That brief visit was an event in our college life, especially to me. How glad I was to see that venerable saint again. How beautiful to see the two aging saints walk arm in arm about the campus and sit together on a campus bench. In the afternoon the host had himself and his guest driven out to Pulpit Rock in Lehigh Mountain. Next morning at chapel we had one of those impressive heart to heart talks which Doctor Passavant alone could give. It was good to be there.

Our last college year was drawing to a close. Our

class was arranging for commencement. I was chosen for class day poet. The poem was published in the *Indicator*. I could not stay for commencement. I was graduated *in absentia*. I had to go home and work on the farm. My college days were over. In spite of the self-denials and hardships that poverty brings, they were happy days. I had learned to bear the yoke in my youth.

Chapter VI

IN THE PHILADELPHIA SEMINARY

I WAS now a college graduate. I had my A. B. diploma. I didn't know just how to feel. True, I did have a feeling of satisfaction. I did feel like singing my Ebenezer. It did come over me with greater force than ever, that to whomsoever much is given, of him will also much be required. During my early college life I had read *Timothy Titcomb's Letters to Students*, one of the books that left a life impress on me. I wanted to measure up. I wanted to be something, to do something, to amount to something, so I mused on my way home from college.

But in this hard, old, every-day, matter-of-fact world one cannot sit and sing himself away in dreamy life of bliss. I had to help to keep my father and his large family. Instead of a new suit with a graduation pin, I had to put on overalls and drive an ice wagon. There were early risings, there were heavy blocks of ice to lift and carry, there were strains and knocks and hurts. Once indeed I fainted away and fell prone in the ice-house door. Is it any wonder that I have always had an interest in and a sympathy for the laboring man? God help and bless the sons of honest toil.

But whether in the stable feeding, currying and harnessing the horses, or in the ice-house prying loose and quarrying and loading the blocks of ice, or driving the team, or fitting the blocks into sundry ice boxes, or making out and collecting the ice bills, I was generally happy. I had a dear little girl whom I saw several times a week. I had the vision of Philadelphia Seminary before my eyes, and after that a home of my own, a blessed life in the ministry. A child of a King! Why shouldn't I sing?

The very thought of going to and living in Philadelphia had its charms. Outside of my journeys to and from and my sojourning in Phillipsburg and Allentown, I had not been away from home. Outside of Pittsburgh I had seen no large city. I had devoured descriptions of Philadelphia, New York, Chicago, Minneapolis, Seattle and the Pacific Coast. And now I was to see Philadelphia, tramp its streets, study its people and live there, live in a Theological Seminary. Life in Thiel Hall had been great. Life in Muhlenberg had, in some respects, been greater. But now! To live in a Seminary. To study under great teachers who were to teach us to see, to know, to understand the other-worldly wisdom of God's Revelation and of everything in its relation to that Revelation, this must be transcendently great! To have for fellow-students, for companions, none other than men who were preparing for the holy office of servants of the most high God, to live in and breathe in daily the sacred atmosphere of a school of the prophets, that seemed to me to be a privilege that a prince might envy.

Well: Things are not always what they seem! As usual, I was late starting. Work had been going in the seminary for several weeks before I arrived. I had to finish up my summer's ice business.

With high hopes I started. I took a daylight train on the Baltimore and Ohio. I was passionately fond

of travel. I like it still. I could not take a parlor car
or eat in a diner. These privileges I could not enjoy
until I had been many years in the ministry. I did
not miss them on that day-coach ride to Philadelphia.
Many people travel and see nothing. At the end of
a trip they cannot tell what they have seen. As for
me, how keenly I enjoyed the Allegheny Mountains,
the descent to Cumberland, Md., the ten cent sandwich there, the setting my feet for the first time on soil
outside of my native state, and Southern soil at that.
Then that long, curving ride down the Cumberland
Valley, along the canal with its mule-pulled boats and
black drivers. Then historic, romantic, tragic Harpers
Ferry. What memories, what scenes, what surprises,
what thrills, what startling stories lie buried in that
little rugged if not ragged old town at the border
line of three states. My heart beat fast as I jumped
from the train during its short stop. Then Washington City! Could it be true that I was being pulled
into the capital city of my country? Was that really
the capitol building that I saw so clearly from the
rear platform of my train? Were my feet standing
within the gates of the grandest capitol of the grandest
nation in the world? It was a great day for me. I
arrived in Philadelphia long after night-fall. By one-
horse street car and several transfers I found my way
to Franklin Square and the seminary.

By previous arrangement I was to room with my
former Thiel and Muhlenberg chum, Mr. Zahn. I was
warmly welcomed by him and Roth, the former
Thielers and my classmates from Muhlenberg. Zahn
and I roomed on the fifth floor. Our window over-
looked the old, homey Franklin Square with its many
stately trees and hospitable benches. I soon got the

42

lay of the city. I loved to walk its streets, study its people, note the manner and customs and their differences from those of Pittsburgh. But most of all I was interested in the seminary and its personnel. I watched and studied the members of the faculty, perhaps more than they studied me when I was before them to be enrolled. As a group they impressed me as stately, dignified and distant. I soon learned to know them at closer range. The three seminary years furnished a growing opportunity for forming a matured estimate of them.

The gentle, scholarly, beaming saint, the oldest in the faculty, was Dr. C. F. Shaeffer. He had the chair of New Testament, Greek and, if I remember correctly, Pastoral Theology. He was quite deaf and had to use an ear trumpet. We had to walk to his chair and talk into his trumpet when we recited. He was really too old and infirm to teach. He could not be a forceful teacher. But I did estimate and esteem him as a clear thinker and a sound Lutheran.

He had completed the writing of a full system of Dogmatics. His son-in-law, Dr. Hill, my former pastor, carried this precious manuscript to the Lutheran book store with the request that they publish it. They never did. There was at that time no good American Lutheran Dogmatics on the market. I never could understand why our book store did not publish it. Since then I have been perplexed more than once by what Lutheran publishing houses would do and what they would not do. There are mysteries. Perhaps sometime I may understand even these.

Doctor C. F.'s nephew was the Rev. Dr. C. W. Shaeffer. He was our professor in church history. At the side he was our once a week critic when we preached before him in turn. He was original. He was unique as a teacher. His like I had not met before nor have I since. His mannerisms attracted attention. His gestures, his facial expressions, his handling of his spectacles, the winking and blinking of his eyes, all these were queer. His droll humor, his sometimes keen, cutting sarcasm, his aphoristic, sententious judgments, his side remarks about Gettysburg Theology, all these were interesting and oft amusing. But he knew church history and wanted us to know it. He was too good-natured to be severe. It was not difficult to bluff and shirk in his class.

His weekly period in Homiletics was peculiar also. He was too easy to give us the criticisms that we deserved. When he did criticize he did it with an apology. This was a mistake. It was a wrong to his students. We needed to be shown our weaknesses, our mistakes and all our faults. To show these up clearly, to make us see and detect them would have been the greatest kindness to us crude tyros in preaching.

Yes, Dr. Shaeffer was odd. He was queer, but he was kind and good. And who knows but what when, a generation later, I became a professor, I did not unconsciously imitate some of the eccentricities of my old professor, for which some of my mischievous ministerial sprouts cartooned me on paper and passed it around at the dinner table?

Doctor Adolph Spaeth was an importation from Germany. He was of aristocratic birth and mien, university bred, widely traveled all over the continent of Europe, especially in the Mediterranean lands. He had become a private tutor in a family of nobility in Scotland. When pastor of a large German Lutheran church in Philadelphia he had taken on the additional work of professor of New Testament Language and Literature. Under him we had Exegesis, or the explanation of the Greek text, Isagogics, or the Introduction to each separate book of the New Testament and Hermeneutics, or the study of the principles of interpretation according to which the language of the Bible is to be explained. The seminary was bi-lingual. Both the German and English languages were read. Dr. Spaeth's lectures were given in both languages. He would give us a sentence in German and then translate ("Upset," we boys used to say) it into English. This awkward method was neither interesting nor satisfying. I learned far more from the books and articles that Dr. Spaeth had written, after I left the seminary than I had learned in his lecture room. Some of his books have been a precious boon to me.

Everything considered, Dr. C. P. Krauth was the greatest Lutheran theologian that America had produced. He knew America. He understood her history, her spirit, her genius and her character. He was at home in her literature, her philosophy, her religion and her theology. He had measured swords with the Nestor of Presbyterian theology, Dr. Charles Hodge. In an extant letter Hodge acknowledges that Krauth had proven his point against him and that Krauth knew more about Calvinistic theology than he (Hodge) did himself.* While he was professor of Philosophy and vice-provost of the University of Pennsylvania Dr. Krauth also had the chair of Systematic Theology in the Philadelphia Seminary. For three years it was my privilege to sit at his feet.

The most scholarly man is not always the best teach-

*See Spaeth's *Life of Krauth*. Vol. II, p. 317.

er. The doctor read his lectures to us from manuscript. He was working out a nine-year course of lectures on Systematic Theology. Each seminary class got one-third of this course. One class got the first third, the following class got the middle third and the next class the last third. In other words, each class got one-third of a full course. My class got the first third. For one whole year we got Prolegomena, or introduction to Systematic Theology. We got nothing on Pneumatology, or the Work of the Holy Spirit. Nothing on the Sacraments, nothing on Eschatology, or the Doctrine of The Last Things. From our viewpoint the Church lost an incalculable boon, because Dr. Krauth did not live long enough to have his whole nine years' course published.

Among the special advantages that the doctor gave us was the occasional Round Table or free discussion on live topics on which we needed and wanted further light. I mention only two. One was on secret societies. The doctor had studied his subject. He knew the literature and rituals of the leading lodges. That hour was worth more than gold could buy. It made clear to me for life that the religion of the lodge is subversive of the Christian religion. How any one who heard or took part in that discussion could ever join a lodge is a mystery to me.*

Another Round Table was on The Galesburg Rule. The rule, or declaration, that the General Council had adopted at its Galesburg Convention was "Lutheran Pulpits for Lutheran Ministers only. Lutheran Altars for Lutheran Communicants only." This rule or declaration had stirred up the whole Lutheran Church.

*See *The Lutheran Pastor,* pp. 122, 237, ff. 360 f.

Controversy was rife. Parties, factions and leaders were pitted against each other. Congregations, communities, families and friends were divided. It was our daily topic among thinking students. We had it for breakfast, dinner and supper. Discussions waxed warm, even hot and sometimes bitter. Doctor Krauth had not yet published his final stand. One of my classmates, in a heated discussion settled it thus for himself: "Well, boys, I don't know yet which way Dr. Krauth is going to go; if he goes to Missouri I'll go; if he goes to the Dickens I'll go!" That sounded too much like a pupil of Doctor Walther for me. Such hero worship, such unthinking subservience to authority I never could abide. It went against my independent spirit!

When Dr. Krauth announced the free conference on The Galesburg Rule and invited all the seminary students, he also invited written questions, opinions and criticisms. I had the temerity to oppose Dr. Krauth. I had written out my objections in a brief paper. As I recall it, I claimed that, while there are serious points of difference between the Lutheran Church and her Evangelical Reformed neighbors, there were also great fundamental agreements on which we Lutherans might fellowship with these other Christians on the points on which we agree, without compromising the points on which we differ. Dr. Krauth's answer was cutting and sarcastic. I did not think it was fair.

I never did agree with the strict interpretation of the so-called Galesburg Rule. I believe its adoption was a mistake and misfortune. It aroused bitter antagonisms. It alienated many weak Lutherans who might have been held and strengthened. It set us in a false light before American Protestantism. I like the

Washington Declaration of Principles concerning the Church and its external relationship better. But even this I might wish to be more explicit in places. In my fifty years in the ministry I never once gave a general invitation to the Lord's Supper. Once only, in my first parish, did I have a minister of another denomination in my pulpit. There was a special reason. My Lutheranism is set forth in my books. It needs no apology.

To come back to Dr. Krauth as a teacher, what I did not get in his class-room I got later from his books. His Conservative Reformation has been studied and restudied. My copy has required a second binding. Doctor Krauth has been a blessing to my life and my work. My whole career would have been different without the contact and influence of Doctor Krauth.

One more of my seminary teachers deserves special mention. I must restrain myself lest I give too much space to the Rev. Dr. W. J. Mann. He was different. He got a peculiar grip on me. He made and left an impress as no other teacher ever did. University bred tho he was, he was not coldly aloof and unapproachable. His students soon learned that he had a big, warm heart, that he loved us and was personally interested in the intellectual and spiritual welfare of every one of us. He invited personal and conversational contacts. His personal counsels were earnest, sincere and sympathetic, and yet, when he felt that it was needed he could and would be cuttingly severe. Some of his rebukes can never be forgotten.

As a teacher, especially in ethics, he was brilliant, magnetic, inspiring. When warmed up in his subject he scintillated brilliancy. In his personal applications and warnings it was no uncommon thing to see big tears roll down his cheeks. Sentence prayers were frequently interjected into his appeals for a consecrated, spiritual, soul-winning ministry. How any student could go thru his course in Ethics and go out into the ministry and be a lazy, cold, slovenly, worldly preacher and pastor passes comprehension. Yet some did. God pity them. Here are a few illustrations of his manner with his boys. I could give more:

We had one Irish student, Mr. H. L. McMurray. When Dr. Mann was proctor of the seminary he kept a record of the boys who missed chapel, which was always held before breakfast. At the first lecture after chapel the delinquents were called up to the doctor's desk and reprimanded before the whole class. One morning McMurray was called up. The doctor held his open record book up to him, pointed to the list of absence marks and said: "Look at that, McMurray! Don't you shame yourself? Doesn't your conscience trouble you?" Mac, as we called him, colored up and looked perplexed. Then suddenly his good natured Irish face lighted up, a broad smile beamed over it and he said: "Why, Doctor, when I sleep, my conscience sleeps too!" Dr. Mann could always appreciate a joke. He laughed at the natural Irish wit and said, "You can go, Mr. McMurray, but don't do it again."

We had a student named Drumheller. He was none of the brightest and did not hurt himself studying. Dr. Mann once asked him a question in class. He got no answer. After several attempts to get an answer, the doctor finally cross-questioned a kind of answer out of him. Then he said: "Well, well, Mr. Drumheller, at last I drummed it out of you, and it isn't worth a heller!" (heller, a small German coin.)

Once a week we had what we boys, irreverently, called Dutch Homiletics, with Doctor Mann. One afternoon one of our would-be bright, conceited students brought in an outline on the text: I am the Light of the World. As I recall it, it was mainly a discussion on the evolution of artificial light from the pine-knot to the grease-soaked rag in a shallow dish to a tallow candle, to a kerosene lamp, the gas light and up to the incandescent electric light. Of Christ as the heavenly, soul-illumining and saving Light there was neither explanation nor application nor appeal.

I saw the doctor's brow darken. I saw the hand vigorously and successively drawn across his forehead. Then a storm broke. It was something like this: "Well! you call that preaching the Gospel? Are you going out with such stuff to convert sinners to Christ?" Then he turned to the student body and gave us one of his impromptu, gripping talks on the responsibility of going out as ambassadors of Christ beseeching men in Christ's stead to be reconciled to God. Then he referred again to the shallowness and emptiness of such a presentation as we had before us. Then his voice broke, he choked up, big tears rolled down his cheeks, he grabbed his hat and said, "Good evening, Gentlemen," and hurried from the room. Did any of us ever forget that lesson in Homiletics? Could any one forget it? I couldn't.

O for such professors of Ethics and Homiletics in all our seminaries! Then would we have fewer loveless, lifeless, cold, wooden preachers.

In after years, as a theological professor, I never forgot Dr. Mann. He was my ideal. In my own weak way I tried to teach like Doctor William Julius Mann.

I go back to life in the seminary. The old building was good for its time. It was not what seminary buildings are now, but we didn't know any better and were happy. There was no provision for bodily exercise, or ventilation except as each student arranged and provided for himself. We boarded together in the basement. A steward had sole charge. He provided the food and the table service and collected the bills. As is natural and usual under such an arrangement, there was dissatisfaction and grumbling. More than once indignation meetings were called in chapel. Descriptive and denunciatory eloquence filled the room. But it did not do much good. As is usual, the steward was informed as to the speakers and the speeches. Then, woe to the kicker who was behind in paying his bill.

It was not a good arrangement. The modern and better way is to have a boarding club managed entirely by the student boarders. If fault is to be found, the boarders must find it with themselves and remedy it themselves.

Chapel service was conducted daily before breakfast. The students took turns in leading. Professors took turns in being present and in keeping a private roll of absentees. The service was short and too often hurried thru. As I recall it, there was a hymn, a short Scripture lesson and a collect-prayer. There was no address. It would have been much more helpful if enough time had been provided to have a ten to twelve minute devotional address and a free prayer. Students cannot have too much practice in making well prepared public devotional addresses without manuscript and in offering public free prayer. Many of our young preachers are lame in these important public functions. Seminaries may be at fault. Some young preachers cannot even offer a sick-bed prayer without a book. I recall how a senior student was supplying a country parish during the Christmas holidays. On the first evening the head of the family that was his host handed him a Bible and requested him to conduct the family worship, to which they were accustomed. The young man colored up, stammered, said he wasn't prepared and asked to be excused till the following evening. How humiliating! Was his seminary without blame? By the next evening the poor student had improvised a sort of a service from Luther's Catechism. Let our seminaries teach their students to pray.

As students we were not overworked. We could and should have had more to do. Idleness is not good, even for theological students. They ought to learn to do persistent, hard mental work. We didn't. There was entirely too much group loafing in students' rooms. Outside of his regular, short recreation periods and his physical exercise in the fresh air, a college and seminary student ought to be kept so busy that he will learn to concentrate, to originate, to persist in his work and master it as he goes along. If he does not learn this as a student, he will be likely to become one of those lazy preachers who are a hindrance to church growth and progress. Of these lazy, loafing preachers we have all too many.

Students ought to learn to use and learn to find delight in using a good, well classified and arranged library. Our library was not so arranged. We were seldom referred to it. We were not required and did not learn to do original research work. This was our loss. But all this has been improved, and now students learn how and are expected to use college and seminary libraries.

As students we did not all do church work. Seniors only were allowed to preach, and that only once a month. I believe that this also was a mistake. I am convinced that a student ought to preach as frequently as possible during his whole seminary course. He cannot get too much practice in preaching and in all pastoral duties before he takes charge of a parish. Might it not be greatly helpful, if the professor of Homiletics would have a weekly hour with all who preached the preceding Sunday, get each one to tell what and how he preached and give him frankly and plainly the counsel he needs?

What all our seminaries need and what has not yet been worked out in a satisfactory manner is a seminary clinic, or a pastoral clinic under seminary supervision. We hope that some one will work out a workable system.

It is a great privilege for students to be in a seminary that is located in a great city. Students ought to have the opportunity to hear the really great, outstanding preachers, first of their own church, then also of other churches. The preacher to be ought to hear great, drawing, soul-winning and soul-building preachers. He ought to study them, the matter and style of their sermons, their method of illustration, application and appeal. How does this man get his message across? Where lies, what is, the secret of his power? Can I, with God's help, get a message of that power? Would that all ministerial students would utilize such opportunities as helps to learn how to preach.

When I entered the seminary Dr. Seiss was pastor of old St. John's, close to our school. During my course he built and went to the Church of the Holy Communion. He was a prince among preachers. He was a preacher of power. He excelled in portraying the sublime. In some of his lofty flights into the regions of the sublime he could make us forget where we were and almost lift us off our feet. His descriptions were captivating. His challenges were powerful. His denunciations were crushing. His appeals were gripping. I could often imagine that I saw the Prophet Elijah challenging the priests of Baal and defying Ahab and Jesebel. I doubt whether in any denomination there was a preacher as majestic, as powerful as Doctor Seiss when he was at his best. And yet the doctor lacked something. One could not help but admire him; but did not feel that he loved him. That gentle, tender, appealing, winning heart power was not there. He appealed to the intellect and to the imagination. He did not melt and move and draw the heart. He could lift the susceptible hearer out of himself up to Sinai or Tabor, but he did not bring helping and healing comfort to the lonely, the sorrowing, the mourning, the disappointed, the broken in heart and in life. He lacked heart-appeal, heart-power. But I thank God that it was my privilege during most of the morning services of three seminary years to sit under the powerful preaching of America's greatest preacher.

The Rev. Dr. Richard Newton was doubtless, in his day, the most remarkable and the most effective preacher to children. He wrote a number of volumes of sermons to children, the best known of which is *Rills From The Fountain of Life*. He was preaching within walking distance of our seminary. I believe it was once a month that he had a service for children in the afternoon. To this Sunday afternoon service the public was invited. With other students I attended many times. His large church, with wide galleries on three sides, was always crowded to capacity.

The service was beautiful, attractive, simple and suited to children. The venerable rector—he was an

Episcopalian—knew how to get and hold the attention of that vast crowd of children of all ages. I recall not a single case of disorder. Dr. Newton knew the secret of interesting, gripping and teaching children. There was no cheap wit or drollery. Sermons, real sermons based on a Bible text, generally a Bible story is what he gave those children. His language was beautiful in its simplicity, his illustrations and stories were short and fitting, his applications and appeals were impressive. It was a privilege to hear Dr. Newton preach to children. God alone knows the amount of good that he did to the hearts and lives of those thousands of children. I advise every preacher to study some of Dr. Newton's books of sermons to children and then, as nearly as possible, to go and do likewise. Any one who can preach interestingly and effectively to children can preach interestingly and effectively to all sorts and conditions of grown-ups also.

The preacher who is not a good Sunday-school man is in so far a failure. Feed my lambs was the Risen Savior's first admonition to the converted and restored Peter.

Here again good example is so helpful. During my seminary years was had in Philadelphia what was supposed to be the largest, the best organized and best managed Sunday School in the world. Bethany Sunday School was under the masterful management of that merchant prince, John Wanamaker. There was a large gallery for visitors. Some of the students went often. The school met Sunday afternoons so as to give an opportunity to attend. Many of our students, I am sorry to say, never went. They never embraced any of these side advantages afforded in a great city. Needless to say that these belonged to that large class that had no holy ambition to make their ministry count for God and for good. They had no vision of becoming a winning and saving influence in their respective communities, no spirit-filled ambition to make the Lutheran Church a great power in America. These are the fellows whose whole idea was and is, "Put me into the priest's office that I may have a piece of bread." Hundreds of them are in our ministry today. Numbers of them are still in our seminaries. Carefree, lazy, always taking the path of least resistance, they strive to disturb or offend no one, satisfied if they can drone off their weekly sermons and get their salary. Higher and holier ambition they know none. They clog the wheels of the Gospel chariot. They have kept and are keeping back the Lutheran Church. They are largely responsible for our losing the third place among Protestant churches. They didn't go to Newton's children's service, nor to Wanamaker's Sunday School, nor to Moody and Sankey meetings. Neither did they work in the Bedford Street slum mission. God pity them.

At Wanamaker's Sunday School we learned much. I had had no experience in a large city Sunday School. I noted how every teacher was in her place. All the literature was at her hand. All the pupils were in their seats when the bell gave one tap on the minute for opening. There was no delay, no moving about, no hum of voices, no confusion or disorder of any kind. Every teacher had come ahead of the class. Every pupil was greeted with a kind word. Every class was ready for the bell and every officer had everything in readiness and in place. The opening service was brief. A kind, clear, cheery word from the superintendent, a hymn sung with spirit and understanding, a brief, heartsome free prayer for the girls and boys, for the teachers and officers, for the school, its work and influence and for the congregation of which it was a part. Then promptly each teacher was teaching. I was impressed with the orderliness, the tact, the absence of all interference between classes. No teacher was loud to the annoyance of another teacher and class. All spoke in a subdued tone and all pupils were attentive. Promptly on the minute at one tap lessons were closed, offerings were taken, noted down and handed to the collectors. No time was wasted. Then again, one tap, an encouraging word of a minute or two from Mr. Wanamaker, a short, spirited hymn and the Lord's Prayer in unison. With military precision the classes went out in sucession and received the Sunday school papers at the door. A model Sunday School. I learned much from it. It could not have been so good if there had not been a weekly teachers' meeting conducted by the merchant prince. When he had become postmaster general he left Washington every Saturday that he might attend his Sunday School, which he had builded up and which he loved as he loved his wife.

CHAPTER VII

IN PHILADELPHIA SEMINARY
Continued

I BELIEVE it was during my middle seminary year
that Moody and Sankey, then at the beginning of
their wonderful career, came to Philadelphia for a six
weeks' Evangelistic campaign. A tabernacle holding
6,000 had been built within easy walking distance
of the seminary. A choir numbering hundreds, picked
from the best choirs of the city churches, had been
trained and was ready for the inimitable leader, Sankey. For weeks in advance the daily papers had given
liberal space to this campaign, the greatest of its kind
that Philadelphia had ever had.

Well, a number of our students went more or less
frequently. Some never looked in! I went two or more
times every week. I can refer only briefly to the impressions and lessons I carried away from those meetings.*

To that great choir, led by Ira D. Sankey, it was a
treat to listen. The hymns were the so called Gospel
Hymns. While many of the best and most Evangelical
hymns in the English language are found among them,
a large part of them were purely subjective and emotional. When Sankey would sing: "Oh, where is my
wandering boy tonight?" or "What shall the harvest

---

*For a full discussion of Revivals see *Way of Salvation in the
Lutheran Church,* pp. 196-256.

be?" the vast audience was moved and was in a peculiarly receptive mood for Moody's message.

D. L. Moody was, beyond doubt, the greatest, the most Evangelical and, all things considered, the best Evangelist that America ever has had. Even at the day of this writing I hesitate to detract from his great work for the Kingdom of God. He believed with all his heart that the Bible is the inspired Word of God. He preached the sinfulness and the damnableness of sin. He preached the all-sufficient, vicarious atonement. He preached the sovereignty of God and justification by faith. God owned his wonderful work. God gave him souls for his hire. Few preachers will have as many stars in their crown as will Dwight L. Moody.

His preaching was so simple that the wayfaring man, tho a fool, could understand. Short words in short sentences. Clear, crisp, keen, cutting, gripping expressions. He knew how to make it clear and drive it home. He made the hearer feel: "That means me, it fits me, it hits me, it hurts me, Oh, I wish I were a Christian." He was full of illustrations and stories. He knew where and how to use them. He could move and melt the stoniest heart. He could bring tears to the driest eyes and the hardest cheek. He could awaken penitence and enkindle faith. Oh, that we had more Moody-like preachers in our dear Church!

I tried to study Moody and learn from him. I counted from three to eight or even ten stories in every sermon. That was overdone. He appealed too much to the emotions. When handkerchiefs would go to the eyes by the hundreds I would often find mine going up. Then, sometimes I would stop and seriously ask myself: "Gerberding, what are you crying for? Are you weeping over your own sins and sinfulness? Not at all. You are weeping for that poor mother whose heart and life were broken by that wretch of an ingrate son. Is there any real religion, any grace in that?"

Not at all. Yet thousands of Moody's inquirers thought that theirs were saving tears. Moody did not understand the doctrine that grace comes thru the means of grace. Had he understood our precious Lutheran Theology he would have been a still stronger and better Evangelist. But I have every reason to thank God that, while a seminary student, I had such a favorable opportunity to attend the Moody and Sankey meetings and to study the men and their methods. The experience has been a blessing to me all my life. I believe it has made a better Lutheran of me.

There were other valuable privileges that we could enjoy because we were in a great city. Great speakers and lecturers of renown frequently came to Philadelphia. To see them, to hear them, to be instructed, stirred and moved to higher ambitions was certainly a blessed and helpful privilege. To study these great leaders, to get an insight into the personality, the individuality, the secret of strength in each one, all this was an education in the broadest sense. "As iron sharpeneth iron so doth the countenance of a man his friends." Contacts with great men inspire to greatness.

We can give only brief impressions left from these contacts:

Doctor John Lord was probably the greatest lecturer on history and biography of his time. He was giving a series of those brilliant, instructive and edifying lectures that became his monumental work, his fifteen volume *Beacon Lights of History*. To read these lectures is an education. I count this set among the best in my library. To hear so many of them was an inspirational and educational treat. The lecturer himself was a study. A thin, spare body with a head of thin, snow-white, rather long hair, piercing eyes, a thin, unmusical voice with unusual carrying power. Such was the man that rose up to speak to us. His lectures were delivered successively, at the noon hour, in a spacious hall in the heart of the city. Business and professional men and women filled the hall every day. Surely any man who could hold such an audience every noon for several weeks must be extraordinary. He was. I count it among the special blessings of the seminary life that I could sit under those uplifting lectures of Doctor John Lord.

Another stimulating lecturer whom I heard a number of times was John B. Gough. He was the great apostle of total abstinence. I think he was the most dramatic speaker I ever heard. A fine looking man with a winning countenance and a musical voice. Wit and humor and pathos, comedy and tragedy, argument and emotional appeal were all so skilfully blended that he kept his large audiences on a strain of attention. He could tell the story, paint the picture, open floodgates of tears and rouse resolution. He did a world of good, saved thousands from drunkenness, prepared the way for the closing of America's plague spots, the saloons. Gough did me good. He helped me in my preaching. Have often thanked God for him.

To me it seems that in those days there were more great orators in the pulpit and on the platform than there are today. Wonder why?

Once I heard Wendell Phillips. He was perhaps the greatest anti-slavery agitator of his day. An imposing personality, tall of stature, an earnest, appealing countenance. A turbulent, fiery spirit. It was an experience to hear such a man. Tho slavery had been dead for a decade, Phillips had not lost his old time dramatic power. He spoke to us on The Lost Arts. His marshalling of facts and their startling disclosures was thrilling. The memory of that experience is vivid today.

Once only did I hear the great, grave Nestor of American journalists and editors, Horace Greeley. He was better as a writer of editorials than as a platform speaker. His lecture was instructive but not inspiring. It seemed to me to have the undertone of a disappointed man. But I am glad that I heard the great Horace Greeley.

Once only did I hear Henry Ward Beecher. In his time and in his prime he was the prince of American preachers. His personality was imposing. A large, well built man. A voice of rare tone and volume, a speaking eye, a clear diction, precise and exact in his enunciation he was an impressive, a natural, born orator. A highly gifted man. One of America's best products. He did much for America and her people. Again I can say that I am glad that I saw and heard him. When I think of him I cannot repress a feeling of deep regret that this great, gifted man should have become ensnared in the insidious meshes of a false philosophy, that led him to throw away the previous Evangelical Faith of which his father had been such a valiant apostle. Poor Henry Ward. His life went out under a cloud. Such is the way of all rationalism and modernism, however sugar-coated and refined. Let him that thinketh that he standeth take heed lest he fall.

I might mention my hearing of the notorious, shallow, sensational, unreliable T. DeWitt Talmage. I have often pronounced him to have been the most spectacular failure of American preachers. Yet, he too was gifted. He was fundamentally sound in his faith. He wrote and preached much that was good. Still a failure, more's the pity.

During most of my seminary time dear old Father Heyer was our house father. As long as he was able to come down he always sat at the head of the table. His presence and his table talk were a benediction. In my time his poor, battered old body was weakening. Ere long he was confined to his bed. He knew that the end was nigh. He was peaceful and cheerful to the end. Volunteer students took turns in sitting up with the veteran missionary until the wornout frame painlessly yielded up the tenant ripe for the house not made with hands. It is one of my pleasant memories that I took my turn in watching by the dying bed of this rare, ripe old saint and soldier of the cross.

In my time we had an epidemic of smallpox. It occurred shortly before the Christmas holidays. The seminary was quarantined. A number of us were not allowed to go home. We took turns in watching by those who were seriously sick. I spent his last night on earth with one who was in a wild delirium. During the holidays another died also. I shall never forget the short and inexpressibly sad funeral service led by Dr. Mann in the Seminary Chapel. A few fellow students were all the mourners present. But the compassionate Christ was there. To this day some of the soul-comforting words of dear old Dr. Mann are with me.

Early in my Senior year an elderly Lutheran layman, one of those good Samaritans of whom we have all too few, a Mr. Vogel, came into our room. He told us how he and a few others from his congregation had been working in a slum mission on Bedford Street. The neighborhood was often called the Bowery of Philadelphia. He wanted a few students to help him. Roth, Zahn and myself, the three Thielers, volunteered. It fell to my lot to speak in the dingy mission hall every Tuesday evening. It was a new experience. What a place! What a neighborhood! Old and young, white and black and darkskinned southern Europeans were there. At first I did not know it, but I learned later that in those motley groups there were criminals, jailbirds, thugs, drunkards, dope-fiends, bad girls and women and what not. A few Christian workers who conducted a Sunday School in the building were always there. These were always a help and comfort to me. They had charge of the music and helped to keep order.

After earnest prayer I had decided that I would deliver a series of short, plain talks on Luther's Small Catechism. It was one of the most valuable experiences of my life. I certainly did have to learn to simplify. I had to talk as to little children. I had to learn to tell stories. Learned argument would not go. I had to learn to speak to and appeal to the heart. I really had little trouble in keeping order and holding attention. Only a few times did turbulent drunks try to break up the meeting. A policeman was always there, and at such times he came in good stead.

I kept up my work till the end of the school year. I learned to love it more and more. I learned to love many of the poor unfortunates, especially among the young people and children. I cannot boast of any great, visible results. This I leave to the Lord. I did receive some touching letters after I had entered on my work as a pastor. Other students carried the work forward, and from Bedford Street Mission a number of members became active in St. Peter's English Lutheran Church.

My two summer vacations were part of my preparation for the ministry. As I recall, I preached only once during my first year. At college it had been our custom, in the English literature class, to write out, commit and recite orations before the professor and the class. It was understood that there would be no prompting. On the occasion of my last effort I broke down completely and felt disgraced for life. It was a severe but valuable lesson for me. I had been warned by my plain old father that he did not want to make a reader but a preacher out of me. In his own blunt way he used to say: "The apostles were not sent out to read but to preach the Gospel." Repeatedly he impressed it on me that if I should turn out to be a manuscript reader he would always regret every dollar he had put into my education. A Presbyterian minister friend of mine had given me this good advice: "Don't ever start reading your sermon, after writing out a full outline. Write them out in full. Don't memorize them. Make yourself thoroly familiar with the sequence of thought; go over that order of thought frequently in your mind and in your own words. You may take a one-page outline into the pulpit, but not the manuscript. Preach from the outline." I resolved to make this my custom. In after years, as a teacher of Homiletics, I gave my students this same advice, insisting that for ten years they should write out in full one sermon a week and preach as indicated above. In the seminary the members of our class agreed together that all would preach before Doctor Shaeffer without manuscript. Ours was the first and perhaps the last class that ever struck out so bold a venture.

When the Rev. W. K. Frick asked me to preach in his pulpit in St. Paul's Church, Philadelphia, I consented with fear and trembling. I certainly did pray and wrestle over that sermon. The Lord helped me thru. This was the only sermon I had preached in a church before I left for home at the end of my first seminary year. That summer I again had to drive an ice-wagon. It went against the grain, but I did it, rising early and doing it all summer long. My neighbors and former Sunday school companions wanted me to preach in the school house every Sunday evening and promised me the collections. I promised. I worked hard on my sermons. Preaching became more and more easy. How glad I was to get the few dollars handed me after every service. That summer's preaching led to the organization of Mount Zion English Lutheran Church, now one of the strongest Pittsburgh churches. As I remember, I preached in a Lutheran church once only during that summer.

My second summer vacation was different and better. Doctor Passavant was supplying Mount Calvary Church at Chartiers, now called McKees Rocks, on the south side of the Ohio River, three miles below Pittsburgh. He engaged me to assist him during the summer. He was also preaching at Baden, Pa., eighteen miles down the river. He had summoned me from Philadelphia to assist him there during Easter vacation. That was a memorable Holy Week. We had service every night, preaching in turn. The days we spent visiting over the hills, up and down the deep valleys and in the village of Baden. Then and there I learned what true pastoral visiting means. Many poor, churchless people live in the valleys. In practically every house we read the Bible and prayed. The doctor's little heart-to-heart talks were touching and moving. By broken chairs, on broken floors we knelt and prayed. The prayers of the Sainted Doctor Passavant seemed almost inspired. How he poured out his heart before God for the family, for father and mother, for the young people, for the children, for the Church and her special services. I was learning Pastoral Theology. I was learning soul-cure. I was learning what true, pastoral, personal work means. I was learning personal Evangelism. I was helping to do the work of an Evangelist. We were preaching publicly and from house to house. That Holy Week with Doctor Passavant was one of the richest and most blessed weeks of my life. It was there also that I had my first funeral. A beautiful, bright, devoted young girl whom we had visited, died suddenly. As the doctor was away, it fell to me to conduct the funeral. That also was an experience.

When the seminary year closed I became student supply pastor of Mount Calvary. I visited every family. I found that the congregation had been torn by factions before Dr. Passavant had come to the rescue. There was still much bitterness in the discouraged little flock. I reorganized the Sunday School, rallied the young people, secured a cabinet organ and organized a choir. But it was, at best, a torn and discouraging field. Where bitterness and strife are, there the Holy Spirit finds scant room.

As Mount Calvary needed morning service only,

Dr. Passavant encouraged me to work across the river, where I had preached in the school-house during the previous summer. I started regular evening services in the same school-house. They seemed to meet with a welcome response. I began a vigorous campaign to gather funds for an English Lutheran church. I visited every house within a radius of about four miles, talking church and getting subscriptions. Doctor Passavant and my pastor, Dr. Laird, contributed personally. They also helped me to get subscriptions in Pittsburgh. Before I went back to the seminary a lot had been purchased, the contract for a churchly chapel was let, and the corner stone of Mount Zion English Lutheran Church was laid. My second vacation summer had given me a rich store of experience whose value could not be computed.

During the last seminary winter I preached almost every Sunday. I even undertook to preach German. There was a vacant German church, not far away, in New Jersey, that wanted supplies. A few of us formed a sort of ring and made ourselves responsible for the supply. As the stipulated pay left the preacher a few dollars over expenses, I fear that our undertaking was partly for filthy lucre's sake. This was not right.

With our interesting senior course, our work in the Bedford Street Mission, the trying to take in as many of our last-chance city advantages, our last winter in school slipped rapidly away. After the holidays I received a call to Mount Calvary, where Doctor Passavant wanted me. The salary offered was four hundred dollars and parsonage. The after-war high prices made living expensive. With the stipulation that I might work across the river, where Mount Zion Chapel was in the building, I accepted the call.

As I look back upon my course in the Philadelphia Seminary, these reflections come to my mind:

We had a scholarly faculty. Every one of our professors was a Christian gentleman. All were sound in the faith. All were dissatisfied with the loose Lutheranism that had spread in the parts of the General Synod. All had hailed with hope and gladness the organization of the General Council. All had written in defense of a historic and confessional Lutheranism. They were zealous in furthering the purpose for which the Philadelphia Seminary had been founded.

There were serious handicaps. The seminary was poor. Salaries were small. Three professors had duties enough outside of the seminary to keep a strong, diligent and zealous man busy. They could not do such work in their class-rooms as full-time men might have done.

Then there was the language handicap. In both the Pennsylvania and the New York Ministerium the large majority of congregations required German preaching. It was taken for granted and expected that the Philadelphia Seminary would provide preachers proficient in the German language. Therefore, as noted above, lectures had to be given in both German and English. This made hard work for the professors and was a serious drawback to the students. In both the Old and New Testaments the lectures were bi-lingual. A poor makeshift.

The courses were those of the old-fashioned European curricula. The conditions and needs of America were not considered. It had not dawned on Lutheran theologians that America's official, governmental, school, newspaper and commercial language was English, all English. Our theologians had not yet grasped either the fact or the tremendous significance of the fact that America had a *Zeitgeist*, a spirit of the times, all its own. It was not realized as it should have been that the Lutheran Church must understand and without compromise of Lutheran principles, must fit itself into, this new situation, influence the prevailing spirit of the land and time and change it for the better. That the Lutheran Church has a great, a grand, a peculiar mission in and for America was scarcely dreamed of. Our courses of study did not take this in.

In our Biblical Exegesis, for example, we were always given the true sense of each passage, but we were not shown how some dangerous sects and cults pervert some of these passages. We were given the true principles of interpretation, but we were not shown how these principles are again and again perverted to the injury and ruin of souls. In fact, the conviction abides with me to this day that, in our seminaries, the far-reaching importance of correct Hermeneutics is not realized. Its history and theory are given. Its practical application to the multiform false teaching of the day is scarcely mentioned. The danger of a false Hermeneutics is not shown as it should be. I recall one instance when Doctor Krauth did stress this point to my life-long benefit. The doctor was thoroly at home in Calvinistic theology. On this occasion he showed us that when a good, clear Calvinist argues against a Unitarian he uses the exact principles of our Lutheran Hermeneutics. But when that same Calvinist argues against the Lutheran teaching on the Sacraments, he abandons his former hermeneutical principles and uses the loose principles that Unitarians use. It was a memorable and helpful hour to me. It seems to me that, in all theological controversies, an agreement on hermeneutical principles ought to be insisted on first of all. And it further seems to me that every seminary course in Hermeneutics ought to point out clearly how this and that and the other dangerous sect, cult and heresy subverts the sound principles of interpretation.

In Church History we got little or nothing on the story, the life or the spirit of the great Reformed Denominations in America and of their influence on American life and character. This omission was a serious loss to us.

Another course that it seems to me was not at all utilized, exploited and fructified as it should have been is Symbolics, or the study of the various church divisions and their confessions and teachings. No doubt what we got as to the history and teachings of the great historic churches was all correct and good. But, was its presentation practical?

The seminary was supposed to make us fit to become useful and successful ministers of our Church in America. That's what we had come there for. We wanted to know what dangers and difficulties would confront us and how we might successfully meet and overcome them. Symbolics should have done much to make us fit. Did it? How we toiled over the errors of Rome, their origin, growth and tendency. Every intelligent minister ought to know and understand all this. But when we look at the young pastor in his parish, bewildered, confused and sometimes scared at the currents, the influences, the wild spirits that surge around him, will his Seminary Symbolics help him out? In how many parishes is the pastor in danger of losing his members to the Roman Catholics?

And how we had to dig thru pages and chapters of

ancient information on the fossilized Greek Catholic Church. But what hardworking and perplexed pastor has ever had to lose sleep over his losses to the Greek Church?

But propagandists, skilful, sneaking, persuasive and plausible enough to deceive the very elect, these are busy all over the land. In city, in village, in the open and lonely country these apostles of soul-destroying errors are present with oily tongues, with deceiving tracts and pictures perverting our weak Lutherans.

How much did our course in Symbolics help us to meet the pernicious and endangering work of the emissaries of Christian Science, of Seventh Day Adventists, of Russellites, of Spiritualists, of Mormons, of Holiness and Immersionist sects, of wild Revivalists of every grade and hue? Ought not every student know these dangers, to be fortified against them and to know the best and most effective literature which will help him over hard places? Is not a seminary efficient and helpful in proportion as it equips its graduates to know, to meet and to overcome these ubiquitous dangers to American church life? Of the history, theory and present status of Home, Inner and Foreign Missions we got little or nothing.

And ought not every student to be given a clear understanding of the basic principles of general Psychology, of crowd and mob Psychology, of materialistic, deterministic, spiritualistic Psychology and all its other wild aberrations? These the young pastor will meet. These are influencing his people. Can he help them? In Catechist and Sunday School work we got no Child Psychology and didn't learn how to teach, to catechise or to test for Confirmation.

The same is true of Sociology in all its variations.

Our seminary grads ought to know them and how to utilize them. And so they ought to know present day variations and tendencies in Philosophy. These reflections are not set down here to find fault with my venerable Alma Mater. She has improved wonderfully in my day. She will improve along all practical and helpful lines more and more. So will all our seminaries. And in proportion will the Lutheran Church influence and win America.

Before I close this seminary chapter I want to make a postscript suggestion:

I believe our faculty made a mistake in the arrangement of its schedule. To some of the major subjects, which required one hundred and fifty hours or more, one or two hours a week were given, and thus the subjects were carried thru three years. I am convinced that this was a pedagogical mistake. In every way it is better to have one hour a day until the course is finished. This begets and keeps up a sustained interest. It would be better if every course were thus carried thru successively. Other things being equal, the student would know his subject better than if he had the old hop, skip and jump method.

CHAPTER VIII

ENTERING UPON THE GREAT LIFE WORK

MY school days were over. I had had a long, hard struggle to get my fragmentary education. All along the way I had felt the pinch of poverty. I was not able to dress like my fellow students. I could not indulge in the pleasures and luxuries that so many enjoyed.

I might have had an easier time. I might have applied for beneficiary aid. I never did. Doctor Passavant saw the evils in the system. He did not encourage it. I never received a dollar of such aid. I was of such an independent spirit that I preferred to skimp and to endure hardness. It was good for me to bear the yoke in my youth. I learned lessons that came in good stead in after life. True, it did gall me often to see beneficiary students well dressed and indulging in all sorts of amusements. Some of them strutted in silk hats and in kid gloves and carried goldheaded canes. I recall not one of this class who attained eminence in the Ministry.*

Now I was ready for the great enterprise. It was with mingled feelings of reminiscence and anticipation that I traveled toward Pittsburgh. I had accepted my first call. My stipulated salary was to be four hundred and house. From mission work at Mount Zion I expected and soon did realize two hundred more. I did

---

*For further views of mine on Beneficiary Education see *Problems and Possibilities,* pp. 129 and 130.

not apply for home mission aid for the same reasons that had kept me from getting student aid. My hopes were high, and my ambition to make my work go was great. It was a good time to enter on my life-work. Ours was the Centennial Class.

After the war's end and after the botched and blundering reconstruction period; after our nation had withstood and emerged from the panic of seventy-three, the whole country was ready for a great forward move. There came a period of growth and prosperity. Immigration, largely Lutheran, increased with leaps and bounds. Big business grew with big undertakings. Capitalistic combinations and great trusts began to be formed. Labor was plentiful and laborers were in demand. Observing men among the toilers began to see more and more clearly that they were not getting a fair share of the abounding prosperity. Discontent was brewing. Agitators were spreading and deepening the discontent. There was just cause. Labor was not getting its fair share. In the great mills and factories toil was strenuous and hours were long. No wonder that trade and labor unions sprang into being, multiplied and grew like mushrooms. Strikes were started. These were often promoted and engineered by conscienceless, unscrupulous and selfish leaders. They hurt the cause of labor. My sympathies always have been and are today with honest labor. I myself had known the weariness and the bitterness of overwork and of unrequited toil. The Church should ever have a sympathizing heart and a helping hand for all who labor and are heavy laden.

In those stirring years when I entered on my life-work our Lutheran Church numbered less than half a million communicants. Lutheran immigrants were pouring in on our shores by the hundred thousand a year. The general bodies in the Lutheran Church felt the pressure, the need and the challenge for more aggressive home mission work. Doctor Passavant was making the Pittsburgh Synod the Missionary Synod. From that synod the Canada Synod, the Minnesota Synod and the Texas Synod were started. From Passavant and his synod efficient help went out to Swedes and Norwegians in the great West. The Lutheran giant was rubbing his eyes and getting awake. Controversy and rivalry were all too rife between the Lutheran bodies. It was a seething, stirring time. It stirred my restless spirit. I was ready for the fray.

The day came when I was to be examined for ordination. The examining committee met the applicants in Greenville, Pa. We had a long, strained session with the committee. I was largely the cause of it all. The question as to the Antichrist came up. In my usual frank, blunt way I told the committee that I did not believe that the pope was the Antichrist. Some of the examiners expressed amazement and asked me to explain. As I recall it today I said something like this: The popes have not all been bad or anti-Christian men. Some had done great good in their day. Their church confessed the three Ecumenical Creeds. The Antichrist cannot confess them but must and does deny them.*

I worried the poor committee. They had to do without supper. They ordained me with my heresy!

I had been busy for some weeks in my work. My father had given me a rundown horse—the best he had. I managed to buy a second hand saddle, harness

---

*For my present conviction on Antichrist, see *Lutheran Fundamentals,* p. 284 ff.

and buggy. I visited the whole countryside round about Mount Calvary. I found the lower side thickly settled by Roman Catholics. They had a bi-lingual church there. On the upper side, the hill farms were largely occupied by Presbyterians and United Presbyterians. Each denomination had a strong congregation. They were a fine, friendly people and good neighbors. On my rounds of visitation they wanted me to call on them also. During my vacation work here, under Dr. Passavant, as his custom was, before Communion, he would announce that on a certain day he would visit in a certain school district and preach in the school-house in the evening. He called on Presbyterians also. I went with him and learned how to do it. These visits were neighborly and there was never a hint of proselyting. The schoolhouses were full of Presbyterians when he preached in them. I was again enjoying a valuable pastoral clinic. Would that all theological students might have like experiences under a like exemplary shepherd of souls.

After I had taken charge of the work I tried to follow Passavant's methods. Wherever possible I did it all my life.

As already intimated, it was a discouraging field. The unhappy controversy between the General Synod and the General Council had alienated some of the best families from our Church, which was weak enough at best. With my emotional temperament, my heart was largely drawn to the General Synod. In my impulsive and inexperienced young heart I had a feeling that that oldest general Lutheran body was more American and more progressive than the new mixed body. I had been instructed and confirmed in the General Synod. The General Council seemed strange to me. Naturally and temperamentally my sympathies inclined to the old and practically all-English body.

But I had come under the magnetic, instructive and persuasive influence of Dr. Passavant. Dr. Jacobs had helped me at Thiel Hall. Dr. Muhlenberg's warm teaching had drawn me, and against my inclinations and feelings, the Philadelphia Seminary had shown and convinced me that confessional and historic Lutheranism is the teaching of Apostolic truth. I entered the ministry, a Lutheran from conviction. The controversies had often been personal and bitter. Much of the preaching had been polemical. This had not been conducive to a healthy spiritual life. Many were the alienations from the Lutheran Church. Hurtful were the misunderstandings and misrepresentations in and by outsiders. The wreckage was sad. I felt it keenly in my hard first field. Controversy is a calamity. I had my share of interesting experiences.

One of my careless, indifferent members had married an Irish Catholic. He was easy-going and not very devout. He took to drink, and, as is so often the case, it mastered him and cut him down in the midst of his days. His wife had remained in her church. She had had all her children baptized as Lutherans. When her husband died she called on me to conduct the funeral. It was a difficult and delicate situation. I was young and new. What should I say? I prayed earnestly and studied deeply. The big house was crowded with Catholics. I preached on the text: "It is appointed unto man once to die, after that cometh the judgment." I never had more attentive hearers. I felt that they were curious and critical. I began by assuring them that these services were not for the dead but for the living, that neither I nor his friends, nor any church could do anything more for or against the dead. He had gone to his last account and the Judge of all the Earth would do right. Then I preached on death, judgment and the supreme importance of preparation and what right preparation means. The good Lord helped me thru, as He has always done.

There was an amusing sequel that made a good class-room story for me. I was driving up the road, a day or two after the funeral. An Irish Catholic neighbor met me and hailed me: "Well, sir," he said, "That was a great funeral you preached down at Jimmy's." I didn't know what to say, so I said: "Well, I hope it will do some good." He hesitated, looked perplexed, brightened up and said, "Indade, n'I hope it will do my wife good!"

Another experience: My first wedding after my ordination was that of one of my finest church girls. For some time she had been coming to church with a rather stiff, starched up stranger. When she introduced me to him I did not like his looks. I met him a number of times. He was affable, self-important and it seemed to me cautious and secretive. I spoke frankly about him to the young lady. She assured me that he was all right in every way. So I married them.

After the marriage I quizzed him more closely about his religious convictions and affiliations. He told me in an offhand way that he was a Spiritualist. My heart sank within me. To make a long story short: In about a year he left his wife and departed for parts unknown. It was discovered that he had forged his employer's name and was fleeing from justice! What an illustration of the text: "If they hear not Moses and the Prophets, neither will they be persuaded tho one rose from the dead." Here was a man who firmly believed that he had conversed with the dead. Did it make a good, other-wordly man of him? Better hear and heed Moses and the Prophets.

While thus working and preaching at Mount Calvary, I was also working and preaching at Mount Zion, across the river. The new church had been enclosed. Home-made temporary chancel-furniture and home-made plank benches had been put in. There I preached on Sunday evenings to good and growing audiences. I saw more and more clearly that not only was there a ripe field here, but there were several contiguous points where work ought to be started.

Meantime, thru academy and college and seminary years and now, thru my initial pastoral months, I had kept on courting the little, modest Methodist girl, Anna Elizabeth Danver, whom I had first met at Gourley's Academy. She was of Irish and Colonial English descent. May I be pardoned for remarking that I believe that my children got much of their wit and humor and smartness from their Irish mother? She had a clear mind, a love for books and education. She had prepared herself to become a school teacher and had taught for a number of years until I butted in and changed her occupation. She had read up on the Lutheran Church and her teaching. I had given her much private instruction. At my first communion in Mount Zion I had confirmed her.

And now, at long last, we were getting ready to be married. Neither of us had any money to signify. She had helped to support her father's family. Doctor Passavant loaned me seventy-five dollars towards furnishing the parsonage at Mount Calvary. With what little my betrothed and I could scrape together, we feathered our nest.

On Reformation Day, 1876, we were married by Doctors Laird and Passavant in Mount Zion Church. Then came the wedding trip. There were no automobiles. The height of style was a two-horse carriage with the driver on top. During the ceremony the bride had been perfectly calm, dignified and was ready to receive the congratulations. The bridegroom was nervous, excited, broke away from the congratulations and entered the carriage before the bride was thru; and called to her to come on in! Once in the carriage and started, he took off his kid gloves and stove-pipe hat and never wore them again. It was a bright, beautiful autumn day. The drive took us along the winding, picturesque Perrysville plank road, around Montgomery's Hill, where one could get an entrancing view of the two cities, the Allegheny and Ohio rivers and Washington Heights on the other side. We passed thru Allegheny City and its spacious parks, crossed the Allegheny River on the St. Clair Street bridge, down thru the narrow, crowded cobblestone streets and crossed the Monongahela on the Point Bridge. Then down thru the great fire-spitting iron mills, for which Pittsburgh was famous. From the mill district we emerged onto the River Road along the beautiful Ohio, crosesd Chartiers Creek and up the high hill to the parsonage. We had had a most delightful, leisurely wedding trip of ten miles. We had paid toll four times. Night was falling when the carriage unloaded us at the parsonage.

We were warmly welcomed by a group of good women who escorted us into our brightly lighted home.

A sumptuous supper was steaming on the table, to which we did full justice after our long ride.

It was presidential election year. A hot political campaign was at its height. A Republican club was pulling off a meeting in the borough, half a mile below the parsonage. I had become acquainted with the captain of the club. He knew that this was my wedding night. He cut his meeting short, instructed his club that they would now march up to the Lutheran Parsonage and serenade the young preacher and his bride. He gave strict orders that there should be no rowdyism and no expecting of a treat. Headed by a fife and drum corps, they marched up the hill, halted before the house and played a number of martial airs. Then they gave three rousing cheers for their candidates, in which I joined lustily, and followed with three more for the bride and groom. While they were forming to steal silently away I came out with a box of cigars which I had provided. This evoked three further cheers. We had a patriotic beginning of our home life. After our kind guests had retired we had our first family worship. With changes and variations this has been kept up these fifty years.

The location of our parsonage was beautiful for situation. It stood on a high hill, overlooking other hills from one side, a steep declivity down to beautifully clear, winding Chartiers Creek on the other side and an expansive view of the Ohio River, of the bluff on the other side clear up to Mount Zion, my other newly built church. Up the Ohio we could see the smoke and fire-emitting mills of my native city, called Iron City and Smoky City. At night time the view was fascinating and entrancing. In all my active ministry, whether preaching or teaching, I have never lived in so romantic and scenic a home.

As already intimated, the home was simply and rather scantily furnished. Some might think that this was a sad misfortune. I believe it was a blessing. I believe it is a blessing for any young couple to begin with the most necessary furniture and furnishings, just enough to make them comfortable. I believe that it is a privilege and a joy to gradually build up and improve the home. To begin on a plain, small scale, to add a new comfort, a new luxury, piece by piece as ability comes to pay cash for it, to see the equipment growing, the comforts increasing, the luxuries gradually coming, this is home building. This is happiness long drawn out. Every new and better kitchen commodity, every new and better picture, every new doily or spread, every new curtain or rug, every new rocker is a new joy, a new source of abiding happiness. How much better than to "Let Hartman Feather the Nest" with cheaply made and painted over stuff —and all on tick!

I recall a case: A young pastor, fresh from the seminary, had courted and won the daughter of a rich man. The father seemed to be very proud that his daughter was going to marry a minister. He purchased a lot on a fine street, planned a house with the help of his daughter, had it built and finished in the best of style, and then furnished it completely and luxuriantly from attic to basement. That nest surely was well made and finely feathered. When I visited the newly weds they took great pleasure in showing me thru their palatial home.

I walked away with some serious reflections. I could not help but think: You poor, young, mistaken mortals, what you are going to miss! All the length-ened pleasure of building up a home will not be yours. Instead of your home becoming more comfortable and more beautiful every year, your furniture will all grow old at once. From year to year the brightness of the beauty will fade. You may tire of the same-ness. How much better, how much happier the grad-ual builders-up of home comforts and home luxuries. Some of this mother-wit wisdom I have tried to teach to my seminary boys. Many of the scamps laugh at the old fashioned simplicity. Oh, well! *So geht's!*

I go back to our plain, simple, happy home. Our contentment could not fence out disappointment. Our home-made honey-moon had hardly been fairly started when the bride groom took sick. It was a peculiar sick-feeling. Breaking out and fever came. A doctor was sent for. He startled us by calmly an-nouncing: "You have varioloid, which is nothing less than a mild form of small pox!"

Of course we were quarantined. The bride had to turn nurse. I feared that she might not be equal to the task. She proved to be one hundred per cent. The most uncomfortable feature of our affliction was that everybody was afraid of us. Inquiries were made and comforts were left at the front gate. Then hasty retreats.

Dear old Doctor Passavant learned of our afflic-tion. One morning an express-man left a box filled with good things. Among them was a package of extra good cigars—such as I was not used to, and, best of all, a short letter of sympathy and encourage-ment such as he alone could write. I have it yet. Yes, God is good. In a few weeks I was out again and ready for more and better work.

Chapter IX

WORK EXPANDING

MOUNT ZION was my new mission. A mission without mission support. As a baby it needed much attention. To my great disappointment an opposition mission was started on the other side of the hill, on what used to be the same farm on which we had built. The aggressive denomination that started this move had a right to do so. But it did not strike me as kind and neighborly. My indignation, doubtless, was not all righteous. It started a bad habit with me. My preaching became more polemic. This was wrong. It did not do me any good, tho it did gratify the old Adam in me. Thru the influence of Dr. Passavant and others I came to see my wrong and mended my ways. I do not believe that polemical preaching ever did build up the spiritual life of a congregation. It took me a long time to learn to preach the truth in love. I pray the Lord not to remember the sins of my youth, nor my many transgressions. My work began to do better, and the growth in spiritual life and health as well as in numbers increased more and more. I also found more joy in preaching.

A request came to me to supply two mission points, Springdale and Natrona, about twenty miles from our parsonage, on alternate Sunday afternoons. The good train service on the West Penn. Railroad made it possible for me to do so and get back to preach at

Mount Zion in the evening. Conducting a Sunday School, teaching a class and preaching three times a Sunday did not hurt me a bit. I really did it during most of my ministerial life. I have often pitied those poor weaklings who think that such service would kill them. I have known some, who, when considering a call, would dicker and bargain for as few services as possible and would persuade the parish to let them have the fifth Sunday free when there were five Sundays in the month! God pity their laziness. They did not make the Lutheran Church a power for good in their communities. They made an easy living, but a poor, barren, spiritual life.

My pay for the afternoon services, as I recall, was five dollars a Sunday. This left me about four dollars above expenses. This pin money came in very good to me. But I did not feel right about these services. I felt that absentee preaching could not build up strong congregations. I felt that such supply preaching was making a convenience of the congregations. I know that is often done by preachers and professors. I know that it helps to increase the income. But does it really give to the congregations what they need to make them grow as they should? I felt that it did not. So I soon gave up this supply work.

About a year after our marriage there came into our home a dear little baby girl. She is now the wife of the Rev. J. R. E. Hunt of Chicago. She is active and helpful in all Lutheran woman's work in the great city. If her oldest daughter had married young I might now be a great grandfather.

Mount Calvary congregation was still discouraging. There did not seem to be a hopeful outlook. I thought I did my best in the pulpit and from house to house. True, I gained some good converts. I often think of this experience: Before my time a good woman had had a quarrel with another woman in the church. Like many others, she felt that she had not been treated right, blamed it on the church and left. For a number of years she never entered the church. I did my best to win her back. She was kind to me, but said she could not come back. Then God called a halt. He laid His hand heavily on the home of a next-door close relative. There soon came a day when there was a coffin in the house and crepe on the door. I had ministered attentively during the sickness. The sufferer had professed repentance for sin and faith in Christ. At the funeral a number of like-minded friends of the alienated woman were present. I tried to magnify the grace of God and the Church of Christ, which offers and mediates that grace. That dying and funeral made a deep impression. The woman in question came back into the church. She soon brought her husband and a number of kindred with her. The grace of God was magnified. I was happy.

I have often told this story: One day when I was visiting the aforesaid woman she said something like this: "Pastor, you don't know how different my life is since I went back to church. During those years when I didn't go, life was very dull to me. I had to work hard every day, was tired every night, and Sunday was the longest, the dullest and the dreariest day in the week. I saw my neighbors go to church while I was bitter and unhappy. But it is all so different since I've gone back. I work as hard as ever. But I now count the days till Sunday comes, when I can go to church again. Monday I go to work again, but I have the sermon to think about, and I feel like taking everybody with me to church." She had experienced the truth of Christ's words: "Blessed are they that hear the Word of God and keep it."

Here is an opposite experience. A rich old neighbor took sick. I had visited him before, and he had frankly told me that he had no use for preachers or churches. When his last sickness came I sent a deacon neighbor to ask him whether a visit from the minister would be welcome. No, he didn't need a preacher. He gradually weakened. On his last night a niece sat by his bed-side. She saw the change coming. She whispered into his ear: "Uncle, do you know that you are dying?" "D—n the difference," he said and died. "Died Abner as the fool dieth."

And still another: A number of times I had visited a poor, forlorn, ignorant widow with a house full of children. She had been a Kentucky mountaineer and had somehow drifted into a shanty in our neighborhood. She was a poor, ignorant heathen. All she knew of religion was that she had once or twice attended a camp meeting in the Kentucky mountains. I read the Word to her, tried to show her what it meant for her, kneeled down and prayed with her. I could not get her to come to church. When I called at another time the house was vacant. Her neighbors did not know whither she had gone. They didn't care. They were glad. For over a year I heard nothing of her. Then, on a raw, blustering evening there was a knock at my door. A frightened, half grown boy was at the door. He wouldn't come in. His mother had sent for me. She had been sick for some time and was worse. Would I come?

It didn't take me long to saddle my "Dolly" and ride away into the night. Several miles away in an almost bare shack I found my erstwhile Kentucky mountain woman. She was lying on a trundle-bed, with scant bedding, coughing away her life in the last stages of consumption. She seemed glad to see me. I spoke to her kindly of her suffering. I read and prayed with her. She seemed comforted. I asked her whether she realized that she was dying. She nodded assent. I asked her why she wanted me. She said she wanted me to help her die. Then she said: "Do you ever sprinkle anybody?" I said, "You mean, do I baptize?" Then I tried to show her as simply and briefly as I could what Baptism means and how it could help her. She must feel that she is a sinner, be sorry for her sin, confess it and see in Jesus her Savior from sin. The poor, weak, dying woman did not want to confess her sinfulness or her sin. She had had no chance, she had not been as bad as some church people. Couldn't I talk to her about heaven? I said, yes, but we had better talk about being prepared for heaven. I spent the night with the poor soul. As the dawn was stealing into the window I kneeled again and then baptized her in the name of the Father and of the Son and of the Holy Ghost. She died that day.

How often have I thought of that poor, neglected soul. Oh, how she had been sinned against. I am glad that at long last our good Lutheran women are taking our teaching Gospel to the poor mountaineers of the South. Let us all pray for and help them.

About six or eight miles west of Mount Zion Church, the Rev. John Muehlheuser was serving the so-called Brants German Lutheran Church. He was an earnest Lutheran and a faithful *seelsorger*. He was a fine scholar, a graduate of a German university. I came to love him as a brother. In his pedestrian visitations he came across a vacant frame church building with a briar-covered graveyard. On some of the moss-grown grave stones he found a number of German names. This induced him to make research among the neighbors. He found an aged German Lutheran who informed him that the old church had been Lutheran. He had been a trustee of the old St. John's Lutheran Church. Among his old papers he found the original charter, fragile and yellowed with age. This was a precious find for Muehlheuser. Thru further investigation he found that the church which had been chartered in 1829 had been served, in short pastorates, by some doubtful characters. For ten years before 1850 it had been vacant. Then the Rev. Mr. Henry Reck, a fellow helper of Dr. Passavant, had reorganized. Again, from 1866 to 1878, all records disappeared, and there was no pastor. During all these sad years, the Cumberland Presbyterians, then active in those parts, held frequent services in the building, and it had become widely known as the Cumberland Church. The Lutherans had never sold, but simply abandoned the property.

Muehlheuser gathered together a few remnants, reorganized a temporary congregation, had the church cleaned and mowed the graveyard, painted a sign, "St. John's English Lutheran Church" on the building. As he did not pretend to preach English, he urged me strongly to take charge and serve St. John's, Pine Creek, in connection with Mount Zion.

I consulted Dr. Passavant, and he also urged me to go and take regular charge. So I notified the mission committee that I could no longer supply Springdale and Natrona. I spent several weeks in a thoro canvass and visitation of the Pine Creek region. I found much carelessness, worldliness and heathenism. The Cumberlanders had also departed from the region. They had not done any real solid and constructive work. The Lutherans were a memory that was not too savory. I saw it would mean slow, discouraging and persistent, hard work to build up a good, influential church.

I had found a few good families and individuals who rejoiced in the prospect of again having a church. With these as a nucleus I completed the organization which elected a church council and adopted a constitution. There had been no congregation to issue a regular call to me. I had to call and gather them and take charge as their pastor. A subscription paper was passed around and several hundred were subscribed toward my salary. A Sunday School was not organized until I could find and partially instruct some teachers. I preached every Sunday afternoon.

It was a long, hard drive of about fifteen miles from the parsonage. After my morning service I swallowed a hasty bite, hitched up my faithful, fast Dolly and was off, up the river road, thru the mills of Saw Mill Run, across the Monongahela, over the narrow cobble-streets of Pittsburgh, across another bridge over the Allegheny River, thru Allegheny City, out to Butchers Run plank road, past Mount Zion Church and on out the Perrysville Road, thru the covered tool-house, round the horse-shoe bend, thru the little town of Perrysville and on to the little white church on the hill. At the foot of the hill, at a road house, I had my horse fed during service so as to be ready to hurry back for evening service at Mount Zion.

On wintry days the drive was specially hard. I had neither fur coat nor fur lap robe. I recall how I was driving out one bitterly cold afternoon to a Christmas eve service at St. John's, Pine Creek. At the Allegheny market I stopped at a coffee house conducted by several good W. C. T. U. women. After a cup of their good, hot coffee, I told the head woman where I was going and complained of the biting cold. She looked at me and said: "Yes, but the one sweet thought of the Day, that ought to keep your heart warm." "A word in season, how good it is." I had my Christmas sermon. I was reproved for complaining, and I was cheered. I did drive out thru the cold with a warmer heart.

As Pine Creek was a hard field, I knew that it required hard work. For weeks at a time I was at home very little. I felt that these people had been left without spiritual food or care. They had been sinned against. They had been practically abandoned. They felt that the Church had not treated them right. No wonder that so many of them were hard to reach. I often thought of a remark that Doctor Laird once dropped at a pastors' meeting: "I would rather preach the Gospel to a people who had never heard it than to a people who had been spoilt under it." This truth will bear many applications. There are barren districts beside those that have been burned over by wild revivalism.

To my great grief I found that two tavern keepers and their families were on the list of those who wanted a Lutheran church. From boyhood up I had had an abhorrence for drunkards and for the saloon that makes them. One of our nearest neighbors was a drunkard. His boys were my schoolmates. His family

was terribly afraid of him. They were poor. All but
he were hard working. One day he ran out of liquor.
After storming about and terrifying his family, he
went out to a woods and hanged himself. I stayed
over night with a boy friend. We slept together in
an attic bed. I noticed that he was restless and would
sit up and listen. I asked why. He said he was afraid
that his Dad would come home drunk and perhaps
beat both him and me. I slipped out of that house
early. When I was grown up I was walking out from
the city on a moonlight night. I overtook a young
man of my neighborhood. I noticed that he was under the influence of liquor, but not too drunk to walk.
I talked kindly to him and warned him of his danger.
He listened in silence. Then he stopped, turned on
me and said: "Henry, do you know who you are talking to? You think you are talking to a man. I'm not
a man, I'm not a master of myself, I'm a beast. You
might as well let me alone." In a few years he had
drunk himself to death. When I was driving a milk-
wagon I found that many milkmen were drunkards.
They would eat at free lunch counters and then drink
themselves drunk. Many times did I see their poor
horses shivering at the hitching posts, and passing
by several hours later, they shivered there still. Oft
in the night time they would whip the horses home
on a gallop. I knew of cases where a whole family
would be driven out into a winter night by a brutal
drunken father. When I first started to preach I won
the wife of one of these drunken milkmen for my
church. I visited that poor home frequently and tried
to win the man from his cups. He generally had his
jug beside him. Once he offered me a drink. I refused
and warned him. He took up the jug and said: "I

know it is driving me to hell, but here goes." I also used to visit a home where the wife and mother was a drunkard. She sent her poorly clothed children to our Sunday School and would sometimes come to church. As a rule, every time she went to town she would get drunk.

I once saw her sitting on a fire-plug with a crowd of grown boys around her, jeering, mocking and insulting her. How often I warned her and prayed with her. She would freely confess her sin and promise to reform. But the demon had her in his grip. One Sunday morning she was found frozen dead in a snow-drift near my church. I had frequently heard John B. Gough. I had read "Ten Nights in a Bar-Room." I hated the saloon. No good ever came out of it. It was the breeding place of corruption, vice and crime. It murdered body and soul. I thanked God when the saloon was constitutionally abolished. Those who agitate for light wine and beer are agitating to bring back the open saloon. It is a disgrace for any church body to vote in favor of the wets.

I was not a fanatic. I agreed heartily with my church when she refused to make that a sin which God had not made a sin. There is no sin in a glass of wine or beer. But there may be danger in it. And because of the evident danger and the untold wretchedness, misery and life-long martyrdoms resulting from the danger, my country has a right to forbid its making and drinking. And when my country so decrees, I am not a loyal American if I break the law and encourage others to do so. It is no sin to do without drink. As the law was made for the weak, I am in harmony with Paul's great law of love, when, for their sake I give up what I might otherwise have a right to enjoy. I give up my liberty when to use it might be a cause of offense to the weakest for whom Christ died. For myself I hope the Eighteenth Amendment will never be modified but will be more and more strictly enforced.

The two tavern-bar-rooms had made their marks on the community. Their presence made harder work for St. John's. But with continuous house-to-house work, my audiences increased. The church gradually regained her standing in the community and became more and more a force for good. I look back with pleasure today on some of the converts that were made. I think of a layman, Thomas Keown, who became a recognized leader among the laymen of the Pittsburgh Synod. In later years I had the pleasure of instructing one of the sons of St. John's, Walter Winner, in the Chicago Seminary. My labor was not all in vain. St. John's is now a self-sustaining church, with a pastor all its own. A new church has been built, and a fine parsonage on Perry Avenue is the home of the pastor. We should never despise the day of small things.

As the work at St. John's grew and the work at Mount Zion expanded and I had my eye on other places where work should be begun, I felt more and more that I should resign Mount Calvary. I did not want to leave this old, historic church to an uncertain vacancy. After consulting with my church council I got them to see that there was more than enough work for one man on the other side of the river. What the council dreaded was a vacancy. I told them that I knew a good, saintly old pastor, who had a helpful family, who wanted a parish of only one congregation. They requested that I have him come and preach.

I did so, and the Rev. A. N. Bartholomew came and preached. He made a good impression. I resigned in his favor. He was elected and called. He accepted and did a good work at Mount Calvary. He was ably assisted by his friendly wife and his two gifted, musical daughters.

I moved to the other side. It was at a considerable financial sacrifice. It was not without a heartache that we bade farewell to our fine parsonage. We now had to rent a small house and begin anew. We were quite poor again. I had learned to do without from childhood up. It was a good thing that I had not married a girl brought up in luxury. My little wife knew how to skimp. She was scrupulously neat and clean about her person and her house. She could make a little go far. We did frequent the five and ten cent stores, some second-hand and so-called "Cheap John" stores. Dr. Passavant had advised me to buy soup-bones and have my wife make nourishing soup. She made it, and we all enjoyed it and prospered on it. A man is rich in proportion to the things he can do without. We should worry!

We were no sooner settled in our rented quarters than I began to plan for a parsonage. My little flock was made up of poor people. As usual, I consulted Dr. Passavant. He encouraged me, wrote out a sub- scription blank, gave me the first subscription and gave me a list of people whom I should see. I went vigorously to work and soon had several hundred dol- lars. I got more names from Dr. Belfour, then pastor of the church in which I had been confirmed. I got the brick and stone donated, borrowed a team, a plow and scoop and did much of the work of digging out and scooping out the basement. In between I was out

96

soliciting money and free labor. Before many months we moved into a small parsonage on the church lot.

Our neighborhood was building up, and there certainly was need of an English Lutheran church. But again I learned more and more that a large proportion of the people had been spoilt under the rationalistic preaching of the Free Protestant churches in Allegheny, sometimes called "the beer churches." All this made my work harder. I gathered all sorts and conditions of people into my mission. Some proved to be unprepared and unfit. They made me trouble and some left the church and went back to the world where their heart had been all along. Much of my trouble was my own fault. In my zeal I was too eager for members and did not do enough preparatory instructing. I also, without proselyting, won some fine people from Methodist, Baptist and Presbyterian families.

Our Sunday School grew rapidly and was a great joy to me. I found some unusually fine young people who made good teachers and workers.

I had some rich experiences: In my inexperienced church council, two deacons had a bitter quarrel. I tried my best to get them reconciled. The better man of the two said: "Yes, I am ready to make up as soon as he confesses his wrong and asks my pardon. That's what God does with us. He doesn't forgive us till we repent and confess." Well, the old deacon had the young preacher fast. I could only go home and think and pray. As far as he went the old deacon was right. But he didn't go far enough. As is so mischievous and so frequent, he told the truth, but not the whole truth. I studied the question for days. Yes, God does not forgive till I repent and confess. But is that all that God does? Does He issue a proclamation, announcing that whoever would come with true confessions and repentance would be pardoned? Is that all? Then not one of us would ever be pardoned! No, no. That isn't all. In every case God comes first to us. He calls. He reasons. He pleads. He sends His messengers to urge, to constrain us to come. All day long He stretches forth His hands to get us to come. Had the old deacon done this with his enemy? Did I always do it? After several weeks of preparation I preached a sermon on Colossians 3:13. I had learned a needed lesson in Christian Ethics.

Another experience: In the school-house where I used to preach, a series of revival meetings was being held. I learned that two of my good girls had attended, had gone to the mourners' bench and "got religion." When I learned of it, my first impulse was to be indignant and to give the girls a good talking to. But I bethought myself of an experience with Dr. Passavant. At Baden one of his young men had gone thru the same experience as my two girls. He had gone a step further and had given in his name as a probationer, i. e., he had become an incipient member of the M. E. Church. Everybody wondered what Dr. Passavant would say or do. The doctor heard about it, bought a nice hand-Bible, went to the young man's home, saw him by himself, gave him a kind, fatherly talk, earnestly entreating him to live near to Christ, gave him the Bible and urged him to read it daily. Then the doctor kneeled down and prayed with him. What could the Methodists say against that?

I met my two girls, talked kindly to them and tried to make them see that they had made a mistake. They heard me silently, then one said, "Well, Pastor, we may not understand it, but I know what I got there

and I know that my heart is different than it was."
What could I say to that? It was doubtless true.
She had made a more full surrender than she had ever
done before. I did not contradict her statement and
expressed the hope that they would remain in our
church. They said that they had no intention of leaving us. They remained true. I do not recall whether
I prayed with them or not. If I did not I failed of a
pastor's privilege. All this gave me occasion for serious self-examination. Had I been clear enough, urgent
enough and appealing enough in my preaching? Had
I shown what that full surrender to Christ means and
how it can be made? I again got a needed lesson.

In going back and forth to the city I had to pass
thru a thickly crowded district called Butchers Run.
There was no church of any kind in the district. My
good old teacher Mr. Dummet was conducting a Union
Sunday School in the school-house where he was then
teaching. I consulted him about holding evening services there on Sundays. He welcomed the suggestion.
Said he would do all he could for the movement. After
several weeks' announcement and urgent invitations to
all he came in contact with, I had my service. We
used the hymn-books of Dummet's Sunday School.
The attendance was encouraging. I announced regular
services. I canvassed the whole district. I found it was
a neglected, wild, worldly neighborhood. Also found
some fine English Lutherans. One of these, Miss Annie
Heckel, became my organist and efficient helper. Later
on she became the wife of my successor, the Rev. W.
P. Shanor. Some fine Presbyterian people also attended regularly and showed an interest in the services. I
preached for nearly a year. I had not yet organized
a congregation when I received a call to Jewett, Ohio.

Chapter X

RESIGNATION AND REMOVAL

UNSOUGHT and unexpected, a unamimous call came from the Jewett, O., charge, a good country parish of the Pittsburgh Synod. I had declined two other calls, both of which offered me several hundred more than I was getting. One of them appealed to me strongly, and I really wanted to go. But I felt that my work was still in the experimental stage and could not safely be given up. So I had declined and labored on to get my infant churches on their feet. Now, after about six years of determined and diligent effort, the work was in a safe condition.

As I reviewed what, with God's blessing, I had accomplished, it was with some satisfaction with the results of my first six years in the ministry.

I had strengthened Mount Calvary and secured for the congregation what the people had needed for years, a resident pastor who would give them all his time.

I had gathered and reorganized St. John's at Pine Creek. It was now a regular English Lutheran Church with some good leaders, a fairly good church council and a going Sunday School.

At Mount Zion, as a student, I had begun with nothing. I had gathered and organized a congregation that was growing encouragingly and had every prospect of further development. We had a band of unusually fine and promising young people, a live and growing Sunday School. The church council was not yet what it ought to be. There was not a man in it that had had experience in that line. But they were learning. We had bought a lot, built a church and parsonage, and the whole debt was only a few hundred dollars. Mount Zion Church had won the confidence of the best people in the community. A goodly number of its members, some of the very best, had of their own accord come to us from other denominations. Several had come over from the Roman Catholic Church. The bulk of the membership had, however, been gathered out of the world. Some of these afterwards proved themselves unfit and left us again. One good woman, Mrs. Harriet Graham, a devout Presbyterian, was one of my best helpers and often gave me encouragement when I needed it sorely. She was poor, very poor, had a large family of children. She often didn't know how she could get the next sack of flour. She had a childish trust in the Lord. She prayed to Him and He never failed her. She was a modern Dorcas, an ungarbed deaconess.

Wherever there was sickness, sorrow or distress of any kind, there was Mrs. Graham, ministering like an angel of mercy. I came across her in homes where there was malignant scarlet fever and where there was black diphtheria. I once ministered in a home from which we buried two children who had been stricken down with this terrible disease. We buried the two in one grave. Mrs. Graham had ministered in the home to the last. Outside of the family she was the only mourner at the funeral. She had a home full of children. She told me that she had never carried home a contagious disease. A life-long Presbyterian, she had never left her church. I never asked her to. She sent her children to our Sunday School. All but two or three were confirmed in our church. Years later I had the pleasure of instructing her grandson in my theological classes in Northwestern Seminary. The Rev. John Booth is an honored minister in the Pittsburgh Synod. Yes, my heart was bound up in Mount Zion Church. My making; my first love; my church baby.

As already noted, I had opened work in Butchers Run. Had labored there about two years. The place was now ready for the organization of an English Lutheran Church. I had also done some prospecting in a neighboring settlement in Spring Garden Run. I called the attention of some of the mission authorities to this place. It was later developed into that most interesting Spring Garden Mission.

Dr. Passavant always advised against hasty organization. His constant counsel was: Preach the Word. Preach publicly and from house to house. Let the Word wake a desire for a church. Let the Word sift out the chaff from the wheat. Thus get to know the people. Then you will be able to pick out the best for leaders and you will be saved from future heartaches. This advice might be worthy of consideration by home mission leaders today.

During our residence at Mount Zion two children had been born. Johnny Myers was our first boy. Poor, dear, saintly child! He came into the world with a lame back. He certainly was one of the children we read about—too good for this world. Good natured, patient, except when he had pain, there was always a sweet smile on his face. He lived long enough to learn to talk, to read, to commit a number of verses, hymns and prayers. He loved to sing and would often say to visitors: "Shall I sing Rock of Ages for you?" When nearly six years he was in a hospital. From there God took him to that upper fold for which he was so perfectly prepared.

Yes, my heart was bound up with my first love. All these years I had had the wise, the goodly and Godly counsel of Dr. Passavant. I often made mistakes and blundered. He always set me straight, restrained my impulsiveness and taught me lessons that gold could never buy. I must tell this one story: I was driving the doctor along in my buggy. He asked me to stop a minute. A Jew peddler boy was walking along the road. The doctor called the boy. The boy came with alacrity: "Buy something, Mister? Matches, blacking, pins, buttons, spenders, shoe-strings, buy something Mister?" The doctor said kindly: "No, I don't want to buy anything. How are you getting along? How much money did you make yesterday? Do you like your work? Good bye. Always tell the truth." Then he told me to drive on. I said: "Doctor, why did you do that?" "Well," he said, "I am interested in these little merchants. Then, too, I wanted to teach you a lesson. Did you notice how keenly that boy is interested in his work? Now I want you to study and learn from all kinds of people. You can learn a lesson from that Jew boy. Are you interested in and do you love your work as he does his?" I had learned another lesson, which is with me to this day.

And now should I leave? Should I separate myself from dear Dr. Passavant? I considered my call for weeks. The doctor really didn't want me to go, but said I must decide it in the sight of God. He advised me to decide it on my knees. I could not decide until

I was satisfied that the right successor would rightly carry forward my work. After conferring with the proper authorities we agreed that the young Rev. W. P. Shanor would be the man. I resigned in his favor and accepted the call.

Mr. Shanor was called, accepted, came, took vigorously hold of the work, promptly fell in love with my organist, Miss Annie Heckel, and son moved into the parsonage with her. He did a blessed work for Christ and His Kingdom.

We moved to Jewett, Ohio. It was a great change for me. Up to this time we had lived on the edge of Pittsburgh, my dear old native city. Every week or so we had errands, visits, marketing or shopping there. I had not been in real country work. The nearest to it was at Pine Creek. Those people had also been in close touch with and had been influenced by the city. Now I was to shepherd a labor among real children of nature. Pittsburgh, their nearest real city, was eighty miles away. Many of the people had never been on a train or in a city. It might have been about one of these homes that this story was told:

A country youth went to a city to live and earn money. Everything astonished and amazed him. He wrote a letter to his mother. He tried to describe the sights and scenes and sounds. He told how there were big yellow wagons full of people running up and down the streets. These wagons had no horses hitched to them! Nothing but a fish pole stuck up in the air! The poor old mother read and re-read that letter. She called in her neighbors. She wept bitterly as she told them: "I was terribly afraid that my boy would be spoilt in the city. But I did not think that he could be so big a liar in so short a time!"

There were four congregations in the parish. Each one was in a little country town. Each town was a true-to-life "Main Street" village. In each one everybody knew everybody's business. They talked about each other. Many knew no other topic of conversation. To us this was new and annoying. Unconsciously we doubtless fell somewhat into the same habit. But unlike "Main Street," there were many thoughtful, noble Christian souls in these towns. These were the saving salt in their communities. Neither were the churches as dead as in "Main Street." The old Gospel was there. It was saving and sanctifying souls. It was enlightening, uplifting and enriching many a life and many a home. Wherever the Gospel is rightly preached and taught and the sacraments rightly administered, there is cleaning and saving salt, there is life and hope, there people are made better, happier and richer.

The four churches were all old and in a manner "sot in their ways." Two were nearly a hundred years old, one about half as old, and the youngest and most progressive about thirty years old. All had been brought up in the old fashioned, easy going, cheap and non-progressive traditions of their fathers. The people from away back wanted a preacher, a common man who could keep their church going. With this they were satisfied. That they were a part of the Kingdom of God, that their church was to help establish and expand that Kingdom, that their churches were to send the Gospel of the Kingdom to the uttermost parts of the earth, of this, for years, they had no conception. Wonder whether they ever sang: From Greenland's Icy Mountains! Of the great Lutheran Church, of her great duty to influence and win

America, during these times of ignorance, they had no vision.

In those days the salaries were small. The pastors were content to live like their people. That "divine discontent" that should drive every pastor to make his people wiser, better, eager for larger service to God, their community and their great church, did not stir these pastors. One of my predecessors boasted that he had never had a stipulated salary; he had always been satisfied with what his people gave him. No wonder that in an old copy of the minutes of his synod I read that this whole parish of four rich congregations had contributed about twelve dollars for benevolence! These primitive preachers lived among the people, would stay day and night in farm homes, get horsefeed and board free and so have a free and easy time. There was a tradition that one of my predecessors would go home only to have his shirts washed! Of regular, systematic study hours they seemed to know nothing. The libraries of middle aged ministers could be hauled away in a wheelbarrow. Their sermons they would often "shake out of their sleeves." Of course there were noble exceptions. But there were all too many of this type. How could the churches grow in grace and in knowledge, be strong in the Lord and in His might be a spiritual power in their respective communities under such shepherds? Of such God's prophets had complained and called them "dead dogs."

My immediate predecessor, the Rev. Mr. D. M. Kemerer, had reorganized all four congregations. The every-member canvass and duplex envelope were not yet known. He had the deacons canvass for subscriptions. He introduced annual congregational meetings

and had deacons and trustees elected and installed.
Also introduced an annual joint meeting of the four
church councils. Thus he brought system and order
out of the chaos. He also brought system into the
Sunday Schools and organized choirs in all the congregations. Then he had all four churches overhauled,
had chancels and chancel furniture installed, stained
glass windows put in, the buildings painted, several
towers built and so made all things new.

Before Kemerer accepted the parish, on the advice
of Dr. Passavant, he had canvassed the best people
in the four churches, had held congregational meetings
and tried to persuade the people to divide the parish
into two. Call two pastors and so have services in
each church every Sunday, instead of having half the
churches stand idle every Sunday. This was too great
an innovation for those slow going, conservative people.
In the way back days they had put up with one service
a month. And when two a month had been brought in
they had an over-abundance. At any rate that had
been good enough for their daddies—and they were
good men—why shouldn't it be good enough for them?
Kemerer used to tell a story of how two neighbors met
and argued the question. One was a progressive and
favored a division. The other opposed; the old way
was good enough for him. The progressive's given
name was Bill, the other's was John. John was arguing warmly for the good old way. Bill said to him:
"Johnny, if the good old ways were best, why don't you
plow with the old wooden mouldboard and why don't
you reap your wheat with a sickle and thresh it with
a flail? All that was good enough for your daddy,
why isn't it for you?" For a moment Johnny was non-
plussed. Then his face brightened and he said: "I

tell ye, Billy, them's the days we raised the crops."
"Nuff sed!"

The conservatives won; the charge was not divided, and Kemerer took charge of and served the four congregations for six years when he resigned and had me called. His good work had certainly made it easier for me.

After we were settled in our new home in Jewett, I preached my introductory sermon on 1 Cor. 15:3, 4. I made the sermon short, and then from the chancel I gave the people a frank, plain talk on what I wanted to do among them and what they might expect of me. It ran something like this: I wanted to preach the best sermons I possibly could. To do this I needed time for study. I would first of all visit all, making short calls to get acquainted. After that round I wanted to spend my forenoons in my study. In my regular visiting I should always go first and most frequently to those who needed me most, the sick, the poor, the lonely, the careless, the backsliders and all the lost and wandering sheep. I should have no time to go out to take big dinners, stay half a day or a whole day. But if ever I was needed by anyone, member or outsider, near or far, storm or sunshine, day or night, I should always be willing to come. But I must be notified. I could not know without being informed. I earnestly requested the members to inform me of such places. This program I repeated in each of the four churches.

To most of the people this was a surprise. They had never heard or seen it on this wise. It was something new. It afforded much village and country gossip.

Then for weeks, with wife and babies in the buggy, we drove over hill and dale, calling at all kinds of homes and habitations, eating when invited and doing without when not invited. In the far congregations I had found out at what places we might stay over night. As far as I recall we had glorious, early summer weather. While there was some hardship for wife and babies, it was a most interesting experience in pastoral itinerating. I had my Pastor's Pocket Record and took down names of all, noted down whether baptized or confirmed or not. After this was all over, we settled down and fixed up our home. We had much to talk about and much to laugh over. We had met all sorts and conditions of people. Some were very odd and peculiar. I followed up this tour of investigation with a more leisurely visitation. I went alone and hunted up the aforementioned needy ones. Many of these were shiftless, thriftless and poor. A number of them expressed surprise that I should come to see them. They had belonged to the church for many years, but I was the first Lutheran preacher who had ever come to see them. These always received my best attention.

It wasn't long before the well-to-do, good, regular members, among whom were church officers, Sunday school teachers and singers, complained that I so rarely visited them. Why didn't I load up the family and come out and spend a day or two? I told them that they ought to feel complimented. I had been busy going out after the lapsed and lost and careless who needed me most. It took some time to get these good people to see into my way of doing. They had been spoiled. Too many former pastors had visited only or mainly the well to do and good, who had comfortable homes, served good meals and were interesting company. This, of course, is all very pleasant. But I submit: Was this the Savior's way? Is this the way of the Good Shepherd? Does He not leave the ninety and nine safe ones and go out after the lost? Did He not send His servants out upon the highways and by-ways, into the streets and lanes to seek and constrain the poor, the lame, the halt and the blind to come in? Did He not plainly say that He came not to call the righteous but sinners to repentance? Oh, for under-shepherds with the mind and heart of the Good Shepherd!

Chapter XI

EXPERIENCES IN JEWETT CHARGE

BEFORE I moved to Jewett I had made several trips to a place called Bowling Green, Ohio. It is now called Osage. There is an old English Lutheran church there. Some claim that it is the oldest Lutheran church in Ohio. This lone Lutheran church had been vacant for some years. The people wanted the Gospel. They had sent to Pittsburgh for supplies and had had one service a month, or rather, one Sunday with two or three services. It was a tedious trip from Pittsburgh; nearly a hundred miles by train, then twelve miles over hill and dale by buggy, wagon or horseback. At the little town we found a devoted flock who loved their church and the Gospel message it had for its people. They could not find the Gospel so clear and so full in any other church. Tho there were only a few families, they paid traveling expenses and twelve dollars besides. The preacher, also, as a rule, went home with a basket or package of good eats. In bad weather, when the clay roads were deep, with here and there a "sink-hole," the horse-back ride was trying. We found there some of the most devoted and intelligent families one could find anywhere. I had come to love the Osage Church and its people. I learned that their church had formerly been connected with the Salem Church, now a part of the Jewett charge. The Salem Church had cut them off and left them to shift for themselves. They could not understand why the

Jewett charge should have four congregations and they should be left alone.

After I had been settled in Jewett I inquired into this matter. The first time I went to the Ohio River Conference I brought the matter up. There I learned how this strange situation had been brought about. I don't like to write it down here. But the truth needs to be known.

The Jewett parish had formerly consisted of three congregations; one in Jewett, one in Rumley and one in Jefferson. The Salem Church, ten miles from Jewett and about the same distance from Osage, had been a separate charge of two congregations. A pastor of the Jewett charge, who boasted that he had never bargained for a stated salary, was casting covetous eyes on the Salem Congregation. Four congregations, by serving two on alternate Sundays, would make a more convenient charge than three. Then there would be the additional income from Salem. Wise diplomat as he was, he won Salem over. But what of poor Osage? That did not seem to trouble him. To this day I cannot understand the conscience of some ministers. They seem to be so sinfully selfish.

Well, I was indignant and told the conference what I thought of such procedure. It was making the rich parish richer and leaving one lone little church helpless and unprovided for. I requested that the conference arrange to have Salem go back to Osage. The conference commissioned me so to arrange. I had a difficult and delicate proposition before me. First I had to get the consent of the three congregations to request Salem to go back to Osage. I did not find an eager response. Only a minority of the more just and unselfish favored my proposition. When all saw that it was a matter of conscience with me and that I was determined, they agreed to the arrangement on condition that they would not have to make up the salary loss that would come from separating Salem. I told them that if the plan was carried out I would preach three times, giving each congregation one service every Sunday. Thus no congregation would have any vacant Sundays. I would have heavy Sundays and I would take whatever added compensation they would give for the additional services they would receive. To this they could not object. They were not enthusiastic, as I thought they should be. And so the matter was left.

I had a harder time to get Salem's consent. Some of them were indignant at the proposal. I tried to reason with them, showed them that they could get more patsoral service and in the season of good roads could have preaching every Sunday. But where could they get a preacher? I assured them that I should do all I could to get them a real good preacher. The best agreement that I could get out of them was that, if I would get them a good preacher, they would try the arrangement for a while with the understanding that if it would not work they could get back into the Jewett charge. I lost many good friends at Salem, but won the everlasting gratitude of Osage. I have never regretted my action. But it does make me sad and discouraged when I see the same kind of injustice that had been committed against Osage, abetted and favored by ministers in other places. God pity them. In after years the same crime against Osage was repeated.

With the help of the proper authorities I secured a good and able young preacher fresh from the Philadelphia Seminary. Also canvassed among the people of both congregations and got enough money to buy the young man a good horse. It did the people good to make this gift.

I now went to work in my diminished field. In that lime-stone country, in spring time when the frost was coming out of the ground, the only way to go was on horseback or on foot. Once my horse's front foot went down into an invisible sink hole and stuck there; the horse fell forward, as I was riding down hill, and I fell over the horse's head into the mud! I was near the church. I was a sight to behold! Before I opened the service I explained my appearance and preached. When a crust that would not bear up a horse, was frozen over the mud, I walked the twelve or fourteen miles and preached to small audiences three times. I made it a rule to preach the same sermon in all three churches. I frankly announced in all the churches that I would do so. Often people from the half way district would attend two churches. They knew in advance that they would hear the same sermon. It did not hurt them.

My three congregations made up about fifty dollars more than they formerly paid, so I had two hundred less than formerly and one-third more preaching. But I was happy that the good people of Osage had a good preacher and regular services.

While in Jewett I helped the neighboring Bowerstown parish, which had five congregations to divide. A new mining town had sprung up at the lower end of the parish. I persuaded them to build a small frame church there—the only church in town.

We made much of a midweek service that is not as general in the Lutheran Church as it ought to be. We did not hesitate to call it a prayer meeting. **Why** should we? Is it against the teaching and example of Holy Scripture for Christians to meet together for a season of prayer? We have not so read our Bible. Let any one take up his concordance, look up the word prayer and read all the passages referred to. As to the young New Testament Church let him read Acts 1:13, 14. Note that women as well as men were at that Apostolic prayer meeting. Thruout that Book of Acts, which is the inspired story of the Apostolic Church, let the reader note how frequently the early believers met together for prayer.

But prayer meetings have been abused. True, so have all public services. So have the sacraments, so has the Holy Scripture, so has every thing that is good. Because a good thing is so often abused, shall we therefore throw away its proper use? Would this be in harmony with sanctified common sense? Overly conservative Lutherans have often blundered along these lines. Because the good words conversion, experience, revival, testimony and others have been abused —often shamefully so—many Lutherans are afraid to use these words! No, no, there is nothing unscriptural or un-Lutheran in having a good prayer meeting.*

We did not have prayer without the Word. We never would dare to put prayer above the Word. I held fast to the Lutheran idea that God's Word to me is more important than my word to God. God must first speak to me. My prayer must be my answer back to God. God's Word is the means of grace. My prayer

*See *Lutheran Fundamentals*, pp. 237 ff. *The Lutheran Pastor*, pp. 294, 295. *Problems and Possibilities*, pp. 57 ff. *The Priesthood of Believers*. Read this booklet.

pleads that I may so use that means that I may appropriate the grace proffers.

We had laymen offer prayer, one each night. I noticed that some good men would not come to our meetings. On inquiry I found that they were afraid that I would call on them to pray. I then made public announcement that I should call on no one unaccustomed to pray in public without getting his consent beforehand. Then they came. I believe we ought to encourage our capable men to learn to pray in public. Why should we leave this function of the priesthood of believers to the less Evangelical sects?

Our general free procedure was this: We would open with a familiar hymn. Then I would read from the General Council's Sunday School Lesson Series the lesson for next Sunday. Then I would give a short, practical exposition of the lesson, such as I hoped would teach our teachers how to teach. Then a layman would pray, and the lesson would be thrown open for question and suggestion. This soon became the popular part of the evening. It was talked about all over town. Out of curiosity others came, and it was not long till we had by far the largest mid-week service in town. Our people became more and more free in asking questions and offering comment. Sometimes we could not get away till toward ten o'clock.

The asking of questions on the lesson or on things directly or remotely related, together with the brief, off-hand answers seemed to interest the hearers most of all. When there was a question that I was not ready to answer off-hand, I would frankly say that I needed time and research and I should try to answer that question at the following meeting. It was at these meetings in my early ministry that I learned the value

116

of the question box in connection with all popular meetings. Numbers of good people have problems and questions on their minds that are never answered. Often too such people go to the wrong places for answers. Perhaps it is to a neighbor or acquaintance who is not at all informed on the subject and only adds more doubt and difficulty to the matter. Or a man may take his question to the country store congress and get confusion worse confounded.

Now, why should not the Church, whose mission it is to instruct, to inform, to teach all things that Christ wants His people to know, encourage all people to bring in all their difficulties and doubts and questions and problems and have them answered by him who is their rightly constituted and qualified spiritual guide? I have used this method of instruction at scores of places, such as summer schools for Sunday School teachers and Church workers, Sunday School and Luther League conventions, conferences and Chautauquas. Again and again I have been told how helpful this question box method has been. And why shouldn't it be? The preacher and leader of groups and conventions and institutes does not always know what peculiar and perplexing doubts and difficulties may trouble some people. The sermons may be Evangelical and edifying and instructive, but they may never answer those troubling questions. Beside all this, people often think that the regular church services are one-sided. The preacher has all the say, and the people have no say. In the early Church we know that the sermon was often a colloquy, the hearers always had the right to interrupt, to question and even to contradict. The custom was simply the meeting of a want of human nature. The question box method satisfies that want. It is good for mid-week meetings. And might it not solve the perplexing problem of the Sunday evening service? Written questions might be gathered with the offering, read off and then answered the following Sunday evening. One benefit might be that it would train the preacher in the difficult art of framing clear, concise and really helpful definitions, explanations and satisfying answers. Isn't the suggested method worthy of trial?

Another service that I had started, under difficulties, in the small congregations of my former parish and learned to utilize more fully in the Jewett parish was the service preparatory to Holy Communion.* As stated above, I had also had the blessed experience of being with Dr. Passavant in these services. I had a feeling that with too many of our people the Communion was not taken as seriously as it should be. I realized more and more that our Lutheran and Scriptural view of the Lord's Supper demanded special heartsearching, self-examination, penitence and confession. I felt that a mere announcing of the intention to commune and the going thru of the service of confession was not enough. A heart-sermon was needed every time. People needed to be shown, before every Communion, their sinfulness and their sins, their guiltiness in God's sight, their need of heart-felt contrition, sorrow and penitence. From this they were to be moved to a heart-felt longing for forgiveness, a real hungering and thirsting for righteousness. Then and then only were they really ready for the blessed, assuring and comforting words of the declaration of

---

*On the nature and necessity of this service, see: *The Lutheran Pastor*, chapter 14; also *Way of Salvation*, chapter 16.

grace in the absolution. Then and then only could they fully realize the unspeakable preciousness of the assurance that now their sins were all forgiven, now they were accepted in the Beloved One. Now, from the heart, they could sing:

> Lord, at Thy Table I behold
> The wonders of Thy grace,
> But most of all admire that I
> Should find thereat a place.
>
> I, that am all defiled by sin,
> An outcast from my God!
> I, that have crucified the Son,
> And trampled on His blood!
>
> What strange, surpassing grace is this,
> That such a soul finds room,
> My Savior takes me by the hand
> And kindly bids me come!

I made much of my preparatory services. I preached on, alluded to and talked on the subject frequently. I got my people so trained that all who possibly could would come to this Saturday afternoon service. With Luther, I also instructed them that if some could not possibly come they should take time for earnest self-examination at home, should confess to God in private and then be assured that they were prepared for and were welcome to the Sacramental Feast. As I write this, I look back with gratitude to God for my Communion seasons in the Jewett Parish. I can still see how on the preparatory Saturdays the plow would stand still in the furrow and the reaper in the field, how the farmers would load their families into their wagons and how the towns would be filled with all sorts of conveyances going to the Lutheran Church. People would ask, What's going on, what's bringing all these people to town? The simple answer would be, "It's Communion Season at the Lutheran Church."

I cannot help but feel and deeply regret that the old-fashioned awakening and refreshing and reviving separate preparatory service has become out of date. We have lost more than we realize. The combining of the confessional service with the Communion service on Sunday morning can never make up for the separate preparatory service we used to have. For this I am deeply sorry. I should earnestly advise all young pastors to earnestly and prayerfully study this question, and if at all possible introduce the old time preparatory service. I might add that I made it a practice to visit every member before Communion.

Before I was ordained I had fallen in love with Holy Week services. Dr. Jacobs always had the full seven-night services with us at Thiel Hall. Our Lutheran churches had them in Philadelphia while we were in the seminary. But the best Holy Week for me had been the one I spent with Dr. Passavant at Baden while I was still a student. Of this I have spoken above. Then and there I made up my mind that I should always utilize and exploit this week fraught with such possibilities for quickening and deepening the spiritual life. In my first charge I had to train my congregations into an appreciation of the services. They had become richer and better attended with each succeeding year. Now in my second parish I had four good-sized and organized congregations. They had not yet learned to value this week and its rich blessings. I

made up my mind while I still had all four congregations I would do my best to make a week of Passion
services a time of refreshing in each congregation. This
would necessitate my beginning four weeks before
Easter. I knew it would be a strain to preach every
week night in addition to the regular Sunday services.
I prepared my sermons for weeks in advance.

When the time came I girded myself for the heavy
task and, in the name of the Lord, went to work. I
usually began in the far congregation. I spent the
days and nights among the people. During the days I
visited from house to house, paying special attention
to the neglected, careless and cold. I tried to conduct
these house visits after the pattern shown me by Dr.
Passavant. I believe that not a few of the backsliding
members were thus persuaded to attend the special
services and thru them were quickened into new life.
I always tried to make the service Evangelistic. New
members were won from time to time. True conversions were brought about by the preaching of the
Cross. More than once such a week was a real time
of refreshing, a true, Evangelical revival. I recall one
when we received nineteen adults into the Communion
of the church on the following Sunday.

Sometimes I struck a whole week of stormy and severe weather. Often I would leave my horse stabled
and would wade deep snowdrifts across fields and climb
fences to get to the people. It was good work. In the
good sense it paid. I verified the old saying that "A
house-going preacher makes a church-going people."
But it must be "preaching from house to house."

I always had seven full nights. I read the seven parts
of the Passion History, one part each night. I
preached every night on some phase or leading thought

of the evening lesson. I tried to give it the background and setting of the whole evening story. As the lessons are long I shortened the other parts of the service. I omitted the liturgical parts, offered a brief free prayer, invoking God's special blessing on that evening service, sang two or three verses of an appropriate hymn before the sermon and preached about twenty-five minutes. Practically the whole evening was given to the Word of God. The service went little beyond an hour. The strain of the weeks was severe. There were heavy hardships. More than half of the nights I slept away from home in "spare room" beds, which were generally cold. And then to "talk for your board," as Dr. Passavant used to call it, day after day and preach every night, certainly was a weariness to the flesh. But as I look back over these weary weeks I count them among the most blessed weeks in my pastoral service. The good Lord always helped me thru. I verified the promise: "As thy day, so shall thy strength be."

One Easter night at the end of the four weeks' strain, when there was not much left of me, I was put to a severe test. While I was preaching I noticed that a rather wild looking stranger came into the crowded church. After the benediction, when I was happy because I was thru, and was ready to tumble into bed, the stranger came forward to speak to me. His sister had been severely burnt. He was afraid she would not live till morning. She wanted to see me. Would I come? I knew the middle-aged sister. She had been a frequent attendant at my Rumley Church. I knew that her family belonged to the United Brethren Church. I asked the brother why his sister had not sent for her own pastor. He said that she did not belong to church and wanted me. Would I come? How could I refuse? I went to the stable, told my Dolly that we had to go again, threw on the saddle and was off into the night, several miles away.

When I arrived at the house it was full of neighbors. I found the woman frightfully burned and suffering severely. She smiled thru her pain, was glad I had come, wanted me to pray with her and baptize her. I was satisfied that she was a Christian, had a brief service of word and prayer and then sat down and explained to her the meaning of Baptism and the Lord's Supper. She had heard me preach on the Sacraments as Means of Grace. Her twitching face had an eager light as I talked to her. I baptized her, administered the Communion to her and commended her to the mercy and grace of God. She was perfectly rational and wonderfully brave. Mid her paroxysms of pain, her face shone as she thanked me and bade me good-bye.

It was with an unusual warmth about my heart that I went out to the hitching post, patted my Dolly on the neck and told her that we were now going home again.

As the morning sun broke into her window the poor sufferer passed peacefully away. She left word that she wanted me to have the funeral. We took her charred body into our spacious Rumley Church, which was overcrowded. I do not recall my text. I know that I magnified the grace of God which had brought pardon and peace to this poor sufferer. That funeral service made a deep impression on the community. The church to which the people of the departed belonged was anything but friendly toward the Lutherans. It was frequently preached there that the Lutherans had no religion and did not know what real spiritual life

is. Here was one of their own who had not found what
she felt that she needed in their church, but had come
to us and found it. My ministration at the dying bed
of this woman had satisfied me that she was indeed
ready to die in Christ and in peace. It was one of the
most satisfactory of all my dying-bed experiences.

This leads me to speak of country funerals. In the
country a funeral is an event. As soon as any one is
dead, word is sent to the church in which he was or
his family are members or which he attended. The
sexton or janitor then tolls the bell slowly one stroke
for every year that the departed had lived. The people at once ask, "Who's dead?" Others count the
strokes of the bell. When the last stroke has sounded
the sexton is besieged with questions. He feels quite
important. Groups gather on the village street. The
news spreads rapidly. The whole country-side is
thinking and talking of the dead, of death! It is taken
as a matter of course that every body is going to the
funeral. All work is stopped. The service is held in the
church. The crowd, however, gathers at the house.
The minister reads or repeats a few verses of Scripture, offers a prayer, and a cortege is formed with the
hearse or the wagon containing the coffin in front. The
funeral processions are generally from a mile to two
miles long. While the procession is moving from the
house to the church the bell is again tolled. This calls
together another crowd of people who live within walking distance. Not all churches have bells. It was quite
a distinction for the Lutherans that their churches had
bells.

The front pews were reserved for the mourners. The
crowd that followed filled every seat, lined the walls,

stood in the aisles, in the vestibules and—on warm days— in groups outside of the open windows.

What an opportunity to preach the Gospel! Here there was always a good sprinkling of worldly people who rarely if ever attended the regular services. Here were unbelievers, scoffers, enemies of Christ and of His Church. At such times and on such occasions only, did the preacher have an opportunity to bring the needed message to such people. What a responsibility! The temptation is to praise and flatter the dead. That is easy, it sounds well and pleases the relatives and friends of the dead. Alas, how many preachers yield to the temptation. It is a frightful thing to preach one Gospel to the living and another Gospel over the dead.*

I always had several funeral sermons that could be adapted to such occasions prepared in advance. Almost invariably I began by saying that these services and this sermon were not for the dead but for the living. I would speak of my responsibility to bring the true, full message of sin and redemption to the living. I would often quote this passage (Ezekiel 3:17-20):

"Sons of man, I have made thee a watchman into the house of Israel; therefore hear the Word at my mouth and give them warning from me. When I say unto the wicked, Thou shalt surely die: and thou givest them not warning, nor speakest to warn the wicked from his wicked way to save his life; the same wicked man shall die in his iniquity; but his blood will I require at thine hand. Yet if thou warn the wicked and he turn not from his wickedness nor from his wicked way, he shall die in his iniquity; but thou hast delivered thy soul." Similarly, Ezekiel 33:7-19.

---

*Read chapter XVII in *The Lutheran Pastor.*

I think I did realize my opportunity and my responsibility. I did pray earnestly that I might be given the word in season, that I might cry aloud and spare not, that I might give such a warning that if the godless hearer would get no other he would not be able to say on the day of judgment: "No man warned me." I did try to make God's way of salvation so clear that no one might say before the great white throne: "I didn't know what I ought to do. No one showed me." I tried to preach awakening, Evangelistic sermons. I look back upon country funeral occasions as among the best opportunities that I ever had to preach the plain, full Gospel to all sorts and conditions of men. I thank God for the opportunities He gave me. I look back with pleasure to recall how sinners were converted, how enemies were reconciled and how whole families were brought into the church by messages to the living over the dead. The city preacher has no such opportunities.

There were some country customs in connection with funeral services that were obnoxious to me; one was that the men among the mourners would keep their hats on during the whole service. An old traditional custom, without rime or reason or recommendation. A relic of the olden time!

A still worse custom was this: After the service the coffin was opened and the whole, large crowd was asked to come forward and "view the remains." This would sometimes take an hour or more. It may be a fault in me, but to thus make a public show of the dead shocked my sensibilities. How much better to have it understood that those who really wanted to take a last look at the departed should go to the house before the funeral. Great public characters "lie in state" before the funeral. Processional gazing is not a part of the funeral ceremony.

And to me the climax of unbecomingness in this whole unpleasant affair was the making an exhibit of the sad, sacred, tender, last leave-taking of the immediate mourners. Surely, surely this solemn, sacred act, too bitter often for tears, ought to be entirely private. In the stillness and loneliness of the stricken home, there let the bereaved and broken-hearted have their last look, their last word, their last caress of love. Let this all be over before others arrive. "The heart knoweth its own bitterness and a stranger intermeddleth not therewith." Except on rare occasions and for special reasons the coffin ought not to be opened after it leaves the house.

In places, in country parishes, there also lingers the age-old custom of serving, after the burial, what Shakespeare called "the funeral baked meats." At the close of the church service the preacher was expected to announce that the friends were cordially invited to return to the house of mourning and "take dinner." What strange, incongruous, unbecoming, if not obnoxious customs! Is this the time and occasion for a feast? And then, at such a time, the labor and expense of it all! I actually knew a poor widow who had her only hog killed and had the after-funeral guests eat up her coming winter's meat. I always kindly declined to give the invitation and kindly gave my reasons.

There are other country customs and characteristics that I found verified in the Jewett parish. These characteristics I have discussed in *The Lutheran Church In The Country*, pages 31-48. One unhappy trait among the country people is the falling-out with one another and the bitter spite-holding. I have referred above to Dr. Jacobs' dealing with Thiel Hall boys along these lines. I have made mention of the quarrel between two deacons in my young Mount Zion Church. To my dismay I found old quarrels that had grown into bitter, chronic feuds in all my country congregations. They seemed to be taken for granted. They were looked upon as inevitable and incurable. To me this situation was intolerable. Frequently I preached over again the afore named carefully worked out sermon on forgiveness of injuries. Also reasoned and pleaded with the guilty parties. Where the quarrel was between men, with few exceptions, I was able to bring about at least an outward reconciliation. I am sorry to write it down, as a terrible warning, that my completest failures were with woman. There is a psychological explanation. Woman, more than man, lives in her emotions. She can and does love more deeply than man. By the same token she hates more deeply than man. There are psychological reasons that explain why this awful sin of spite-holding is much more prevalent in the country than in the city. Read more fully in *The Lutheran Church In The Country*. The grace of God can overcome it. The sinfulness and damnableness of this sin is to be preached with power. The unspeakably tender and loving heart of Christ, His weeping over, seeking, calling, pleading, bleeding, beseeching offers of full and free forgiveness to all who will repent and forgive are to be most earnestly pressed home on the impenitent and unforgiving.

Another evil that I saw among country people as I had never seen it before was the frequent marriage between blood relations. Too many cousin-marriages. And never before nor since have I seen in the offspring of such unnatural and unscriptural unions, such frightful fruitage. There were physical defectives, there were mental defectives, whole families of idiots, and there were moral degenerates, morons. The Laws of nature are the Laws of God. God is not mocked. Whatsoever a man soweth, that shall he also reap. He that soweth to the flesh shall of the flesh reap corruption.

Before I leave the Jewett charge I must refer to an experience which was, in some respects, among the most important experiences of my life.

Our Lutheran congregations, especially in Jewett and Rumley, were close neighbors to old-time rivival churches. Every year these churches would have a protracted meeting. Every night, for weeks, sometimes for five or six weeks, wild mourners'-bench revivals would hold sway. The whole community would become more or less wrought up. It was not an uncommon thing for revival leaders to publicly denounce the Lutherans by name as sad examples of spiritual deadness. Public prayers were often offered up for the Lutherans that they also might "see the light," "get religion" and be "truly converted." Some of our Lutherans were really disturbed and uneasy. Over against the bold, loud assertions of the revivalists, some of our people were timid if not helpless. They sometimes apologized and expressed the modest hope that even tho they were Lutherans, they might still be saved. This strange situation grieved and stirred me. I think I had a righteous indignation. I wrote a rather scathing article on False Revivalism. I painted the picture and told the story of what had come under my own observation. I told of some of the wild scenes and of some tragic results. This article was published in Passavant's *Workman*. The copy containing it was passed

129

from house to house in our neighborhood. A scurrilous reply, full of personal abuse, was published in a local paper. I wrote a quiet answer in the same paper. I appealed for fair play. I invited my opponents to public or private discussion, if they would reason and discuss in a Christian spirit. This ended the matter. As far as I know the revivals, after this, were never again so wild and abusive as before.

I had learned something. I had seen that my own people were not clear on what their own church holds and teaches as to becoming Christians and growing as Christians. The experience was the best thing that ever happened to me. It made me write my first book: *The Way of Salvation In The Lutheran Church.* Perhaps because it was wrung out of the deep convictions of a troubled soul, that book at once struck a popular chord. It met a real need. It not only clarified, strengthened and comforted thousands of Lutherans, but it won converts by the score. About fifty thousand copies of the English edition have been sold. It is still going. It has been translated into the main modern tongues and into a number of the languages used by the natives in our foreign mission fields. Dr. Passavant used to say: "Well, Brother Gerberding, I guess the good Lord put you down there among those howling revivalists to compel you to write *The Way of Salvation.* I also preached a series of sermons on Conversion. This series made the book, *New Testament Conversions.*"

During those six years in Jewett we had our own family experiences and changes.

Not long after we were comfortably settled, on August twelfth, 1881, there came to us a bright, curly-headed little girl. We often called her our sunshine.

For more than a score of years our Mary Emma has been a missionary in Japan. Her oldest daughter, Faith, is a commissioned missionary in the same land. The Lippards are well and widely known in missionary circles.

On November twenty-seventh, 1883, Josephine Henrietta was born. The good Lord called this bright little brunette home on March thirteenth, 1886.

On the day on which she died another little girl came as if to take the place of the one who just left us. On the same day we had a doctor and an undertaker in the house! We called the unexpected arrival Annie Comfort. She surely was a great comfort in the stricken home. But again, as if to impress indelibly that our abiding Comfort must come from the sinless and deathless home on the other side, God called Comfort home before she was five years old.

On May third, 1887, Ruth Danver was born. As the wife of Field Missionary W. C. Stump, she has for years been a directing and inspiring leader among the Lutheran women of Milwaukee. Our Jewett home had three births and two deaths.

I look back upon my six years in Jewett, Ohio, as a valuable experience. I had learned to know, at close range and by personal contact, that real country people are, as a class, different from the dwellers in the city. They are children of nature. They have lived close to nature. Nature has been their teacher. They are natural. They are not glossed over and artificialized as so many city people are. Country people are not so apt to pretend to be what they are not. They are more apt to be unspoilt and frank—often brutally frank. From nature they have learned to be narrow, to move in the same tracks or grooves. As Nature never forgives, always collects her bills, is no respecter of persons, makes all pay penalties to the uttermost farthing, so country people are in danger of becoming hard and unforgiving. These psychological traits are set forth, as already mentioned, in *The Lutheran Church In The Country*. It was worth while to get to know them at first hand. Every country pastor ought to know and understand country people. He cannot expect to improve and uplift them until he understands where they are, what they are and why they *are* thus. Only then can he broaden their outlook, soften their hearts and give them higher culture.

In the country as in the city there are always those who are of a finer strain. Their nature is cast in richer mould. By nature they are more highly gifted than their neighbors. Instead of succumbing to their environment they rise above it and make it better. We find such everywhere, in city slums, in barren wastes, in heathen lands. These are intended by God to be the uplifters of their fellows. As there is, in nature, no push from below, these brighter and better people are to be God's uplifters to give the pull from above. Happy is the pastor who knows how to use them.

I found many such superior natures in the Jewett parish. They were the saving salt, the burning and shining lights among their neighbors. They gave standing and strength to their congregations. They were the Aarons and Hurs for their pastors. How often they refreshed my soul. What hours of precious converse and social communion I spent in their homes. How they helped me. What needed lessons I learned from them. God be praised for them. They are bright pictures on memory's pages. They made my work easier. They restrained me where I needed it. I could not have done the work I did without their prayers and their help. God bless them.

Before I leave my Jewett work I feel that I should still refer to a rather unusual experience. It was after a hard winter and an unusually strenuous four weeks of passion services, that I felt that I must have a rest.

It was in 1884. A centennial cotton exposition was going on in New Orleans. Attractive excursion rates were offered. We talked it over in our home. Wife said she would be glad to take three children and visit her and my people in Pittsburgh. I secured a promise from Father Roof, a former pastor, now retired, to supply the congregations for five Sundays. I laid my request before my church councils. They consented. Of course I had to bear my own expenses. When the matter was talked around, a bright, enterprising young man whose family belonged to my church and who himself attended regularly, but whom I never could win to membership, offered to go with me. I was glad to have his company. For years I had cherished a strong desire to visit the Southland. How glad and grateful I was to go. As I did not have much money, I had written a Missouri pastor to secure lodging in a private home. We did not travel by parlor or Pullman cars. We were young and did not need these luxuries which the old ought to have. I never was in a Pullman until I had been in the ministry for nearly twenty years. We traveled by train to Memphis, Tenn. Then by Mississippi steamer to New Orleans. How I did enjoy the novelty and the romance of this river trip! Every hour was an event.

We soon found our simple quarters. We were close to Canal Street in the heart of this most typical of all southern cities. To me the city itself was the most interesting exposition. Its sights, its sounds, its scents, its varied, blended and mixed humanities were a never ending study. The out-door life, lines of men sitting on the curb-stones with their feet in the gutter, breakfast tables set on the side-walk with families eating as unabashed as we in our dining rooms. Lunch counters on side-walks, the strange, unkempt, crowded, noisy French market where white and black and yellow mingle and jostle in happy abandon. The old St. Louis Cathedral, where I happened in on Confirmation Sunday and saw the hundreds of black and white confirmed together. The crooks' rendevous, where hold-ups and thugs and pick pockets openly plied their trade on the river bank where General Jackson had routed the British army. These and scores of other scenes and sights, all of entrancing interest to me, I cannot dwell on here. The great cotton exposition was brimful of interest. I barely glimpsed it a number of times. What I wanted above all else was to study the negro problem. And here again I can mention only a very few striking incidents. I watched these strange people among whom I had never lived. They were a study and an amusement to me. Going to church in groups, loitering and loafing in groups, women carrying great bundles of laundry or full market baskets on their heads, laughing and talking as they stepped along; men carrying packages, sweeping walks and streets, pushing wheelbarrows or driving mule carts and donkey carts. Not often would I see one walking alone. If so he would often be whistling. Where two or more were together they were talking and laughing loudly, sometimes clapping hands, nodding heads and gesticulating gleefully. Their dress was interesting. All shapes and colors were worn, without the least idea of matching or blending. The red bandana turban was much in evidence. Rags and tatters and dirt did not seem to disturb them. Here and there some strutted in fading finery—no doubt handed out to them! Especially at the French market and on the broad plaza before St. Louis Cathedral these happy, carefree, oft barefoot children of nature could be seen acting out their native traits unabashed and unrestrained. On bright, moon-light evenings street blocks would be swept, chairs and banjos would be carried out and a merry unconventional street dance would be automatically started. Couple after couple would join in. The banjo thrummers would twang more vigorously, the curbstone audience and wall-flowers would guffaw and clap and cheer. Again the whole crowd, dancers and audience, would burst into song to which banjos and dancers would keep time. The weird, wild voices would fill the street, the open houses and corridors with mirth and melody. Isn't there always something quaint, mystical, a far-awayness in negro voices and melodies? Don't we seem to hear it in a minor note? A strange harking back or leaping forward? Even underneath their jollity is there not a lost chord, a something intangible, unexplainable, mysterious? So whether at the free and spontaneous street dance, in front of the cabin on a summer night, at the loading and unloading of steamers at the wharf, in cotton planting, hoeing or picking, in boat salon, in hotel lobby or at a minstrel show—is there not that same mystic, minor undertone of sadness? And when we go to their churches, their " 'vival meetin'," it is there. I have often imagined that I could hear the wail of a wronged and down-trodden race.

What a wonderful compensation of a good God that He has given to just these people such a large measure of good humor, lightheartedness and ebullient happiness.

An amusingly interesting sight too, was to see and watch the black nuns, in their cloister garbs, walking the streets. We know that white nuns always carry a serious if not sad face in public. It seems to be studied and put on. But these Catholic, black sisters couldn't put it on. The cloister face is alien to their nature. They chatted and laughed and looked about from under the veils as was natural to them. It seemed to me the cloister garb and calling did not and does not fit the darkey nature. At any rate, those that I watched did not bear it out. Nature asserted herself.

On a Saturday afternoon we were out to one of the many beautiful and interesting parks of the city. This one is at Lake Pontchartrain. While there I noticed a big, well-built negro sitting alone on a bench. He was dressed up in a clean-cut clerical suit. I spoke to him and said, I see you are a minister. Yes, he was a Methodist preacher. I introduced myself as a preacher from the North and told him that this was my first visit to the South, and I was specially desirous to get a clear and right understanding of the situation and condition and hopes and prospects of his people. We had a good, frank, free and informing talk.

As we rose to go he said: "Say, Br., won't you come and preach for my people tomorrow afternoon? I'se got a good big congregation. They likes to hear a preacher from de Norf. Won't you come." "Yes," I said, "I'll come." I had him write the location of his church and what street cars would take me there. Next day at the appointed hour I was there. It was a hot Sunday afternoon. I found a good-sized, plain, square

church, well filled with all sorts and conditions of black
people. I found my preacher friend of yesterday in
the chancel conferring with some of his deacons. I
went forward to greet him. He looked at me and
seemed puzzled. Then his face brightened as he said:
"Oh, yes, dis is dat Br. from de Norf. But say, Br.,
I forgot dat today I promised to compliment my young
men fo' fixin' up de church. Jes see how des done gone
and cleaned and decrated. I mus' gib dem a compliment." I was provoked. I said, "Now, look here. You
asked me to come and preach. I am here prepared to
preach. This is my only chance." He brightened up
again and said: "Das right Br. I jes tells em dat here's
a Br. from de Norf, way up from Ohio, he wants preach
fur us. Now me, ye have always, But him ye has only
today, so I'll compliment de young men nex' Sunday
and de Br. fom de Norf he preach today." There was
a hearty vocal response from all over: "Das right, let
him preach." So I was duly elected and called. I took
an old familiar sermon which I could adapt to almost
any occasion on the text: "Blessed are they that hear
the Word of God and keep it."

I believe I had never preached to a more responsive
audience. I never had a more responsive service. The
responses were not all liturgical. But they were all
hearty. Here are a few: "Das so Br. Hallejujoy.
Das good. Tell us some mo. Das not so. Wite fokes
been stuffin you. Wite fokes do dem tings too." Yes,
I said they do. We preach against it all the time just
as I'm doing to you. "Das rite Br. We needs it."
Sometimes there would be a loud laugh as some would
voice a loud "Amen." Dr. Passavant once told me
how, when the General Synod met at Chambersburg,
Pa., provision had been made to fill the pulpits of all

the white churches, but not one had been appointed to preach to the large colored congregation. The doctor was to preach in the church where the synod met. He notified the officials that he would preach for the negroes. He did. He told me about it and said, "We had a great shout in the camp." So had I, on that hot Sunday afternoon in New Orleans. Looking back to that service, I have often thought: How natural is a responsive service! That whole darkey service from opening hymn to benediction was abundantly responsive. True worshippers want to take part in the service. If their church does not provide for them a liturgy, they make one up as they go. It is not all churchly. The responses are not always in the correct form or in the right place. A hearty Methodist service is responsive. It is a human argument for a liturgical service.

Before I left the black Bethel Church the big preacher asked me to attend a black M. E. preachers' meeting on the morrow. "Yes, Br., come to our meetin'. We always likes to hear a Br. frum de Norf." I took down the address and time and said I'd come. I found a noisy, happy crowd of about thirty preachers. Not all were dressed as finely as my new friend from Bethel. Some had shabby and shiny suits, but all had white neckties and all seemed to feel their dignity as preachers. My friend introduced me to some of the leaders. All were glad that I had come to their "meetin'." Several of them informed me that they had been slaves. One told us how he had been sold on the auction block for fifteen hundred dollars. (I afterwards saw that auction block. It had a gruesome interest for me.) While we were freely chatting a fine looking, tall, gray-haired white man walked in. He took his place at the desk and rapped for order. They sang a hymn, in that same plaintive tone, with that same undertone of a far-away wail so characteristic of the race. There were wonderful voices. All the parts were there, the easy blending and the soft cadences were pleasant to hear. The white presiding elder offered free prayer for the brothers present and for the work in which they were engaged. There were many and varied responses. They were not all liturgically correct. But they were spontaneous and hearty. After roll-call and minutes my friend of yesterday addressed the chair something like this: "Mista President, we has a Br. here frum de Norf. He preached fo' me yestidy. Preached a powful sermon. I asked him to meet wif us. He wants to talk to us." The president smiled and said quietly: "Now, Br., haven't I told you all more than once that isn't the way to say it? You ought to introduce the Br. and then say, 'I move that we request him to speak to us.'" "Oh, yes, yes. Beg padon. I move dat we request de Br. to speak to us."

I had thought out an address along these lines: After telling who I was, that this was my first visit to the South, that one thing I had come for was to study the situation and the problem of their people and especially of their church work, I told them of what I had been seeing and noting in their wonderful city. I frankly and plainly told them of the dangers I saw for their race, that they were yet young in their freedom, were untrained, were weak and exposed to fierce temptations of the flesh and I feared that many of their people were being swept into immorality by these temptations. There were frequent responses from the start. But when I plainly pointed out their sins and dangers there were vigorous and indignant protests. Some were

quite angry. These were the slanders of the white
people. Their slanderers were worse than they themselves. I requested quietly that they hear me thru,
spoke kindly, said I was willing to learn and wanted
to help them. But I had nearly raised a riot. There
was fire in some of those black eyes. But I got them
quieted. Then I reasoned with them, assured them that
the only hope and help for their people and for my
people was in the religion of the Gospel. That this did
not mean that if they would have big meetings and
excitement and shouting in their churches they were
all right. What they and all their people needed first
and most of all was instruction. They must learn,
learn to know what sin means, what sin does, what
sin brings. They must get clear ideas about Jesus,
who He is and what He did to redeem them and how
the Holy Spirit must bring this redemption into their
heart and life, make new creatures out of them and
strengthen them to lead more and more holy lives.
That's as far as I could go in that one address. The
presiding elder said a few kind words, was glad that
I had said what I did and told his auditors that they
needed my message and he hoped they would take it
to heart. He also assured me that it was part of his
work to introduce a system of catechization in Wesley's Catechisms in all the colored churches over which
he presided. As the conference now had business matters to attend to, I excused myself and was glad to
get out into the open. In these two days I had learned
much. I had much to think about. I am thinking
about it yet.

Up to the time of which I am writing the Lutheran
Church had done very little for the millions of colored
people in our own land. For poor, benighted Africa

the great Lutheran Church of the World had poured out money and men without stint and done a most blessed and wonderful work. But for the children of Africa at home we had done practically nothing.

From his youth up Dr. Passavant had had a deep concern for "Our brother in black." Read of it in *Life and Letters of Passavant*, pages 529-534. Read there what a wonderful opportunity God gave to the Lutheran Church in the East to do great things for a needy people. A great and effectual door had been opened to us. We did not enter in. We lost a golden opportunity. It is one of the many sad "might have beens" in Lutheran history.

All honor to the Missouri Synod. In this great work that synod has done far more than all other Lutherans combined. I had read of their work. I knew of that wonderful man, the Rev. Mr. Bakke, who was the leader in the great Lutheran work among the colored people. He gave his life to and for it. The work he started and organized is going on all over the South. The Colored Lutheran Theological Seminary at Greensboro, N. C., is his creation. He was one of God's noblemen.

I hunted him up in New Orleans. I spent precious hours with him. He was a Norwegian who had taken his theological course in Concordia Seminary, St. Louis, Mo. I went with him and sat thru a half day in his colored parochial school. I attended his Sunday School and heard him preach to his little black flock. I went with him to a conference of Missouri ministers. They received me kindly. It was all German, *Gemuetlich* and free. Cigars and beer were free for all. They talked over *Casual-fragen*, i. e., questions brought up by any one. (Missourians believe in the question box.)

141

I received social recognition only. There could be no ecclesiastical fellowship. I did not expect it.

I received a surprise and a shock. Pastor Bakke asked the question whether in his preaching to his little flock, made up mainly of catechumens and those recently confirmed, he ought to tell stories? The unanimous answer was No! I was shocked. They said it was un-Lutheran and was beneath the dignity of the pulpit! Well, what fools some Lutheran mortals be! Had these men never read the story-parables of our Savior? Had they not read that the common people heard this story-telling Preacher gladly? Had not even His enemies said, "Never man spake like this man." Alas for the unreasonable and unscriptural stiffness of some Lutherans! How it has hurt our cause and hindered our progress! My conference with these brethren had been spoiled. I spoke my mind freely in private to Bro. Bakke. He agreed with me. I believe that in my own body we have some Lutheran ministers as stiff and magisterial as these with whom I met in New Orleans. Let us hope that they are exceptions and will soon become extinct!

There are many other matters of interest that I might mention in connection with my first visit to and my first glimpse of the Southland. But the above must suffice. All too soon I felt that my time was up. I must get back to my people and my work. I was rested, refreshed and enriched in knowledge and experience. I went back to my work with new heart, new hope, a broader vision and a greater resolve to make our dear Church count more in and for America. I had found not one single English Lutheran church in the great city of New Orleans!

By and by I received an urgent call from the home

mission board of the General Council to go and plant an English Lutheran church in the far away frontier town of Fargo, N. D.

Chapter XII

OUT TO THE FAR FRONTIER

THRU my intercourse with Dr. Passavant, my experience in my first charge and my membership in the Pittsburgh Synod, called "The Missionary Synod," I had conceived an interest and love for the English home mission work of the General Council. Dr. Passavant was the first president of the Council's Home Mission Board. His paper, *The Workman*, had kept the home mission fires burning in my soul. I had become interested in the great West and in the pioneer Lutheran work that was being done there by Scandinavian and German Lutherans. As I have shown in his *Life and Letters*, the doctor was deeply interested in these Lutheran pioneers. He had made several laborious missionary journeys to them, had counseled with them and helped them. He had often talked to me about them and about the great future that awaited the Lutheran Church in the West. He had helped young W. K. Frick to begin English work in Milwaukee. He had helped the young Revs. G. H. Trabert and A. J. D. Haupt to start English missions in the Twin Cities. The doctor had a prophet's vision. He knew how the Church of his love had lost thousands of her most promising youth in the East by not giving them the Gospel in English. He did not want the Lutherans of the West to repeat the mistakes of those in the East.

When the call came for me to leave Jewett it impressed me. It laid hold of me. I felt that I must go.

I arranged for my family to remain in Jewett while I went ahead to prepare the way. The Rev. W. F. Ulery, of Greensburg, Pa., had been doing pioneer work for English Lutheranism under the auspices of the General Council for about two years. When he saw the need and the possibilities he had gone east and solicited money for an English mission in Fargo. He returned and purchased three lots at the corner of Fourth Ave. and Eighth St. North. There he had erected an attractive little frame church which had been finished, all but the chancel furniture, and dedicated before I came. A preliminary organization had also been effected. The number of charter members, I believe, was ten.

When I alighted from the train in that little, windswept prairie town on a July afternoon it was with strange and mingled feelings. My first impression was one of disappointment. I had read the boom literature about the beautiful little gate city. I did not see it. An inflated western boom had been on some years previous. It had collapsed. Big frame buildings with flimsy fronts were standing empty. Brick veneer business blocks were unoccupied. There wasn't a block of paved street in the town. Broadway was a wide mud street. Pacific Avenue and Front Street crossed it and flanked the Northern Pacific Rail Road. These main streets had plank sidewalks. Cement walks came a few years later. The town had about five thousand people. It was scattered over a wide space. Vacant lots and blocks abounded on every street. On the south side were a few short residential streets with substantial and comfortable homes. But Fargo was a good business center. The wonderfully rich soil, producing from forty to sixty bushels of number one spring wheat to the acre gave assurance that this would soon be a rich and prosperous country and that the Gate City must become a strong, flourishing city. The deflation of the bursted boom could be only temporary. Eastern financiers, business men and promoters had faith in the future of Fargo. Manufacturers of farm implements and machinery were erecting large and costly warehouses and sales rooms. The two transcontinental railroads were building branches, improving road beds, rolling stock and equipment. Several strong banks were doing a good business. The post office, in rented quarters, was doing a big business. Large wheat elevators were raising their bulky forms skyward on the outskirts of the city and at almost every little station. Real estate men and loan sharks were busy. The latter, with their chattel mortgages, were robbing the pioneer farmers at a shameful rate. While there my heart often bled for the poor farmers who had to bring in their farm machines because they could not make the last payment on the mortgage, with the robbery interest. Acres of vacant ground were piled up with this farmers' property, more than one-half or three-fourths paid for. These robber loan sharks and chattel mortgage men were sowing the seeds that in later years fruited into rural socialism.

There were plenty of retail stores where every necessity and commodity could be had. Prices were exorbitant. Often from one-third to one-half higher than in Minneapolis. The merchants made it pay to live in Fargo. Greed and graft abounded on every side. City improvements, such as water, sewers and light were as yet confined to a few central blocks.

But there was a spirit of enterprise, of optimism, of

hope and big promise everywhere. Initiative, energy and push were largely in evidence. The devil had come with the earliest settlers. The open saloon had the best corners and was pushing its body and soul destroying work. Gambling dens were wide open and plentiful. Bad women had a certain quarter of the city assigned to them, and there they openly and fearlessly did their devilish work. Yes, the devil had an easy reign and rule. Satan's throne was there. We had two daily papers, one morning and one evening. Their editorial tone was not what it ought to be. They catered largely to the lower elements. Corrupt politics and politicians seemed to flourish in that rich virgin soil. The two Dakotas constituted Dakotah Territory. Carpet bag officers held rule in the big empire. They were not living in blizzard-land for their health. The territorial capitol was located for a time at Pierre in the South. Fargo was the largest and best situated town in the Northern section. Naturally it became a sort of a sub-capitol. Here was a group of bold, conscienceless politicians. Here they hatched their schemes, laid their plots, bought and sold office and privilege and raked in the sheckels. Later on I became acquainted with some of these birds. The stories of trafficking in franchises and offices that they would gleefully tell were enough to bring a blush to a denizen of the lower regions. Such was external and official primitive Fargo when I arrived as a young tenderfoot home missionary. No wonder that, while I was trying to get my bearings I was bewildered. I was in a new world. I have often thought that I had something of the old Athenian in me. I was and am fond of seeing and hearing some new thing. I liked the shocking novelty. To live and to love and to labor in this new wild winter world was

147

an exhilarating prospect. And so I turn to a more attractive side and study the people among whom I was to live and to labor. And these were as new to me as was the country, its climate, topography and external condition.

Up to this time I had not come in contact with the Scandinavians as a people. I had met a few students in the Philadelphia Seminary and had formed a good opinion of them. Have always been glad that Dr. Lindberg, the almost life-long dean of Augustana Theological Seminary, was a classmate of mine in Philadelphia. After I had landed in Fargo I found that I was in a new Scandinavia. Hardy Norsemen made up the bulk of Fargo's citizens. There were two Norwegian Lutheran congregations, one Norwegian Baptist. The Swedish Lutherans, as yet, had no church in Fargo. Across the Red River, which we would have called a creek in Ohio, was the little town of Moorhead, Minnesota. One Norwegian and one Swedish Lutheran church were there. Many Scandinavians were unchurched. I learned that Norwegian Lutherans owned the bulk of the rich land in the Red River Valley. On a clear day I stood out on the open prairie. In that clear, rare, dry atmosphere one can see ten and twenty miles with the naked eye. The country is perfectly flat. Not a hill nor a tree obstructed my vision. Never before had I felt so really out of doors. Never had I seen so much of God's footstool and of God's heavens. On a crisp, clear night the expanse of the starry heavens is a sight to behold. It astounds and overawes one. At first I feared that I should weary of the flat prairie. Its monotony might pall on me. It never did. The wonder of the vastness impressed me more and more. It brought over me a feeling of the majesty of God and of the wonders of creation. It made me feel the littleness of myself.

This was God's country. It was owned by Lutheran people. On that day of my first vast vision, a Norwegian minister was with me. I counted ten large, frame, steepled and belled church buildings on the prairie spread around us! Every one was a Lutheran church. There was not one that was not Lutheran. What a scene of Lutheran strength! What visions of future possibilities.

On another day I was riding across the prairie in a Norwegian pastor's buggy, who was at home in that country. In nearly a day's drive we passed only one farm that was not owned or tenanted by a Lutheran! Any wonder that, with my sanguine temperament, I grew enthusiastic for a great, growing, coming, rich Lutheran Church in the Northwest. Any wonder that I wrote colorful letters to Passavant's *Workman* about this promising, wintry wonderland of the Northwest, whose chief products were number one hard spring wheat and young Lutherans.

I studied these people, so new and so interesting to me. I could write a book about them. Others better able than I have written such books. I like to read them. Here I can only mention a few general characteristics as they impressed me: Physically they are well-built, strong, tall, hardy, healthy, fair haired, fine looking people. They have an open countenance and look you fairly in the face. The fear of men is not in their eyes. Neither are they afraid of hardship. Stories of long, hard, bleak, blizzardy winters do not keep them away from a fertile soil that promises a heavy harvest. Inured to privation and toil in the home-land, they do not fear hardship in a land with promise of better remuneration. They are just the people that the new Northwest needed. They have made the erstwhile bleak and barren prairies bloom out like a great garden of God. America owes them an incalculable debt of gratitude. They are gifted with a fine mentality, a good mind, a quick insight and perception, ability to think, to reason, to reflect clearly, naturally and logically. We can safely call them a bright people. Exceptions, of course, there are. I am speaking of their general traits and characteristics. I believe I am safe in saying that the leading educators in America agree with my estimate. And how they love education. How they will plan and how ready they are to sacrifice and to suffer that their children may have an education. I actually saw large families living in sod shacks on the open prairie sending a boy or girl to Concordia College. Am sorry to say that I have not seen anything like this among the Germans. Noble exceptions of course there are. But the rank and file of the German common people want the boys and girls to earn money as early as possible. The Scandinavian lands have the smallest percentage of illiteracy of any in the world. The state superintendent of North Dakota Schools, a middle-aged, New England Yankee, told me that it was a constant surprise to him how these Scandinavians love education. That accounts for their wonderful, recent nearly three million dollar drive for their colleges and seminary. They love education. St. Olaf College is known and admired the world over. These people love liberty. They also respect law. I believe it has been statistically established that they furnish the smallest percentage of criminals of all the nationalities in America. As a class they are honest. A merchant from New England, whose business was mainly with farmers, told me that he did a large credit business and that he had never had business with people who as a class were so honest. Here is a striking illustration. The charter of the iniquitous and disgraceful Louisiana Lottery Company was about to run out. The shameless robbers who made up that company wanted to find a state that would grant them a charter. North Dakota had had several successive crop failures. The farmers were very poor. They didn't know where their next seed-wheat would come from. The lottery company sent a smooth-tongued rascal, with a million dollars, to Bismarck, where the North Dakota Legislature was in session. This company had drawn up a carefully worded, deceptive bill, "A Bill to Provide Seed Wheat for North Dakota Farmers." There were twenty Norwegian Lutherans in that legislature. They were largely farmers. The lottery men had figured that if they could buy the Norwegians they could get their bill thru. They did get one Norwegian, named Sandager. With his permission they called their lying bill "The Sandager Bill for Providing Seed Wheat," etc. The bill would really grant a state charter to the lottery company. O the villainy in politics! A storm of indignation swept the state when the devilish scheme was published. A committee of ministers of whom I was one went from Fargo to Bismarck. In the governor's office he said to us: "Gentlemen, I could now retire and be independent for life if I'd promise to help to put that bill thru and then sign it." When it came to a vote, of the twenty Norwegians, one, Sandager, voted for the bill, two refused to vote, and seventeen voted against it every time. It was hopelessly defeated. The lottery men had not known how all Lutherans have had drilled into them, in confirmation

151

class: "Thou shalt not steal." They did not know Norwegians. The sturdy Norsemen saved our state.

As a class they hate the saloon. Under the Local Option Law they voted their state dry. Like the lottery men the liquor men poured in money like water. They didn't know the Norwegian Lutherans. After election they didn't know what had struck them!

These industrious, thrifty lovers of the soil are a model to the whole Lutheran Church. The whole Church should glory in them. They are getting rich by leaps and bounds.

Speaking of the general religious traits of these people, I learned that as a class they are deeply and sincerely pious. The emotional element in them is strong. They have a heart. They feel. They want their feelings touched and moved. They like it. In this the Swedes, as a class, are probably more pronounced than the Norwegians. Both are open to the emotional appeal. Both are in danger of being swept from their own church moorings by waves of excitement from the outside. The fundamentally heretical Waldenstrom led a large section of the Swedish Lutheran Church into his own dangerous sect. Many of his followers, who call themselves "Mission Friends," are superficial, indifferent to doctrine, one-sidedly subjective, bitter and unfair against the Lutheran Church. They have greatly weakened the Augustana Synod. I may be wrong, but I have often felt that it would have been better for Augustana if her ministers had imitated the activity and the personal soul-seeking of these unsound rivals, and if they had put more warmth and heart-appeal into their own preaching. In a lesser degree, the same thing is true of the Norwegians. They too are Scandinavians. They too are more emotional than

the Germans. I am speaking of nationalities as a class.
The Germans live more in their intellect. The Scandinavians in their feelings. The German Lutherans, in
the home land and in America have been hurt and
weakened by rationalistic leaders and movements. The
great Evangelical Synod, which represents the Prus-
sian Union in America, is rationalistic and averse to
Confessional Lutheranism. It has troubled German Lutherans as Waldenstrom's movement troubled the
Swedes. The Scandinavians have been much more ready
to be influenced by emotional sects and movements than
the Germans. Methodists, Baptists, Moodyites and the
Salvation Army have scarcely touched the Germans.
All find ready recruits among the Scandinavians. It
seems that they find many more among the Swedes
than among the Norwegians. The Norwegian Lutherans have been seriously divided among themselves.
Among their early immigrants were the followers of a
layman, Elling Eielsen. They organized themselves into a synod. Later on most of these went into the
Hauge Synod. They represented the more emotional
Norwegians. There has been a tendency to split off
and split up among these people. Today there are two
other bodies more or less akin to Ellingites and
Haugians: one is the rather large so-called Free
Church, the other is the Brotherhood Union. The former has Augsburg Seminary, Minneapolis, as its school,
the other has the so-called Bible School at Grand
Forks. To my mind neither of these two bodies has a
valid and justifiable ground for a separate existence.
The great, historic, scholarly and confessional Lutheran body was the Norwegian Synod. This body had
great leaders. They loved education and insisted on an
educated ministry. In all their strong settlements they

established schools and soon had good colleges. Their large, profusely illustrated *School Calendar* of eight hundred pages has been an eye opener to all Eastern Lutherans who are progressive enough and broad enough to examine it.

The "Synod Lutherans," as they were called, had troubles of their own. Their native tendency to individualism and free thought brought disagreement as to the theological education of their ministers. Some of their leaders conceived a great admiration for the stalwart German Missouri Synod. They induced a growing stream of their students for the ministry to get their theological training at St. Louis. When I became acquainted with Norwegian character, characteristics and temperamental traits I became more and more convinced that the Missouri straight jacket never did and never could fit the free Norwegian back. The Norwegians found it out to their sorrow. They could not swallow Walther's doctrine of Predestination. They followed Ohio and separated from the Synodical Conference. In later years they united with the other Norwegian bodies and formed the great "Norwegian Lutheran Church of America." As other Lutheran bodies, both East and West, had done to the incalculable injury of Lutheranism, these people held on to the separatistic, nationalistic adjective "Norwegian." But they can't carry the irritating, hampering load much longer.

I have gone into all this historic and descriptive matter because it was so new to me. I was shamefully ignorant. As I came to understand my new human environment I studied these people and their history. It was intensely interesting to me. It became more and more a fascination. And the more I came to know the

Scandinavian people as a whole, I am frank to say, the more I came to admire and love them. Not all of them, of course. Why, some of them were foolish enough not to agree with me!

Among these good people I had come to gather and organize an English Lutheran church for the General Council. Why should that Eastern Lutheran body want to come away out here and plant a new and lonely mission? That is a big question. It deserves an answer. It has not always been answered as frankly as it deserves. As usual, I want to be very frank.

We Lutherans from the East had a century and a half of history behind us. We had made our mistakes, our blunders. As we look back we feel like calling them criminal blunders. I do not hesitate to say that because of our stupid shortsightedness on the language question a million of children and youth had been lost to the Lutheran Church. It is a tragic story. We did not want the Scandinavians of the West to repeat the suicidal blunders of Germans and Swedes in the East. We wanted to help them save their children in the Lutheran Church. From Doctor Passavant I had learned to see a great future for our Church in the Northwest if she could hold her children. We wanted to help in this vast undertaking.

Not that we few, scattered General Council men expected to do all the English work needed out here. That was never my idea. Others, among us, had that idea. I believed, first, that in many of the important centers the foreign speaking Lutherans were making the old mistake of not providing English for their children. I saw in Fargo, Moorhead and in the neighboring towns that I visited that Lutheran children were in Reformed and Union Sunday Schools and in Christian

Endeavor societies. To me the saddest part was that neither parents nor pastors seemed worried. They did not and would not realize the bearing, the force and the danger of this movement toward English. Here are a few factual experiences. When Grand Forks Lutheran College was dedicated, by invitation I made the English address. Before that large audience of ministers and leading laymen I related some of the deplorable mistakes that Eastern Lutherans had made and of the consequent losses to our Church. I tried to make my hearers see that their dear, bright children, born in free, English speaking America, brought up in our public schools, where the whole atmosphere and spirit and language are of America, could not be Norwegians like their parents but would be Americans. I told them that these children were thinking and talking and scrapping and sleeping and dreaming in English. Some of my hearers looked grave, others smiled skeptically, still others shook their heads and seemed annoyed. They had never heard it on this wise before. I spent the night in the hospitable home of a prosperous Lutheran merchant. It was one of those still, bright, piercing Dakota winter nights. As we sat by his big, red-hot "Radiant Home" heater, my host said to me: "Pastor, you made that too strong today, that about English. My children are just as Norwegian as their mother and I." "Well," I said, "I know you think so. You ought to know; but pardon me, you don't know it all." As we were thus good naturedly arguing, while we smoked our cigars, one of his bright, sweet little girls, about six years old, sleeping in a room open to the living room where we were sitting, had a bad dream. She screamed and called Mama, and all she said in English. Her mother quieted her in English. I said to my host: "Did you hear that, Mr. E.? Why didn't the little girl talk Norwegian? Didn't I tell you that the children sleep in English and dream in English?" He smiled and said: "I guess you've got me now, I didn't know that." "Yes," I said, "But some of us have been watching these things for twenty-five years and we know."

I was invited to preach a number of times in a Hauge Synod church in Mayville, N. D. It was a prosperous little Norwegian town. There was a Congregationalist mission there, supported by Eastern money. I investigated carefully. I found that in that church the Sunday School superintendent was a Lutheran. Every teacher was a Lutheran, the organist and the whole choir were Lutheran. Of course the Sunday School was made up of Lutheran children. And that was going on in a hundred towns all over the great, coming Northwest!

We, Eastern, English Lutherans were needed to plant English Lutheran missions and organize English congregations where our board had money to send us. But the sporadic and isolated work that we could do in "these empires yet to be" was only a drop here and there in the great big buckets that were leaking so badly. We couldn't begin to do even a moiety of what was needed. But while we were putting in our sporadic little plants which were to become fruitful trees in God's great garden, we were doing these other sorely needed things: First, every purely English mission was a trumpet call to the Lutherans all around us, proclaiming to them that it is high time to bring our pure, Biblical message to all the people in the language of the land. Second, our work was an ocular demonstration, an obvious object lesson showing that it was possible to be a good Lutheran and to do pure, sound Lutheran work and preach and teach and worship and sing in English only. Third, we showed our neighbors how to do it. We brought with us our literature. Its English was classic. It was the fruitage of a hundred years of experience. For its style we could rightly claim that it had "the ring of the chimes of the church bells." Its Lutheranism was unimpeachably sound. It had taken our best scholars twenty years to make our Common Service. Our matchless graded Sunday School series also had been in the making for twenty years and has been in the process of perfecting ever since. Yes, we could be Lutheran in English. We showed our neighbors how. In so far as they were willing to profit by our experience they did more and more excellent English work. For this we thank God and take courage. I hope they will not forget what they owe to us.

My mission then in Fargo was to gather and build up an English Lutheran Congregation. By so doing I was to herald out, up and down the Red River Valley and to the regions beyond, the need of English Lutheran work. I was to demonstrate the fact that it is possible to be thoroly sound and orthodox and to speak and worship entirely in English. I was to help to show how such a thing, hitherto unheard of in the Northwest, could be done. And all this was to be an encouragement to my neighbors, far and near, to go and do likewise.

With this motive and this vision, what did I expect in Fargo? Well, I did think that of all the people who read their daily papers in English, did their marketing, shopping and trading in English, went to shows, entertainments and social gatherings where all was English, I did think that many of these would be glad to come to a soundly Lutheran Church that was entirely English and belonged to an English Lutheran Synod. But they didn't come. They were all kind and friendly and wished me well. But they went to their own foreign-tongued churches just as before. They let me and my little mission gloriously alone. I had to depend on those who were unconnected anywhere. Some of them called themselves Lutheran but were attending Reformed churches, Sunday Schools or ladies' aids. Other ex-Lutherans were going nowhere, still others had neither Lutheran blood nor tradition. They were outsiders—heathen in a Christian land. Out of such material I had to build my mission. It was painfully slow and discouraging. In Ohio I had preached to full houses. To move out here, advertise my services and then preach to ten or a dozen or at best to fifteen or twenty for a whole year—this made my heart sink within me. I was humbled in the dust. Perhaps I needed this. True, some of the young pick-ups developed into substantial church members who became a great comfort and help to me. Likewise did some of those who had been originally Lutheran, had joined Reformed churches and had come into our little flock. It was slow, trying and often vexing work. I often felt like running away. But I was not a quitter. I had the growing conviction that, for reasons stated above, our church was needed in Fargo.

The Sunday School work went better. We began with seven pupils—three from our family. I recall the first Sunday, when I arrived there were several boys and girls in front of the church. One boy had climbed into a box-elder tree. I greeted all kindly. The boy up the tree was not a Zaccheaus. He made me a speech. He informed me that he didn't want to come to Sunday School, but his mother had told him to come and see what we had there. He predicted that our Sunday School wouldn't go anyhow, that Rev. Ulery had tried it and had given it up, that our church wouldn't go either. That his parents were German Lutherans, so were his uncle's folks, that there was no German Lutheran church in town, but they all said they wouldn't go to that English church nohow. That boy became one of my best and most regular pupils. His older brother became superintendent, deacon, and one of my best helpers. Our Sunday School grew rapidly and was a surprise to our Lutheran neighbors. We knew how to conduct a Sunday School that was thoroly American and yet soundly Lutheran. We knew how to make it both attractive and instructive, both lively yet helpful. We had both pep and sound doctrine. Ere long our Lutheran neighbors, who would not worship with us, sent their children to our Sunday School. Our Sunday School was our hope and encouragement. I might mention here also that as our curly-headed missionary Emma was rapidly growing she developed a great love for Sunday School work. By and by she gathered a Sunday afternoon, summer, wood-shed Sunday School which beat the Sunday School in "Mrs. Wigg's Cabbage Patch" all to pieces. How that wood-shed Sunday School would sing the Lutheran hymns out of the Sunday School Book! Well, it helped our Sunday School and developed our Japan Missionary.

To come back to our slow church growth. Why couldn't I realize my expectations? I had several things to learn. I didn't know as much as I thought I did. People who would talk English and trade in English and gossip with their neighbors in English were not so eager as I thought they would be to worship in

English. If they were real, devout, Lutheran Christians they had two languages. One was a heart language, the other a head language, one was an every day language, the other was a church language, one was for making and spending money and being neighborly, the other was for converse and communion with God, one was secular, the other was sacred. The one they had picked up or gotten in school. In the other their mothers had taught them to pray and to sing. In it they first read and heard read the Bible. In it they heard the minister preach. In it they had been instructed, catechised and confirmed. All their life they had talked with God and God had talked to them in the mother tongue. That was sacred. That was religion. That I didn't know. So foolish was I and so ignorant. I learned the lesson unwillingly. I thank God I learned it. Many English Lutheran ministers never learn it.

And so my church work was slow, disheartening and disappointing. The best Lutherans were anchored in their own churches. They remained there. They ought to, I never tried to pull them away. On their own accord they did not come as I had expected that some would. It was a hard lesson for me to learn that, out here, our English missions do not get the best Lutherans. We would have to be content with what our neighbor Lutheran churches could not hold. We had to be content with the crumbs that fell from their tables. These were sometimes begrudged us. Then we were here also to go out into the streets and lanes, seek out and bring in those whom no church had sought or found or won. The heathen at home we were to seek and save. Thank God for all that our English missions have done and are doing in this line. The home missionary who is not doing such work is faithless to his trust and will have to give an account for souls lost whom he might have saved.

Now that I have frankly confessed how ignorant I was and what mistakes I made, I want to be just as frank as to the ignorance and the mistakes and sins that the foreign speaking Lutherans are guilty of. Because the good who came from a land across the sea, or were brought up here in a foreign tongue community, have that feeling of reverence and piety toward their mother-tongue they believe that their children ought to feel just as they do. This is a mistake. It is ignorance. It is wrong. As shown above, those children, born here, reared here among English speaking neighbors, educated in our public schools, cannot be Germans or Scandinavians. They are English-thinking, English-feeling, English-speaking Americans. To expect them, to force them to be and feel like the parents is to expect the impossible. It is against their nature to be and to feel other than English speaking Americans. If their parents and their pastors do not see that they get their religion in English they sin against them. This is one of the hardships that comes from emigrating from fatherland and immigrating into a new land with a new tongue. Such a big move brings many and great blessings. But it requires and demands many hard and painful sacrifices. For the children and children's children, the old precious faith needs not to be sacrificed. But the language needs to be sacrificed. The rising generations must have the faith of the fathers in the language of the children. The parents are sacrificing for their children in many ways all the time. They make this great sacrifice also. As I said above: My father united with the English

162

Lutheran Church for his children's sake. Had he not done so, in all human likelihood I would not be a Lutheran today. Here is the greatest lesson that our foreign Lutherans must learn. Here is the great sacrifice foreign speaking parents must make. Make it for Christ's sake, for your Church's sake, for your children's souls' sake.

CHAPTER XIII

LIFE AND EXPERIENCES IN FARGO

WHEN I arrived in Fargo I, at once, began investigating the possibilities of bringing out my family and making them comfortable. I found the cost of living was fully fifty percent higher than in Jewett, Ohio. Rents were one hundred per cent higher. It did not take me long to be convinced that I could not pay rent and keep a family of five on a thousand a year. It would take over a hundred a year for fuel alone. We would all have to be re-clothed from undergarments to over coats before we would be able to be on the streets in winter.

I saw only one way out. We must build a parsonage at once. I contracted for a small, five-room frame house. Water pipes and sewers had not yet reached our end of town. We could have no inside plumbing. Our cottage must have a cistern, under the kitchen, and a small, deep cellar. The cement cistern must catch all the rain-water from the house roof and one side of the church roof. It must be filtered thru charcoal. I hired contractors by the day and arranged for the purchase of material. Then I wrote dozens of letters to friends back East soliciting help for this enterprise. I went out on the street and presented my cause in office and store and bank. I frankly told the story of the need of a purely English Lutheran Church, of what we stood for and what we hoped to do. I also told them that we did not expect to pester the town with requests to buy tickets for suppers, sales, fairs, bazaars and cheap shows. My straightforward plea met with a kindly response. I did not expect large contributions. On this and several subsequent rounds I gathered upwards of a thousand dollars on the streets of Fargo and Moorhead. I was contractor, collector, paymaster, janitor and man of all work. Some money came dribbling in from the East, but not as I had hoped. I learned over again what I had learned before and have learned ever since, that to get money for the cause of Christ it is not enough to send out circular letters from office or study. The inspired Paul tells us to "charge them that are rich," i. e., those who can give that they be "rich toward God." Charge them, see them personally, button-hole them, plead with them to give. That's the Bible way. That's the way that Doctor Passavant, singlehanded and alone raised more money for his wonderful work than the whole General Council raised for benevolence in the same length of time. I was with Passavant on several of his soliciting tours. Oh, how he could appeal "by the mercies of God." But he also was often coldly turned down.

Well, I paid my bills for labor and material regularly. In less than two months the little house was ready for its occupants. I had a hand-pump to bring water from the cistern to a kitchen sink. A similar pump to bring water to a little up-stairs bath room for which I had purchased a second hand bath tub. I purchased the necessary furniture from a good Lutheran firm, Beck and Weight, in Moorhead. From a Fargo Lutheran hardware firm I purchased a cook stove, a sheet-iron heating stove for the living room and a smaller heater for the bed-room study up stairs.

The girls' bed room, above the living room, was kept livable by a hot air drum from the stove below.

The good wife had had a public sale of the household goods, except the books, in Jewett. When all was ready I went to meet the tender-foot pioneering family in Minneapolis. We put up at the ever open, hospitable home of the Traberts. Then, off to Fargo for a new home and a new life. Little did we know what was before us. But we were young. We had the blessed good fortune of having learned to bear the yoke in our youth. We expected hardships. But we were ready to take the new life, hardships and all, as an adventure. I believed that I had been called of God. From Doctor Passavant I had learned that this assurance would ever be my safest capital, my comfort and my stay.

It was early autumn. Esther and Emma were started to school. Even then the schools were excellent. Our two babies, Comfort and Ruth, were at home. We had heard gruesome stories about the terrible winters. They were not all exaggerations. On the twelfth of October we had a twelve-hour blizzard when we could not see across the street. Then the bitter, biting cold! For weeks at a time the thermometer would hang at about twenty below. Sometimes thirty. Rarely forty. I walked to Moorhead and back one day when it was forty-one below. I had a good, long, coon-skin fur coat and cap and gloves. Arctic over-shoes and other clothes to correspond. Sometimes we would see a farmer crawl out from under the buffalo robes in his bob sled and throw the robes over his horses. He would look almost like an animal. Buffalo trousers with feet to them, buffalo coat, cap and gloves. What cared he for forty below?

Here are a few true stories. I met a Norwegian

166

preacher from Cooperstown, N. D.—sorry I can't recall his name—who told me how he was caught, with
his team, on the open prairie by a sudden blizzard. It
was mid-afternoon and he had to face the driving,
stinging wind and blinding snow. He hoped to reach
home before night-fall. But night fell early and quick-
ly. His ponies refused to face the storm. He saw that
he was lost. He spied a gulley with several stunted
trees. He turned his ponies into the gulley, got out
of his sled, tied the Buffalo robes securely on the ponies
and tied them to the back of his sled. The gulley
afforded some shelter from the wildness of the wind.
But the snow was piling in around him and his team.
He saw that there was danger of himself and horses
being buried out of sight before morning. He also
knew that he must keep in motion to keep alive. He
began to tramp a circle around horses and sleigh. Thus
he kept the snow down. And so he tramped, tramped,
tramped the weary hours away. After a while the
wind ceased. He had purposely avoided looking at his
watch for fear it would disappoint him. Now he struck
a match. He knew how. I could never have done it.
It was three o'clock. He girded himself and tramped
for two hours more. The bright stars of the prairie
heavens were shining. He hitched up his stiff horses,
got his bearings and drove home to his frantic family
for breakfast. Another Norwegian pastor told me he
had covered and tied his horses and dug himself under
the snow, wrapped around with buffalo robes and actually slept till he dug himself out in the morning. At
St. Olaf College I like to hunt up the statue erected
to the memory of a young preacher—graduate, who
was frozen dead when on his way to carry the Gospel
to an outlying congregation. There are modern Ameri-

can Lutheran martyrs. They counted not their lives dear unto them. God knows them all.

I found a young man without hands—only iron hooks strapped to his wrists—selling newspapers on a street corner in Fargo. I inquired as to the cause of his pitiable condition. He told me that his hands had been frozen off. He was averse to talking about it. Afterwards I found his mother. She told me this tragic story: The family had been living in a "claim shack" on the open prairie in Cass County. Fargo was the county seat. Her husband, a thrifty German, had built a better house on another part of the one hundred and sixty acre government claim farm. On an afternoon of early winter they were moving to their new house. The husband and oldest boy had hauled one load with the mother and baby into the new house and had hurried back after the remaining goods. It seems that he had neglected to put up the stove and bring in wood. The mother had hastily set up a bed and then tried to set up the stove. She had trouble, grew faint and had to give it up. She had put the baby—less than two years old—to sleep on the floor. By this time a blinding blizzard was raging and it had grown inky dark. The sick woman crept into the bed. It grew killingly cold. Early in the night a new baby was born! The poor little boy was moaning beside the bed and pounding his frozen arms like hammers on the floor. The mother, in birth pangs, could not move. She was praying for her husband to come. He never came. He and his boy and the team were frozen dead not many rods from the new house. The mother kept the new born baby alive. God kept the baby on the floor alive. His two hands had to be amputated. He became the husky newsboy, helping to keep his mother with his daily earnings!

I could tell more true blizzard stories, but these will suffice. Into such a clime we had come to build up a home, to rear a family and to plant and build the first English Lutheran Church in the vast empire of Dakotah territory. God was good to us. We kept our house comfortable. We were all warmly clad. The two school girls had lots of fun hitching their new sleds on behind the many vehicles on runners that were driven on the streets.

As it doesn't rain during at least six months of the long winter I was afraid that we should pump our cistern dry. Fur-clad men were driving bob-sleds loaded with great, heavy chunks of ice along the streets. They were offering this ice for sale at fifty to seventy-five cents a load. I bought a big new dishpan and a pair of ice hooks or tongs. Then bought a load of ice which we piled up, like cord wood, on the shady side of the house. As I had been an ice-man I knew how to handle ice. I kept the dishpan full on the back of the stove. We had plenty of water. Every vehicle in town was on runners; even the fire engine and hose cart. We lived thru it and counted it an adventure.

My first task was to make myself and my mission understood. I was a rare bird. Before the Rev. Mr. Ulery, an English Lutheran minister had not been heard of in those parts. The English speaking Americans knew the Lutherans in a foreign tongue only. A lawyer stopped me on Broadway one day and said: "Are you really a Lutheran preacher? Why, you speak pretty good English for a Lutheran!" Many Scandinavian ministers had never met a Lutheran who preached in English only. They had serious doubts whether pure Lutheranism could be preached in English. I visited them and cultivated them. Fortunately for me I had written *The Way of Salvation.* I kept a stock on hand. I gave them away freely. They were eagerly read. The book established my orthodoxy. They also gradually came to understand that I did not want to proselyte what they could hold; that I did not want to weaken them but wanted to help them. They came to see that I was there to make the Lutheran Church understood and to help them to make sound Lutheranism strong in the new Northwest.

From the beginning of my ministry I had believed that the Lutheran Church was entirely too modest. She seemed to shun publicity. I felt that this was all wrong. I made myself known to the editors of morning and evening papers. I published all Lutheran doings. I wrote short, informing paragraphs as to Lutheran teaching and Lutheran strength. I kept my own services before the people all the time. Lutherans sat up and took notice. They liked it. The town was learning that they were here and that they were somebody. And so little St. Mark's was letting the big light of Northwestern Lutheranism shine. Lutherans were surprised to find themselves before the public. They were being introduced to themselves. Publicity was doing its work. But with all that, St. Mark's was growing, oh, so slowly. My impetuous spirit often chafed impatiently. But I was beginning to do a wider work.

My neighbor Lutherans were finding out that they could use me. I was willing to be used. I really felt that I was not earning my salary from the board. My St. Mark's results were so meager. Fargo was not a ripe field for English. The feeling also grew on me that the whole North Dakota and especially the Red River Valley needed a Lutheran Evangelistic campaign. The Scandinavian churches needed to be enlightened and warned against their dangers. Because of the swelling stream of immigration from their homelands that was pouring into this new land of promise, their churches were growing with leaps and bounds. New members were pouring in by scores and hundreds. This was the time of their prosperity. Their prosperity was their danger. They were satisfied.

A generation was growing up that had been born here and was being reared in our public schools. As shown above, these young Americans could not have the same feeling for fatherland and mother tongue that their parents had. More and more they were thinking, talking, playing, scrapping, sleeping and dreaming in English. As they had the every day school in English, they wanted English in the Sunday School.

The rich, far sighted and aggressive home mission boards of the strong Reformed Churches saw an opportunity. They would gather these promising children and youth into their Sunday Schools and thru the Sunday Schools into their churches. Glowing reports of the new fertile lands in the West, of the inflowing stream of settlers, of the fact that they were Protestants—rarely did they say that they were Lutherans—that their children were growing up without Sunday Schools, that they must be Americanized or would grow up as stupid aliens who might become a danger to our country and our government. Men and money were poured in. Back there in the eighties, North Dakota had over a dozen denominational Sunday School secretaries and home mission superintendents who gave their whole time canvassing communities, building neat and attractive churches with Eastern money and organizing Sunday Schools and congregations. A full time pastor was placed in every little town. Sometimes there were two or three of rival denominations. The little churches were equipped with music and all sorts of attractive cards, charts and literature. This was going on all over the middle Northwest and clear out to the Pacific. The children liked these bright, cheery Sunday Schools with their welcome atmosphere and kindly greetings. They always carried home a card, a picture paper, a lesson-leaf or booklet. Why shouldn't they like it?

Here, then, was an organized, a well planned, well-manned and well-financed work that was threatening the future of the Lutheran Church. What was going on at Mayville, as shown above, was going on in hundreds of places. The same nefarious, proselyting work is going on still.

As this sad situation became more and more clear to me, it grieved me sorely. To me the saddest part was that it did not seem to worry the Scandinavians. I felt that they must be aroused and helped. I felt that I should like to help them.

My dear friend, W. A. Passavant, Jr., had the whole situation before him. Together we planned that the board should send students from the Philadelphia Seminary into several important Northwestern centers for the summer. I wanted one so that I might travel among the Lutherans of the Red River Valley. They sent me a splendid Philadelphia middler, Mr. Geo. Gebert. He spent the summer in our Fargo home. He was an Israelite without guile. He was eager to learn and ready for any work that might be assigned. A good student, he prepared good sermons and preached them well. He was ready for Sunday School and Luther League work. He went with me as we visited from house to house. In our home we all came to love him. I soon saw that I could safely leave my St. Mark's work in his hands and go out into the larger work.

By this time my Norwegian brethren had come to know and trust me. They were no longer afraid of my Lutheranism. I had preached and spoken in their churches. They came to see that it would be a good thing to have an English address or paper at their *kredsmøter* or circuit meetings and at mission festivals, cornerstone layings and consecrations. Their program committees would say: "Well, we must have Gerberding along." And Gerberding was always willing.

I found no trouble in making out a summer itinerary while Gebert took care of Fargo. I visited and spoke in twenty-one churches. I had good and attentive audiences. The majority of the congregations had never seen an English Lutheran minister or heard an English sermon. I tried to tell them something of the greatness and the superior goodness of the Lutheran Church; of the wonderful opportunity that God was opening for their Church in this new land. I showed them their own strength and tried to make them see that God had given them the rich Red River Valley as really and as truly as He had given the Promised Land to His people Israel. I showed them how Israel had lost their Canaan and how Lutherans might lose theirs. I showed them that their new home land had a new language. That English here is the language of law, of government, of business, of the public schools and of social life. That their children and children's children would want and would use that language.

That they would want it in Sunday School, in confirmation class and in the pulpit. That the little English churches around them were not Lutheran, that their teachings were unscriptural and often dangerous. That these heretical churches wanted their children. That they offered them the Gospel, such as they had, in English. That their children would be drawn in by the English and would thus be lost to the Lutheran Church. I showed them what terrible losses the Eastern Lutherans had sustained and gave many concrete examples. I warned them against the proselyting Reformed churches around them, showed them that if the Lutheran Church wants to hold her children she must give them English. I told them where they could get English Lutheran Hymn Books and Lesson literature for their own Sunday School. As was my wont, I spoke out plainly. I did want them to see their danger. I did want to scare them, and I sowed good seed up and down the fruitful valley.

My greatest disappointment was the coldness and apathy of so many ministers toward the American Sunday School. They said that it is superficial. That it amounts to nothing. That it is an American humbug, that it is not worth noticing. I freely confess that many so-called Sunday Schools are but poor excuses for schools, and yet, when I look at the American Sunday School movement and organization I cannot help but admit that it has been a mighty influence in American church life. It has probably drawn more Lutheran children away from their church than all other agencies combined. You cannot laugh a movement like this out of existence. It is attractive. For children and youth there is a fascination about it. It draws them. It holds them. It weans them away from the church that has no Sunday School, or, at best, a lifeless, dull, dry, unattractive, compulsory gathering. There is only one way to successfully meet its drawing away power, and that is to have a better, a more helpful and at the same time more attractive Sunday School of our own. This is possible. It can be done. It has been done and is being done in hundreds of places all over the land. The whole Lutheran Church must learn how. To this I have repeatedly referred in the foregoing pages. I repeat that it pained me to see how Norwegian Lutherans were losing their children. It pained me still more to see that they would not believe it or did not seem to care. And what is still worse is, that this is still going on. Several years ago I looked up in the minutes of the latest convention of The Norwegian Lutheran Church the statistics for North Dakota. The figures frightened me. Over one-third of their congregations had no Sunday Schools at all! Too sad to tell! Proselyting sects still have a rich field and open doors in North Dakota and all over the great Lutheran Northwest. Our Eastern, foreign speaking Lutherans had made the same fatal mistake. I wanted to save the Western Lutherans from repeating these blunders. I hope I did some good. They need district Sunday School secretaries everywhere.

Time came all too soon for Geo. Gebert to leave us. It pained us to see him go. He had done a good work. He had endeared himself to our people. He and I had spent many happy hours together. He has done good work for Christ and for His Church ever since. He has never shirked hard work, self denial and sacrifice. He was not always appreciated. But God knows. May His richest blessings abide with him to the end.

My Fargo life was rich in varied experiences. I can briefly mention but a few.

We had an unusually pleasant surprise when we received word that Dr. Passavant was going west on the Northern Pacific and would stop with us over Sunday. I got busy at once to make arrangements to get the most good for Fargo Lutheranism from the visit of one whom I considered our greatest and grandest Lutheran leader. I called on all the Lutheran ministers and informed them of the rare privilege of having such a visitor. I proposed a mass meeting for all Lutherans in the skating rink, our largest public hall, on Sunday evening. All the ministers responded, promised to make announcements Sunday morning and urge all their people to come. We also arranged for a chorus made up from the various Lutheran choirs. Then I wrote half a column for each of the dailies. I gave a brief account of who Doctor Passavant was and of the wonderfully Christian charity work he had done and was doing. I invited all good people out to the Rink on Sunday night to hear him. He arrived Saturday morning, and it was a benediction for us to have him in our home. On my study-table he saw my write-up about him and his work. He took me to task for doing this without his permission. He said that he never gave himself such publicity. That such bragging is all wrong. He reminded me how the Savior after working a great miracle went away and hid Himself. On Saturday afternoon the doctor inquired about the county hospital, our only one. He asked me how often I visit the patients. I told him that I go whenever I am sent for. Then he gave me one of those never to be forgotten kindly reproofs. He showed me that here was an opportunity for doing good right at my door.

That I ought to visit all the patients at least once a week. I took his personal sermon to heart. I deserved it. I arranged to take a few singers every Sunday afternoon, have a short service and a few words with every patient. I came to enjoy and to profit by these visits more and more. I had some blessed experiences of good coming from this work. Thanks to Doctor Passavant. I most heartily commend such work to all our ministers. At his request I took the doctor to the hospital. I introduced him to the matron, a noble Christian Methodist woman. She and the doctor had a pleasant and profitable visit. Then the doctor went from bed to bed, talked to the patients as only he could and knelt by their bed side and prayed with them. I was again learning needed lessons from him who did me more good than any other man in the world.

At the doctor's request I invited the Lutheran pastors to meet him in my study on Monday afternoon. There he talked to them about the need of a Lutheran hospital in Fargo. Possibly that little gathering sowed some of the seeds that years later fruited out into the great and good St. Luke's Lutheran Hospital, which is a blessing to thousands and a pride of the city. A Lutheran chaplain ministers there at all the sickbeds. I must not forget to mention that at that little gathering of ministers Dr. Passavant had all that were there kneel down with him as he prayed for them and for their work. I may have mentioned this before, but I never heard a man pray like Dr. Passavant. What wonder that he prayed hospitals and orphans' homes and academies and colleges and Chicago Seminary and mission churches into being. No wonder that his answers to prayer were fully as remarkable as were those of George Muller of Bristol, England.

The doctor preached to our little flock in St. Mark's on Sunday morning. It was a rare spiritual feast to all who were there. In the evening we crowded the Rink. It was probably the largest and most representative Lutheran gathering that Fargo had seen up to that time. That was back in the eighties. Many of the leading citizens from other churches were there also. Like Paul who spoke of his wonderful experience in the third heaven in the third person, so our doctor spoke of "a man whom he had known." He gave a graphic account of some of the wonderful things that God had enabled him to do. That meeting made an impression, especially on the Lutheran people. Passavant's visit was a benediction.

Another experience not so pleasant was a brush with a bishop. When North Dakota was made a state, Bishop Ireland, of St. Paul, constituted it as a separate diocese or bishopric. A diplomatic and eloquent young Irish priest was consecrated as bishop of North Dakota. Unlike Dr. Passavant, Bishop Shanley had his coming heralded with trumpets and banners. A great public meeting of all citizens "regardless of creed or confession" was called. A procession with brass bands playing "Hail to The Chief" escorted the bishop from the station to the Rink. The governor of the state, the mayor of the city and other civic dignitaries gave him generous welcome. "Tell it not in Gath, publish it not in the streets of Askalon, lest the Philistines rejoice and the daughters of the uncircumcised triumph." A Methodist minister welcomed the Romish bishop in the name of the Protestant churches! The bishop felt flattered and honored. He made a characteristic, flattering speech. He praised the new state and its people. He promised that *the* church would bring great help and blessing to all, as the Catholic Church had always and everywhere done! The crowd seemed to drink it all in and swallowed it whole. The papers gave great headline articles and editorials. The Roman Catholic Church had a wide and warm welcome into Lutheran North Dakota! This was too much for my Lutheran blood and conscience.

On the night after the glaring newspaper publicity I couldn't sleep. I arose, ransacked my *Kurtz Church History* and my *Encyclopedia Britannica*. I learned over again how the Roman Church had always kept her lands and peoples in ignorance. I gave facts and figures from Italy, Spain, Portugal, Central and South America and Mexico. I contrasted Protestant lands on the percentage of illiteracy, especially the Lutheran, Scandinavian lands. I recalled the unsavory facts of adulterous and heretical infallible popes. I referred to the inhuman, brutal cruelties of the Inquisition and of St. Bartholomew's Massacre. I wrote these facts in an "Open Letter to Bishop Shanley" and had it published in *The Fargo Argus*. In my letter I also appealed to the people of our young state to consider well whether they wanted to welcome the bishop's church to power and influence among them. My letter caused some stir. It was widely referred to in the press. I received many commendatory and grateful letters. There were several scurrilous and slanderous attacks on me. To these I paid no attention. It was, of course, beneath the dignity of the bishop to reply!

But why, why are Lutheran ministers so timid? Why don't they get themselves into the papers where they can, and speak out. Metropolitan papers will not publish their articles. Smaller papers will. Romanism is a deadly menace to America.

At one time our town was shaken by a great Union revival. The Union Ministers' Association, made up of all English Protestant ministers, of which I was a member, had an offer from a professional Evangelist. He wanted to come to Fargo, hold a three weeks' big meeting to revive and strengthen all the churches. He was willing to accept, as remuneration, free will offerings to be paid to a treasurer chosen by our association and to be handed in on the closing days of the revival. The offer provoked a lively discussion. The Episcopal minister and I opposed the movement and declared that we could not conscientiously cooperate. Others had their doubts as to its expediency, but would go with the majority. The Evangelist was invited. A committee was appointed to make all arrangements. The Rink was rented. Choirs from all cooperating churches were joined into a mass chorus. Soloists were picked out, and practice under a chosen leader was begun. The daily papers were easily persuaded to grant liberal amounts of free space to the furtherance of the project. A printer was found who was willing to furnish several thousand handbills free of cost. The town was circularized and all things were ready. I was waited on by a special committee and urged to sit on the platform with the other ministers and cooperate in the work of the meetings. I gave the committee my reasons why my conscience would not let me take an official part. I told them that I would not publicly oppose the movement, that I would attend some of the meetings and would thank God for every true conversion that might result. I also tried to show them as I had to the ministers' meeting that I believed that our Lutheran Church had a more Scriptural and more excellent way of making disciples. To my own congregation I made a similar but fuller explanation of my stand in the matter. I knew that probably a majority of my people would attend the meetings. It would have been folly for me to oppose them. I said to them that if any of them wanted to go they should go prayerfully, pay strict attention, prove all things and hold fast what was good. I assured them that many good things would be said by which their own souls could profit. But they must beware. They must hear critically. Many things would be said and done that would not be in harmony with the teaching of God's Word and of their own Church. I strongly urged them that if some things said and done there would trouble and perplex them they should come to me and I would help them. I also informed them that I expected to go myself as a hearer and observer, but would not sit on the platform or take any part in the meeting. This seemed to satisfy all my people. I never lost a lamb. But I gained some members from the cards on which inquirers had indicated their church preference. These cards were handed to me.

The revival was not as wild, nor as boastful, nor as sacrilegious and insulting as some that I had known. It was not a brilliant success. Fargo was too Lutheran a town. Here are a few sequels: My stand did me good. It still more improved my standing with my Lutheran brethren. It helped them also. We had a number of good talks about the whole American Revival System.

The Presbyterian minister came to see me. He informed me that he was thru with the whole business. He would never go into such a movement again. That

I was right in my position. That he was sorry that he did not take the same stand. Waxing earnest, he said in substance: "Do you know what this fellow did? We ministers had cultivated the trees and ripened the fruit. He came along and shook down the fruit that we had ripened and that we would have gathered without him. But he claimed all the credit and all the glory. And he got more pay for his three weeks' work than many preachers get in a year!"

I met the Congregational Mission Superintendent. I inquired about the fruits of the revival. He was enthusiastic. It was wonderful. A manifest blessing of God. The Holy Spirit certainly was in it all! But, I said, show me some specific fruit. "Yes," he said, "I'll give you one striking instance. Do you know the editor of the Sun?" "Yes," I said, "I know him, and if he is truly converted I centainly thank God for it." "Well," he answered, "He certainly is. He not only made a public profession of faith and joined our church, but he has erected a family altar and has family worship every day." "Good," I said, "I'm glad."

A few weeks later I was sadly disillusioned. This same editor had secretly left town. His distressed family did not know what had become of him. He had left behind a raft of unpaid bills and his family unprovided for! Now I know that such sad things happen in our Church also. The human heart is deceitful and desperately wicked. All that glitters is not gold. At any rate we prefer to keep on making disciples by baptizing and teaching.

In Moorhead the Augustana Synod had a strong congregation. The Rev. J. O. Cavallin was the wide awake and aggressive pastor. He believed that his church ought to have a school in the Red River Valley, which had twenty-five Swedish Lutheran churches. He organized a "Lutheran Benevolent Society of the Red River Valley." A fine hotel property was offered for sale at one-fourth of its original cost. The Benevolent Society bought the hotel, remodeled it and opened a school called "Hope Academy." They secured a fine, capable young schoolman in Professor Challman for principal. I took much interest in this movement. I advertised it and helped it to get a start for a library. The school opened auspiciously. There seemed to be promise and prospect for a growing Lutheran academy. If my recollection is correct the synod did not adopt it. The center of the Swedish population was farther north. In that Northern region a good, strong school was planted some years later. No doubt Hope Academy, which was merged with the Northern school, gave the first stimulus for its starting. Hope did a good work, and its fruits are still growing.

The Norwegians were the great, strong, controlling people in the Red River Valley, especially on the Dakota side. Of their numerical and economic strength and influence in North Dakota I have spoken above. In 1890 a number of the Norwegian Lutherans had agreed together that they ought to have a church school of their own. They had formed themselves together into a "Red River Valley Lutheran College Association." The association invited bids for locating. I agreed that there ought to be such an institution. But I believed that it ought to be located in Fargo. This was the political and commercial center of our young state and of the Red River Valley. We were at the juncture of the two great trans-continental rail roads. We could take trains in nine directions

every day. I tried to stir our Fargo brethren. They
were hard to move. But we did get the matter before
the Fargo Board of Trade. It was favorably received
and committees were appointed to secure the college
for Fargo. The College Association received bids and
offers from Crookston and Grand Forks. Our Fargo
Board of Trade made the best offer. They offered
eighteen acres of land inside of the city corporation
and ten thousand dollars. Crookston and Grand Forks
combined against Fargo. The majority of the members of the College Association were from the neighborhood of these two towns and would not accept Fargo's fine offer. I succeeded in getting the brethren
from Fargo and vicinity to call a meeting. At this
meeting it was decided that a school at either Crookston or Grand Forks could not meet the demands of
the large Norwegian population contiguous to Fargo.
Measures were therefore taken to try to establish an
institution here, regardless of what the Northern towns
might do. We did not have the right men to push the
Fargo interest. The conditioned subscriptions and
offers that had been made were allowed to lapse. The
board of trade was disappointed at the lack of interest and push and dropped the matter. Fargo Lutherans failed.

Then came a fine offer from Moorhead across the
little Red River. Eight years earlier the Episcopalians
had started the so-called "Bishop Whipple School."
They had erected a fine, large three-story building
at a cost of twenty-eight thousand dollars. The school
had failed. Money alone cannot make a school go.
The architectural beauty had stood vacant for several
years. It was offered to the Lutherans, with six acres
of ground, for ten thousand dollars. Moorhead citi-

zens offered to raise one-third of the price. This was surely a tempting offer. I still believed that the proposed school ought to be in Fargo. I was convinced that the great majority of students would come from the Dakota side of the river. Besides, Moorhead had a Lutheran school in Hope Academy. I believed that with a proper, energetic effort Fargo's flagging interest could be revived. But the path of least resistance was chosen, and Concordia College was located in Moorhead. As soon as it was so decided I threw my whole force in favor of Concordia. A "Northwestern College Association" was organized of which I became an active member. They made me vice-president of their first Board of Directors. This memory has been a joy to me ever since. I took a lively interest in every forward movement. I made many trips with brethren and made many addresses in which I tried to rouse an interest in every forward movement and in the coming school.

God prospered the movement. I got a place for my friend Prof. E. D. Busby on the faculty. His excellent and capable wife became the first dean of women. I was glad to have a part in the dedication of the building, the inauguration of the first president, Prof. Grose, and the opening of the school. I had the privilege of making many chapel and other addresses to the students. I have watched Concordia with deep interest thru all its history. Its growth, prosperity and efficiency have been a constant source of joy and gratitude. Dr. Aasgaard, now the efficient and progressive president of the great Norwegian Lutheran Church of America, brought up Concordia and gave it a name and a place of honor among the many ambitious colleges of the Northwest. The new president,

Dr. Brown, a man after my own heart, whom I cannot help but admire and love, with the aid and influence of his efficient helpmeet, has already shown himself to be the right man in the right place and has worked wonders in his first year. Yes, I am glad that I had a humble hand in starting Concordia.

The zealous and often jealous Reformed denominations knew and appreciated the value of the young Lutheran tribes that were growing up out here. They wanted to catch this young Lutheran stock. Their secretaries had, by tongue and pen, carried glowing reports of this great country, of the "foreign hordes" that were filling it and of the great, crying need of Evangelizing and Americanizing them. At Wahpeton, thirty miles south of Fargo, in a region that was densely Norwegian and Lutheran, the Methodists were building a "university." They were canvassing among the Norwegian farmers for students. They were promising that they would have a Norwegian professor. They owned eighty acres of land and had contracted for a thirty-five thousand dollar building— The Great University never amounted to anything.

I was present all day at the dedication of Memorial Hall, the first unit of Fargo College. This Congregational institution was fostered, builded and endowed with Eastern money. Rich New Englanders had been made to believe that out here were thousands of thrifty settlers, raising large families. That they were all foreigners. That Fargo College was needed to save the coming generation and make intelligent and cultured American Christians out of them. Orators of national repute had been sent for. They came from Boston and other classic centers. It was an intellectual treat to hear these great men. Their appraisement of educa-

tion and culture was good to hear. The addresses were
eloquent and forceful orations. There was, however,
what seemed to me to be a sinister undertone, a false
note underneath it all. There was a lumping of "the
foreigners" which struck me as unworthy of intelligent
men. Foreigners to these New Englanders were foreigners. No distinctions were made between those who
came from Northern and those who came from Southern Europe. No distinction between Protestant and
Catholic Europe. If they didn't speak English they
were dangerous. They needed Fargo College. This
college would make the Red River Valley safe for
America. Without this college, oh, my! What a
threatening future! It was gruesome to calculate!
This was the story and the picture that these brilliant Yankees brought to us from away down East!
I went home and wrote a column for the Fargo Argus.
Among other things I said in substance: "The new
president of the new Fargo College made the serious
mistake so often made by uninformed and hasty
writers and speakers of measuring all foreigners with
the same yardstick. The great Dr. Strong in his great
book *Our Country*, from which I have received much
information and inspiration, makes the same inexcusable mistake. These men need to learn that there
are foreigners and foreigners. For the comfort of
President Barnes and his congeners I would inform
them that these foreigners who inhabit the Red River
Valley and the Dakotas are practically all Scandinavians. They are stalwart Lutheran Protestants. They
are children of the Mother Church of the Reformation. The percentage of illiteracy in their home lands
is smaller than in any other lands under the sun. From
childhood up they are taught to know the Holy Scrip-

tures. They will compare favorably in this with the
very best New Englanders. They believe in and love
education. They want the heart educated as well as
the head. That there is found among them as much
earnest piety and spiritual life to the square yard
as among the best of the sons and daughters of the
Puritans. These Lutheran Christians have in Minnesota alone five academies, four colleges and three theological seminaries. In these seminaries they have about
two hundred and fifty young men studying for the
Gospel Ministry. They will preach a Gospel free from
any New England Unitarian taint. These people make
up more than half the population of the Dakotas and
Minnesota. They voted North Dakota dry last year.
They will do the same for Minnesota. Seventeen
Scandinavian Lutherans were in the legislature at Bismarck last winter. A quarter million dollars in cold
cash was there to buy up the legislature to grant a
state charter to the Louisiana Lottery Company. The
seventeen Lutherans voted against the bill every time
and so saved our young state from shame and ruin.
These people are preparing to open Concordia College
in Moorhead. The medium of instruction will be the
English language. Its course will be full as high as
that of Fargo College. It will have many times over
the number of students that Fargo College will have.
The Word of God and Luther's Catechism will have a
prominent place all thru the course. These people are
going to do a work for Christ and His Church for
which even the sons of New England will yet rise up
and call them blessed. The writer of this paper is
not a Scandinavian."

This open letter was widely commented on. It gave
me further confidence among the Norwegians. Among

many others I received a fine commendation from a Norwegian Congressman in Washington.

The same patronizing tone that was voiced at the Fargo College dedication was heard at the county and state Sunday School conventions. "We must help to Evangelize and Americanize these Foreigners." This really meant that we must proselytize them away from the Lutheran Church. The ignorant, baseless and dishonest assertions made me tired. They made my Lutheran blood boil. I got myself put on the programs of a number of Sunday School conventions. I embraced every opportunity to tell these unctuous Sunday School leaders the facts that I had written to the *Argus* on the occasion of the college dedication. There were many good, sincere and earnest Christians among these Sunday School workers. They had been misinformed and misled. What I told them about these Scandinavians was a revelation to them. They were surprised. They were gratified. They thanked me profusely for my information. It was simply letting the Lutheran light shine. It was bearing witness where it was sorely needed. Oh, that all Lutherans would do more such public witness bearing. Make the opportunity and use it.

On the other hand I used the information I gathered at such Union meetings to further enlighten and warn my Lutheran neighbors. They were entirely too innocent. They were too ignorant of what was going on around them. They did not know of the plans that were made and of the nets that were spread to catch Lutheran children and wean them away from their church. They did not know of the hundreds of thousands of dollars that were poured into this fruitful land to proselyte Lutherans. What I told these Lu--

therans about the proselyters was as much a revelation to them as what I told the Sunday School conventions and the *Argus* readers about the Lutherans was a revelation to *them*. I hope the mutual enlightenment did good on both sides.

As to Fargo College, there is a sequel. In spite of their fine plant, their buildings and the City Park for campus; in spite of their liberal endowment they could not make it go. Lutherans established their own, better college. Lutherans began to see thru the underhanded purpose of the Reformed colleges. These colleges had no field out here. This country was Lutheran soil. As I often said, its chief products were number one hard spring wheat and young Lutherans. At this writing Fargo College has been dead for several years. Its fine buildings are vacant. Concordia is flourishing like a green bay tree. God be praised.

There is another side of Fargo life that I cannot pass over. It is unpleasant. I do not like to tell about it. But it is true. The reader would not have a complete picture of Fargo life without seeing the darker side. As in all new western towns there was a rough element here. Lewd fellows of the baser sort were a plenty. There were Scandinavians among them. There were adventurers, jail birds and criminals from the East. Bad women, pimps, drunkards, gamblers and hold-up men were there. The socalled "under the hill" region was the red light district. Shantytown was an unsafe place to pass thru at night. As usual, corrupt politicians were there. They knew how to exploit and use the baser elements. They did. In several wards they were in power. They were a serious menace to our fair Gate City.

In my righteous indignation I once wrote for the

190

Argus a scathing expose of the dark doings. I told the story of the exploits of our Catholic chief of police. I related some disgraceful doings of several city aldermen. I threw a flash-light into some of the dens of vice and crime. I was told that it was the most daring exposure that had ever been made public. I wonder to this day how I escaped violence and persecution. God has always been good to me. At a future city election we elected a reform administration.

Here is an account of a public Fargo funeral which I attended and described in a letter to Passavant's *Workman*. I give it here just as I wrote it thirty-five years ago:

"A few weeks ago we had a typical western funeral in our town. A man who had been one of the pioneers of Fargo, a boomer of the early boom days, who had been a reckless real estate speculator and at one time owned a good part of the young Fargo and was worth a quarter of a million, died. He was Fargo's second mayor. When the wild boom burst he was stranded and not only lost his all, but involved and wrecked a number of others. For the last eight years he lived on the charity of his former friends. He became sick, went to St. Paul to be treated and there committed suicide. He was not only an unbeliever, but a scoffer at the Christian religion.

"After his untimely end he was brought to our city, where he lay in state for a day. Then a public funeral was arranged. By proclamation the stores were requested to close. A public hall was secured, an orchestra and a glee club were engaged, an ex-congressman and a colonel were invited to deliver orations. There was no minister, no Word of God, no hymn, no prayer, no hope for the beyond. 'Died Abner as the fool dieth.' Buried like a heathen! It reminded us of the funeral of Julius Caesar, with the oration of Mark Anthony. Such is the heathenism of the West, a heathenism encouraged by the public and glorified by public sentiment.

"These people have outgrown the old Gospel, and call themselves the Apostles of Progress! But really it is a retrogression, back to the corrupt and debasing heathenism of the Roman empire.

"The popular churches seem to fear to attack and expose this materialistic and sensual spirit. The kindred religions of the lodge and the Unitarian are threatening to carry all before them. Indifference and latitudinarianism are the popular types. During the winter the Presbyterian church was vacant. A Swedenborgian preached for them twelve times. Shades of Knox and Calvin, where are ye? At some of the services several Presbyterian ministers sat in the congregation, listened to the Swedenborgian teacher, and uttered never a word of protest.

"It has been said that beyond the Missouri there is no Sunday and beyond Miles City there is no God. The longer we are in this Western country the more are we convinced that the hope of this region is in the old Lutheran Church. May she continue to lift up the Banner of the Truth, preaching repentance toward God and faith in our Lord Jesus Christ as the only help and hope for poor, lost, ruined and restless humanity."

One of the smallest of the many nationalistic Lutheran groups in America came from the little, bleak, frozen, icy Iceland. The immigrants from the most interesting Lutheran land are worthy of special study. While in Fargo it was my privilege to get acquainted with this unique little group of Lutherans. The Rev. Mr. Bergman came to see me. I found him a most interesting companion. He had taken his classical and also part of his theological course in his native land. That little land, by the way, is in the front rank for education, intelligence and culture. Mr. Bergman had been wise enough and foresighted enough to take a full course in the Philadelphia Seminary. We found that we were kindred spirits and had many interests in common. Thru him I learned that the headquarters of the Icelandic Lutherans was in Winnipeg. Several counties in North Dakota also had a strong Icelandic population. At Gardar, in Pembina County, Mr. Bergman was ministering to a number of Lutheran congregations. Thru him I became acquainted with the work, the leaders of the Icelandic Lutherans both in Winnipeg and in North Dakota. In after years it was my privilege to help to prepare a number of their bright young men for the ministry in the Chicago Seminary. The Icelandic Synod officially adopted that as their seminary. At the twenty-fifth anniversary of their synod is was my privilege to bring the seminary's greetings. To my delight, Doctor H. E. Jacobs was also an invited guest at the festive celebration. It was an agreeable surprise to me to find that full three-fourths of the ministers of the little synod were graduates of Chicago Seminary. As a whole they were among the keenest intellects in the seminary.

There is a sad sequel to this little Icelandic story. By reason of his brilliant intellect, his broad culture and scholarship, the Rev. Mr. Bergman had become quite a leader in his synod. Next to President Bjarnason of Winnipeg he was probably the strongest man among them. Bergman went astray. He made the mistake that has been the undoing of many brilliant men. In the great discussion among theologians and church leaders he read one side only. He was perfectly at home in the German language and literature. He read regularly several scholarly German theological periodicals. They were all from the Harnack-Ritschlian school. Had he kept and read *Luthardt's Evangelische Kirchenzeitung* he might have been saved. He fell in love with Tolstoi. This remarkable Russian nobleman had many attractive and excellent traits. He was the friend and the strong advocate of the downtrodden Russian peasantry. But he was a rationalistic modernist. He professed great admiration for Jesus. Jesus was for Tolstoi a great social Reformer. He did not know Jesus as a Savior from sin or a Soul Redeemer. As is usual with such advanced leaders—Fosdick, for inst.—Tolstoi drifted farther and farther away from Evangelical moorings. He became dangerous to good morals. Perhaps unconsciously he was drifting back to Rousseau's fundamental principle: "Back to human nature." This really means: Let the lust of the flesh be our guide! Tolstoi became so corrupt and corrupting that some of his later books were forbidden the United States mail privileges. I don't believe that Bergman adopted these corrupt conclusions of Tolstoi.

Bergman also found Reginald Campbell, the founder of what he called "The New Theology." It was old Rationalism revamped. My Presbyterian friend and neighbor in Fargo, the Rev. Mr. Pike, was likewise carried away by Campbell. Bergman devoured Campbell. So often to dally with Rationalism is like dallying with vice:

Vice is a monster of such hideous mien
That, to be hated, needs but to be seen;
But, seen too oft, familiar with her face,
We first endure, then pity, then embrace.

And so poor, brilliant Bergman became a Modernist.
He expected his synod to follow him. Not more than
three or four ministers did. Of all the Chicago Seminary graduates he won but one. A number of laymen
were led astray. They built a big tabernacle in Winnipeg for Bergman. Bergman died suddenly a few
years ago. So did the one Chicago Seminary apostate.
The tabernacle now is a big, orthodox, Lutheran congregation. Bergman's followers went to the Icelandic
Unitarians.

Chapter XIV

A MISSIONARY JOURNEY AND A NEW SYNOD

WHEN the General Council met in Minneapolis in 1888 the Augustana Synod delegation from the Columbia Conference officially invited the council's home mission board to establish English churches in the principal cities on the Pacific Coast.

In several respects the Minneapolis Convention was the most important up to that time. Numerically it was the largest. Many of the Eastern delegates and visitors had never been so far west. To them the beautiful, prosperous and progressive Twin Cities, the majestic Mississippi, its Falls that turned the wheels of the largest flour mills in the world, its factory-lined banks; all these were eye openers. Among the industries was the largest sawmill in the world, owned by the Lutheran Lumber King, C. A. Smith, who became a great factor in the development of our English work. In Minneapolis were the then beautiful Minnehaha Falls, immortalized by the poet Longfellow. Some of its ten beautiful lakes are large enough for steam pleasure launches. No other city in the world has this distinction. In this respect Minneapolis is the most attractive city in the world.

The convention was epoch-making for other reasons than because it was sitting for the first time beyond the Mississippi. It was the great Home Mission Convention. President Doctor Spaeth preached an opening sermon such as had never been heard in any previous convention. He surprised the staid and sober Eastern delegates. He made the crowded house sit up and take notice. It was a picturesque portrayal of the powerful possibilities and probabilities that were looming in the great Northwest. It was a bugle-blast to awaken the church to the hitherto unappreciated importance of immediate English mission work from the Great Lakes to the Pacific. Many hearers said, Dr. Spaeth must have been reading Strong's stirring book, *Our Country*. And that was true. The doctor, in his rousing sermon referred to the book and pointed out its one mistake in that it does not discriminate between desirable and undesirable immigrants. Others said the preacher must have studied the letters to the *Workman* from Fargo. I hope he had. That great sermon bore immediate fruit. How often one great, good sermon, a sermon worked out in the intercessions of a soul in close communion with the Lord of the harvest started or turned a tide in the affairs of the Kingdom. Think of Wichern's sermon at the Wittenberg Congress. Why don't we have more such convention sermons?

That convention instructed its board to elect a superintendent of Home Missions. The board elected the Rev. W. A. Passavant, Junior. Before he accepted the call he insisted that he must have the board's consent to start English missions in the principal cities of the North Pacific Coast. Official consent was given, and young Passavant, as was his wont, at once took vigorous hold of the work. The board was reorganized and put on a working basis. New life was put into the whole Home Mission situation.

In February of the follownig winter a telegram came

to me from the new Home Mission superintendent. It requested me to drop everything, hurry out to the Pacific Coast and preempt its cities for the General Council. This was on a bitter cold Friday evening. I put on my fur coat and hunted up Prof. Challman at Hope Academy and arranged with him to supply St. Mark's pulpit for four or five Sundays. I remained to attend to my services and explain the situation to my people on Sunday. Monday evening, when the thermometer was twenty-nine below, I bade farewell to my little family and was off for a four-night and four-day trip. To save expense for the Mission Board I never took a sleeper, but sat in a day coach all the way. I did not take a single meal in the diner, but ate at lunch counters along the way.

One reason for young Passavant's haste was that he had learned that a commission from the General Synod's board was on the way to plant missions in the cities to which he was sending me. His message gave me this information. I purchased a ticket to Portland, Oregon. On Saturday I had dispatched letters to the Augustana pastors of Portland, Tacoma and Seattle, informing them of my coming. I requested Pastor Anderson to meet my train at Tacoma, so I might consult him during the brief stop. When I greeted him on the platform, my first question was, Had he seen or heard anything of the General Synod men, Barnitz and Clutz, in these parts? He had not. I thanked God that I was ahead. I had Bro. Anderson make appointments for me in his church and was soon aboard for Portland. Before I debarked I saw buttercups blooming on the banks of the Willamette and heard thrushes sing in the leafing trees. It made my heart glad. At Portland I was met by the Swedish pastor. He helped me to find a comfortable room at a dollar a day hotel whose proprietor was a Norwegian and a nominal Lutheran. He treated me kindly and made me comfortable. I was in the greatest fish region of the land. I loved fish and largely lived on it for over a month. For five weeks I walked the streets, climbed stairways, rapped on doors from mid-forenoon till early bed-time, hunting and tracking Lutherans. I found many who were not ripe for English and had not been found by the German or Scandinavian pastors. These I reported to them. I can do no better than to insert several letters that I wrote to *The Workman*:

"Dear *Workman*: We are now ready to report our operations and progress at Tacoma and Seattle. Both of these towns are on the top wave of a wild western boom. Real estate speculation is a veritable craze here. Speculators, with glowing and extravagant circulars, met our train east of the Cascade Mountains. On trains, on boats, in the street-cars, in hotel lobbies, on street corners, everywhere the talk is of town lots, additions, booms and golden opportunities. The newspapers are ablaze with advertisements, items and editorials on these all-absorbing topics.

"This is the food that people feed on and the charm that they dream on. Out here the god of this world repeats over and over again the acts recorded in our first Lenten Gospel. Here the believing man is told how these stones can be turned into bread! Here the seeker after wealth and its pleasures is shown the kingdoms of this world and their glory! Here the ambitious man is pointed to pinnacles on the temple of fame, from whose heights he can cast himself down into the intoxicating whirl of flattery and fame and power!

"Thus worldliness is stimulated, the spirit is keyed

up to an unnatural tension, and life becomes more and more artificial. The materialistic strain and spirit are indeed appalling. One who visits these reckless young coast cities for the first time sees much that is deeply interesting and often quite ludicrous. The town-lot craze strikes one as supremely ridiculous. Here in Tacoma the surrounding country is laid out in lots for eight or ten miles. Out in the forests primeval, where the giant fir trees, six feet in diameter, nod their heads to the clouds, suburbs of Tacoma are platted, streets and avenues surveyed and lots all numbered. We are told that there is enough ground plotted for a city of two millions of inhabitants.

"Seattle is, if possible, worse still. We took a cable-car, rode seven miles thru deep cuts, up and down steep grades, over lofty trestles, across ravines and gulches thru a wilderness of trees and stumps and logs. Out there in the woods we actually saw a real estate office perched high up in mid-air on the trunks of four massive trees. These wilderness lots are only five hundred dollars apiece, trees, stumps, roots, rubbish and all. But the end was not yet. The cable begins near the docks on Puget Sound. It ends on the shores of Lake Washington. There we are met by a ferry-boat, which takes the passenger across the lake for two miles, and yonder on the other shore, the hills and forests are all plotted. That is East Seattle. We return and stroll to the docks on the Sound. Here a ferryboat runs westward across the bay. Those far-off wooded cliffs are West Seattle. And so it goes. We pity the gullible people who are persuaded that in this new and undeveloped country, they can at once have a New York and Chicago.

"But they are beautiful and romantic cities withal.

We were specially pleased by Seattle. Standing on one of its many heights in the sun-set glow of a beautiful spring day, we had a view never to be forgotten. At our feet westward lay the business part of the stirring and ambitious young city. On its edge it was fringed by the gleaming waters of Puget Sound, dotted with many a sail and plowed by many a keel. On the western shore there towered up against the evening sky the wild and craggy heights of the Olympia Mountains, dazzling with eternal snow. Turning towards the east, we could see the placid fresh waters of beautiful Lake Washington, fringed with sombre cedars and shadowed by giant firs. Northward lay the smaller lovely Lake Union, whose shores are being rapidly built up, and which is to be girt about by a pleasure drive. Looking southward we could also see the familiar, massive and colossal Mount Tacoma towering far above and dwarfing the Cascade range, holding communion with the clouds.

"But—here we are writing a booming letter, while we intended to speak of our church work—pardon the contagious enthusiasm!

"We have preached and spoken in Tacoma ten times. On Sunday, March 3rd, Pastor Anderson went to preach in the country and kindly granted us the Swedish church for all day. We had the house comfortably full in the morning. In the evening it was so crowded that some did not get seats and went away. On Sunday, March 10, we returned from Seattle and made an address at the corner-stone laying of the new Swedish church, an account of which will be found elsewhere. In the evening we preached in the German Lutheran church to a comfortably filled and attractive house. We also preached several times on week evenings in the Norwegian church. We have been kindly received and heartily welcomed by the pastors of all these churches. All have lent us their active co-operation and all recognize the immediate need of an English church.

"The outlook here is quite encouraging. We have found a dozen Lutheran communicants from English churches in the East. Also a number who were once English Lutherans, but have grown careless or gone into other churches. There are also a number of young Germans, who are no longer familiar with the language and whom the German pastor will be glad to recommend to an English church. The Scandinavians are generally newcomers and therefore need no English. Still there are some of them also who are attending English churches, and many of their children will grow up English.

"Among the English Lutherans here we have a family that comprises in itself an excellent choir, and a number of good Sunday school teachers. Had we had such a family in Fargo, its value would have been incalculable. This field is ripe and waiting. Expressions of joy at the prospect of an English church are heard on every hand.

"Seattle is even more promising. We only spent six days there and preached five times. We had only one Sunday service, as we hurried back to Tacoma for the corner-stone laying. We had goodly and attentive audiences. Were especially delighted with our Sunday morning congregation. There were over two hundred people present. We were pleased to find a seemingly excellent family from Dr. Fry's church in Reading, Pa. There are three young people in the family who will be an excellent Sunday school force. Found altogether twelve English Lutherans from the East. Several are careless, but all may become reinterested.

"We found in Seattle a larger number of Swedes and Norwegians who want an English church than in Tacoma. A few of them are quite influential. The last words we heard were, 'Send us a minister. Send us a good one. Send him soon.' Seattle also is a good field ripe for the harvest.

"And now our preparatory work is done. The way is clear for occupancy. The call from the three cities where we have labored for over five weeks is urgent. The Lord has many people in these cities for our English Lutheran Church. May the whole Church assuredly gather that the Lord has called us to occupy this coast land of promise. Under God, everything will depend on getting the right men for these fields.

"Tonight we leave again for Portland, where we preach once more to-morrow evening, making our twenty-eighth sermon or address since we left home. The next day we start for a leisurely trip homeward over the Union Pacific..—G. H. G.

"Tacoma, Wash., March 11, '89."

I relate one only of my many rich experiences: It was rumored that the General Synod's superintendent of missions was on his way with a companion to plant missions in these same cities. I was stopping at a cheap, dollar-a-day hotel. On a Thursday morning the pastor of the Swedish Lutheran Church, who had helped me most heartily and encouraged us most cordially, came hastily into my room. He was evidently excited. He almost stammered out the news, "B-B-Barnitz is here! He and Clutz are at the Esmond Hotel." "Well," I said, "we'll go to see them. You must go along to testify of our call here by Augustana men and of our work thus far." The good brother was timid. "I'm afraid you'll fight," he said. I assured him that I had been acquainted with Bro. Barnitz for years, had preached for him in Wheeling, and would certainly not fight. We went to the telegraph office and wired appointments in Tacoma and Seattle for Friday and Saturday nights. We had made an appointment in the Swedish pastor's Portland church for Sunday afternoon. Then I went alone to the Esmond to hunt up our General Synod brethren. The Reverend Mr. Clutz had not yet arrived. I found Bro. Barnitz in the dining room, slapped him on the shoulder and said, "Well, Bro. B., I'm glad to see you, but am not glad to see you here." He finished his dinner and we took a walk. We had a very frank conversation. Each one knew for what the other was here. I informed him that I was there at the request of the General Council's Home Mission Board, which board had sent me because the General Council, at its Minneapolis convention, had received an earnest request from the Augustana men on the North Pacific Coast to come out and plant English missions in the principal cities and centers there; that I had canvassed and preached in the three cities; had found material in each city for a future church; had thus staked my claim; would protest to the whole Church if he "jumped my claim." I reminded him that the General Council had all the English work on the Northern Pacific; that the General Synod had the Mid-West states to the coast; that English missions were needed in a score of places in these regions, especially in California, where but a bare beginning had been made, and that he and Bro. Clutz had better go to California and leave the Northwest coast to us. He agreed to talk it over with Bro. Clutz.

I took the night train for Tacoma, canvassed there Friday and preached at night, did the same at Seattle Saturday and made further appointments at both places. Meanwhile I was more or less apprehensive, not knowing what was going on at Portland and I was back there by noon Sunday. After dinner our Swedish brother met us with a beaming face. "They leave for California tonight," he said. We thanked God and took courage. Then we met the two brethren and had satisfactory, but unofficial, agreement as to the division of territory. This agreement was recognized and kept inviolate for over twenty years. Both bodies found more than they could rightly do on their respective sides of the unofficial boundary line, which was in after years made official by a joint committee of the two bodies at Lancaster, Pa., in 1911.

At that historic meeting at the Esmond Hotel in Portland, Oregon, we had a most cordial conference. We invited the two brethren to go with us to our afternoon service and speak to the good people. Both of them went, and both of them spoke. Both of them cordially commended our work and we bade them God speed at their steamer as they sailed toward the sunset land at the Golden Gate.

"Dear *Workman*: After our work in Tacoma and Seattle, as reported in our last, we left for Portland again and preached in the Swedish church on the evening of Tuesday, March 12th. It had rained all day, and at nightfall it came down in torrents. But we still had something over a score of devout and attentive worshipers present. After the service we received several new names and many warm words of encouragement and promises of assistance and co-operation. Our last service convinced us more than ever that

205

the Lord has many people in that city for an English Lutheran church, and that He has opened to us a great and effectual door. Let us hasten to enter in and occupy. 'The King's business requireth haste.'

"And so we closed our work on the Northwest coast. We labored about five weeks, preached and spoke twenty-eight times. We were met with nothing but kindness and sympathy in the work at every turn. We received everywhere the kindest co-operation from Lutheran brethren, whether Germans, Norwegians, Swedes or Finns. We realized that the good Lord was with us all the way, and His hand had led us on every step of our journey. The same has been true of the journey thus far homeward.

"We bade farewell to Portland early on the morning of the 13th, taking a Columbia River steamer for the Dalles, distant two hundred and thirty miles. Altho the day was somewhat dark, and we could not see the royal Mount Hood, the graceful St. Helena, the entrancing Multuowah and the frowning Horn, it was a trip never to be forgotten. It is claimed by tourists who have steamed up the Hudson, the Rhine and the Danube, that for beauty, magnificence and grandeur of natural scenery, the Columbia excels them all.

"The scenes of beauty and grandeur pass before the observer in one continuous procession of bewilderment. Here to the right are the 'Pillars of Hercules.' These are two queer rock-formations, several hundred feet high, in shape like huge, slim haystacks. A railroad runs betwen them, and one is topped out by a tempest torn cedar, striking its roots in the crevices of its rocks. Then comes Rooster-Rock, a queer, isolated, tall formation, rising abruptly from the water's edge. We saw a number of such fantastic rocks. Sometimes they appear like a file of granite guards, standing in line, like silent sentinels of the passes. Then comes Cape Horn, a towering cliff one thousand feet high, striped with a number of crystal waterfalls, washed at its base by the ever-rolling stream. Then comes Castle Rock, split off from the mountain side and pushed down into the water, where it rises one thousand feet high. Yonder are the famous Multuowah Falls, pouring over a cliff high up the mountain-side and dashing in spray upon the rocks eight hundred feet below. There again rises a mighty crag crowned by fir-trees, under whose sombre shadows lie the red men of these primeval wilds. Those ancient chiefs and their followers evidently rest where the soughing of the winds in the firs and the rushing of the waters beneath would soothe their last long sleep.

"At the Cascades, where the river dashes down its steep and rocky channels, we debark and take a narrow-guage train for several miles. The scenery, the falls, the ride on a flatcar are romantic and exhilarating. We re-embarked on the 'Middle Columbia' for 'The Dalles.' The wild and ever-varying scenery continues. The mountains rise up perpendicularly, at times 2,800 feet from the water's edge. All imaginable shapes and forms and colors present themselves as we steam by. In the evening twilight we leave our steamer to take the next train for Salt Lake City, distant about 1,000 miles. Of our forty-eight hours' ride we cannot speak in detail. We crossed the Blue Mountains, rode thru stretches of snowsheds, traversed the reservation of the Mintah and Snake Indians, saw many curious and amusing sights, ran along the Snake River, afterwards thru the rich Larche valley, along the ranges of the Wasatch Mountains into the famous Utah valley.

"We had been passing thru well-cultivated farms, grove-embowered and widely spread villages, orchard-hidden and vine-covered homes, all made to blossom and bear by irrigation, when we came to Logan City. We were informed that most of the farmers, stockmen and villagers of the valley were Mormons. At Logan City we got our first sight of a Mormon temple. Of course we were on the qui vive and intensely interested. After passing thru Ogden—a Mormon city—we caught our first glimpse of the deep blue waters of Great Salt Lake. What thoughts and impressions crowd upon us as we rush along! The curious desire of years, running back to the romantic days of boyhood, is about to be realized! We are whirled thru the suburbs, all excitement and interest, as the train slows up and the brakeman calls 'Salt Lake City!' We alight, and with strange sensations tread this historic ground.

"But how shall we describe this famous and notorious town? We begin with the words of a noted traveler—Phil. Robinson: 'I have described in my time many cities, both of the East and West; but the City of the Saints puzzles me. It is the young rival of Mecca, the Zion of the Mormons, their latter day Jerusalem. It is also the city of the "Honey Bee," "Deseret," and the City of the Sunflower—an encampment, as of pastoral tribes—the tented capital of some Hyksos, "Shepherd Kings"—the rural home of a modern patriarchal democracy; the place of the Tabernacle on an ancient prophet-ruled theocracy.' "

"The notorious Brigham Young laid out the town on a generous scale. The streets are one hundred and thirty feet wide and cross each other at right angles. The lots are an acre and a quarter each. They are planted with shade and fruit trees. The houses are covered with vines and, for nine months in the year, surrounded by a profusion of flowers. All this gives the city an attractive, quiet and rural appearance.

"City Creek, a pure mountain stream, flowing down from Emigration Canon, supplies the city with water and irrigates the ample gardens and surrounding farms. This stream is so divided that a clear and limpid brook flows down the regular grade on either side of the street. There is no underground sewerage. Instead of filthy gutters are these swift purling brooklets. Many of the inhabitants dip up this crystal water for drinking and domestic purposes. These rills from the mountain also water the roots of the large, luxuriant locust and box-elder trees that shade all the residence streets on either side. The widely-dispersed city must look like a veritable paradise in summer. It lies in the basin-like valley girt about by the Wasatch and Nintah Mountains.

"This whole region was mapped and modeled after the Holy Land. The city represents Jerusalem, and is called 'Zion,' 'City of Saints.' Great Salt Lake represents the Dead Sea, Lake Utah the Sea of Galilee, and the Jordan River runs thru the latter into the former. Mount Nebo stands out bold and prominent, overlooking the lakes, the Jordan valley and the City of Zion.

"We never got tired wandering thru the wide and quiet streets and looking at the many objects of interest. We stood at the shrine of the great—false—prophet, Brigham Young, whose grave, with those of a number of his wives, is enclosed with an iron fence. His own grave is overlaid with a marble block of seven tons' weight. We stood before his house, from whence he ruled the duped 'Saints' with a rod of iron. We looked in on the strange-looking 'Beehive' house where he kept most of his thirty-one wives. And so we viewed the 'Gardo House' home of his favorite wife Emily, the tithing house, where the faithful must bring in one-tenth of their income and produce. All these and other important buildings are surrounded by high walls, surmounted by numerous round turrets. The arched Eagle Gate was once guarded by the armed 'Danites,' who kept the city under a reign of terror by their wholesale assassinations.

"But most interesting of all are the Temple, Tabernacle and Endowment House. The Temple has been thirty-five years in building, is of solid Utah granite, walls eighty feet high, to be surmounted by two massive towers. It is a labyrinth of small rooms, secret and underground chambers. It was intended for infamous ceremonies of 'sealing' and 'endowment' and other secret horrors.

"We hope that now, that the United States government has laid vigorous hold of this abominable and treasonable despotism, the Temple may never be used for the intended purposes. The Tabernacle has often been described. It looks like a huge turtle. It seats 10,000 people. Its acoustic properties are perfect. We looked in also at Assembly Hall, another large building seating thousands. A school examination was in progress. We could not suppress a tear as we looked over that sea of children brought up in that horrid and fanatical delusion. Of course, we became deeply interested in this modern apostasy. We were struck with the prominent place which the sensuous occupies in this religion. The appeal is to the senses. Music takes a very prominent place in their religion. Singing is assiduously cultivated. In the ward meeting-houses the church provides weekly dances, where the young of both sexes are encouraged and even commanded to assemble and dance together. Thus the church tries to interest and hold her young. Are we not reminded of some others also?

"Of course we attended a tabernacle service. There were probably 5,000 present. A grand pipe-organ, said to be the third largest in the world, and a choir of one hundred voices furnished grand music. Pity that it should be prostituted to such a cause! Bread and water were passed thru the large audience—a weekly ordinance—and during the distribution, which lasted for an hour and a half, a rambling, incoherent and dribbling speech was inflicted upon the patient and sleepy audience.

"We studied the faces of the crowd. And what countenances! Such a degradation and vacancy! We couldn't help contrasting that with a Christian congregation. A long-felt desire to attend a tabernacle service has been gratified. We have enough of it! We would like to speak of the quaint old adobe houses, low and long, with many front doors—one for each wife—in former days; of several moonlight walks in the suburbs, and an inspection of ruins of the old walls that used to surround the city. But our letter is becoming too long for even the long *Workman*.

"For the noble work of our Brother Kratz, pastor of the Swedish Lutheran Church, we have no space. Suffice it to say, that this earnest brother's work has been greatly blessed of the Lord, and that he is probably doing more to enlighten and bring back to the true faith many of the poor, deluded wretches, than any of the other churches of Salt Lake City.

"Neither can we describe our memorable trip over

the grand scenic route of the continent, the Denver & Rio Grande. The wonderful, inspiring and sublime scenery of that ride is beyond description. The crossing of the Wasatch range; the famous Castle Gate, with its crested pillars five hundred feet high; the steep and winding ascent and descent of the Squaw Mountain; the far-famed Black Canon of the Gunnison River, thru a narrow gorge of rocks, guarded by Courrucanti Needle, with perpendicular walls 2,000 feet high; the world renowned Marshall Pass over the Rockies, reaching an elevation of 11,000 feet, after the most inconceivable curves and loops; and then, most wonderful of all, the Grand Canon of the Arkansas, whose walls and crags seem heaven-high, as we look up from our open observation car. Here are perpendicular walls that loom straight up 3,000 feet. Here is neither blade nor leaf of vegetation. Here are crevices that the sunlight never kissed. Here are solitudes where for ages nothing was heard but the soughing and dashing of the waters of the Arkansas. It is sublime, stupendous, overpowering.

" 'Great and marvelous are Thy works, Lord God Almighty. In wisdom hast Thou made them all.'

"We are here at Denver, the 'Gem' city of the Rockies. Here we expect to rest—in several pulpits—over Sunday. And then for—home, sweet home.

—G. H. G.

Denver, Colo., March 22, '89."

An important part of my errand to Denver was that I might meet the Rev. H. P. Shanor. As noted above, he had become my successor in my first parish on the edge of Pittsburgh. At this meeting it had long since been a part of Pittsburgh. Shanor had done fine work

212

in that parish. He had a strong pastoral charge of it and was greatly beloved there. His health had broken. He found that tuberculosis was working in him. He was advised to spend some months in the Colorado mountains. He was tarrying in a mountain town near Denver.

I had tarried in Salt Lake City for almost a week. Had preached in the Augustana Church and discussed the feasibility of an English mission. We agreed that an attempt ought to be made. I arranged with Bro. Shanor to go to Salt Lake City, preach there, drive a stake and preempt the ground for the General Council. We did establish an English church there. After several years we found that missionating among these American Moslems was too slow and expensive. So we turned our work and property over to the Augustana Mission Board. The Swedes are doing valiant work there today.

I count my missionary journey to the Pacific Coast as one of the many blessed privileges of my life. I like to think that from the then driven stakes there has grown up the brave little Pacific Synod. And from that synod has sprung "The little, lone seminary in the West." That heroic pioneer school of the prophets will not always be little, neither will it remain so lone. The heroic service and sacrifice that planted, sustained and developed it thus far will not be in vain in the Lord.

When I arrived back home I found all well. Truly God is good to Israel. I found that St. Mark's had not suffered under the able and kindly supply work of Prof. Challman. To this day I have a twinge of conscience. All thru my journey I had been scrupulously careful to save expense for our needy home mission board. I had made no agreement with the professor as to remuneration. I should have done so. It is always best to have a clear understanding. I did not give him enough for his services. Have been sorry over and over again. We have always been good friends.

It had been Dr. Passavant's idea that the English congregations planted in the Northwest would gather in people from all nationalities and outsiders of all sorts. The doctor foresaw that such congregations would not fit into any synod composed of one nationality and speaking a foreign language. The only proper thing for such congregations to do would be to band themselves together into an English Synod of the General Council.

The leaders of the Augustana Synod, which was a part of the General Council, had a different idea and a different vision. They had the conviction that all the congregations established by the General Council should belong to the Augustana Synod. This conception would have been sound and sensible if the new, English congregations had been working among and with Swedes only. The English churches had a broader vision. Even before they knew anything about Dr. Passavant's idea they were working it out. There were two congregations whose membership was made up mainly of the descendants of Swedes. These were St. John's of Minneapolis and the church in Red Wing. This was not the case with the congregations in Fargo, St. Paul, North St. Paul and West St. Paul. Neither was it true of Milwaukee or Duluth. The pastors of these congregations felt that both we and our churches would be out of place in the Augustana Synod. To be tied up with a body whose official language was a foreign tongue would certainly hinder and hamper our mission work. By correspondence and by word of mouth, when we could get together we discussed our anomalous situation. Of this group the St. Paul pastor was the only one who belonged to the Augustana Synod. He was not only ready but eager to ask for a letter of transfer to an English synod that would soon be organized. The other pastors of this group belonged to different synods back East. We all came to see more and more clearly that we needed and must have an English synod. Our pioneer pastor, the pathbreaker of English work, the Rev. G. H. Trabert, was not ready to join our movement. He hoped that a plan agreeable to the Augustana Synod might be worked out. A few years later, when he was fully persuaded that this was impossible, he became an enthusiastic member of our young English Synod.

The rest of us drew up a petition to the Home Mission Board of the General Council. That board not only gave us permission but encouraged us to form a district synod of the General Council. We called a preliminary meeting, resolved to organize and appointed a committee to draw up a constitution and prepare for a meeting for official organization. That meeting was held in Memorial Church, St. Paul. I had been requested to preach the opening sermon. My theme was: "The Lutheran Multitudes; Their needs and how to supply them." When the roll was made up it was found that we were seven pastors and six congregations. Salem Mission, Minneapolis, was not yet organized. The election made me president. The Rev. W. K. Frick, who, by common consent, became the "Unmitred Bishop of Wisconsin," was the first secretary. I freely confess that I could scarcely have guided the young body safely if it had not been for my splendid secretary. His executive ability, his keen insight and foresight and his wise counsel were a great help to me and were highly appreciated. Our baby synod had its difficulties. We were scarcely launched on our official career when we had an unpleasant case of discipline to deal with. The case touched an Augustana congregation. The Swedes were not slow to note this. It gave occasion to ugly talk. I took the stand that we must respect the discipline of sister congregations. The synod sustained me. It became my painful duty to temporarily suspend from membership our only self-sustaining congregation and its pastor.

The synod made application for membership in the General Council. At the Buffalo convention in 1891 our application was laid before the body. We knew that some Augustana men would oppose it. Before it came to a vote, on the advice of friendly leaders, I requested the privilege of withdrawing our application for the present. The privilege was granted. We had not been received.

We knew that many of the Augustana brethren had a haunting fear that our English churches would draw away their members and so weaken their work and their synod. At the advice of young Passavant every congregation of the synod drew up a carefully prepared table showing exactly how many of its members had come out of Augustana congregations, how many out of congregations of other Lutheran bodies and how many had belonged to no Lutheran congregation. The tabulation of these reports made interesting reading. It showed that only a negligible number of our members had come out of Swedish congregations, a small number out of other Lutheran churches and the great bulk had been gathered from the streets and lanes, from the great outside. This tabulation I read to the council convention in Fort Wayne in 1893 in connection with a renewed request for membership. The tabulated report made an impression. It showed that we were not a proselyting body but were doing missionary work in the real, original sense of the term.

When our application came before the convention a leading Augustana official arose and said that he wanted to have the privilege of moving that the application of the Synod of The Northwest for membership in The General Council be granted. Another recognized Augustana leader arose and said that he wanted to have the privilege of seconding the motion. The motion was adopted unanimously. We were in. I am not going to retell the story of the early days of our synod. That has been done and well done three times. When the synod was ten years old Dr. Haupt edited a story. When twenty-five years old Dr. Rubrecht did the same. Doctor Trabert has written the story in full in *English Lutheranism In The Northwest*. I insert here a part of what I wrote for Dr. Rubrecht's *Reminiscent Sketches*:

"We were seven. We were a varied, an individualistic, a characteristic, big-visioned little bunch of English Lutherans who found ourselves in the midst of a stalwart and strong Lutheranism that was speaking to its own people alone, speaking in tongues foreign to America, trying to hold its own people, with no message that the English-speaking American could understand. We were American born. American bred, American trained. We loved our distinctive Lutheran faith as well as the distinctive spirit and the distinctive life that ought always to grow out of, manifest forth, and propagate that faith. We knew by experience and by observation that it was possible; that it

217

was easy; that it was natural to be an orthodox Lutheran, and at the same time an ardent, a patriotic and up-to-date American. We believed fervently that all America ought to know Lutheranism; that all America would learn to respect and to love Lutheranism in proportion as all America would come to know and understand the genius, the teaching, the spirit, and the life of true, confessional Lutheranism. We did not believe that in coming out into regions where the Americans did not know our Church we needed to apologize for our faith and practice, or modify them, and so make them more palatable to our American neighbors. We also had sanctified common sense enough to know that we should not come with a club to knock down all who did not agree with us. Our common sense showed us that it was not the fault of these Americans, but their misfortune that they did not know us or our Church. Sanctified common sense made us realize that it would be unscriptural, un-Christian and un-Lutheran to despise and denounce our neighbors for what they could not help. We tried to put ourselves in their place. Who made us to differ? Not ourselves, but our heredity, our training made us what we were. In the place, with the heredity and the environment of the others, we should have been where they were. And so we felt that while we must be true to our convictions, we must preach the truth in all its realism and in all its reach; we must ever preach it in love. This was our vision and our mission to Northwestern America.

"We also had a conviction that we had a special mission to the great horde of unchurched Lutherans and to those who were becoming unchurched on account of the language question.

"We did honestly believe, as a body, that we were not there to pull members out of existing Lutheran congregations. We did believe that they all had a right to all whom they could gather in and hold. Neither did we, as a body, believe that it would be right for us to undermine or subvert the discipline of existing congregations. Our history clearly proves this contention. If any individual pastors in later years became disloyal to these our first principles, they were responsible as individuals who did not carry out the principles of their synod or of the then Chicago Seminary, which has been so closely bound up with our work in the Northwest.

"On the other hand, we did believe and do believe that we had a right, yes, a duty, to gather into our Sunday Schools the Lutheran children who were not attending a Lutheran Sunday School, but were attending or were likely to attend a Sunday School of another faith and another spirit. We knew from our sad history and from our own observation in the East what becomes of such children. We had the same conviction as to those of or past the confirmation age who were not in other confirmation classes. Also of adults who were not communicants in existing Lutheran congregations. All these were considered legitimate material for us to gather in. We believed that we were on the ground to put an end, as far as in us lay, to the losing of this ungathered Lutheran material to our church. And right nobly has the Synod of the Northwest pursued this mission and followed this vision. Could the full story be known of the thousands of souls gathered in who would otherwise have been lost to the Lutheran Church, if not to the Kingdom of Grace, every true Lutheran would thank God for this blessed ingathering, upbuilding and using of these sons and daughters of God.

"We had another mission of which we were not fully conscious. We were the pioneers, the path breakers for sound Lutheranism in the English tongue. It had been a settled tradition in the foreign synods and churches that when the mother tongue was given up the mother church must be sacrificed. There is a tradition that when a daring young preacher had the courage to speak English on the floor of the old mother synod, in the early days, he was called down with the words: 'Unser Herr Gott ist ein deutscher Gott'! Our God is a German God! A western tradition says that when the students of a theological seminary petitioned for an occasional chapel service in English, a scholarly professor exclaimed: 'Was? Englisch singen und beten! Das ist doch kein Gottesdienst!' We ourselves have heard prominent Scandinavian leaders, in those earlier days, express the fear that if their people should ever worship in English they would of necessity have to sacrifice the real spirit of Lutheranism. They had a haunting fear that sound Lutheranism could not live in the English tongue.

"It was the mission of the little English Lutheran Synod of the Northwest to not only tell these foreigners that they were mistaken, but to show them that Lutheranism can be sound, true, devout and filled with a living zeal in a purely English church. The large and strong synods who at first feared and opposed our little body have learned much from it. They not only were forced to open their eyes to see and to acknowledge the need of English, but they were shown how to do English work and do it so successfully that it would both maintain its own purity and would draw to itself many thinking people who had not a drop of Lutheran blood in their veins. These erstwhile foreign synods, which are now introducing English services and organizing English churches so rapidly, owe a great debt of gratitude to the English path-breaking Synod of the Northwest. And all the English synods owe these other synods congratulations and thanks for following the good example set by the Synod of the Northwest. Let us all be Lutheran enough to rejoice and thank God for true Lutheran growth and prosperity wherever found. And let us all be broad enough as Lutherans to love the Lutheran faith first and our own organization second. Such was our mission and our vision.

"Who were the members of this little band who had to dare, to do, to unlearn, to learn, to experience, to settle so much and to make such important history?

"Beginning in the eastern end of the synod, there was the versatile, enthusiastic advocate of good English, the Muhlenberg grad, the founder of St. Paul's, Philadelphia, the professor of English in Gustavus Adolphus College. He became the first secretary, our booster in old Pennsylvania, the father of the synod's slogan, "The Faith of the Fathers in the Language of the Children." Happy, sunny, punny, cheering on his brethren and ever since turning visions into realities, the Unmitred Bishop, Dr. Frick.

"At St. Paul lived and labored his cousin, The Rev. A. J. D. Haupt, a Pennsylvania university man, with his sorrel, 'reiseprediger,' who gave many a missionary a free ride while dreaming dreams and seeing visions in the old top-buggy, of the future St. Paul and the future power of English Lutheranism in its expanding borders. A planner, designer and builder of new churches; a happy big boy; a cheerful, cheering, hope-inspiring companion, whose stories and puns helped us laugh away many a fear and many a perplexity; a lovable brother, whose heart was always right, even when his judgment erred and needed correction.

"His young colleague in the same saintly city was the Rev. Willard Smith, fresh from the Philadelphia Seminary. A Thiel man, earnest and faithful, he pushed the work in his hard field early and late until a fatal fever laid him low. His early death was deeply mourned. It was the first break in our ranks. He was not, for God took him. His labor abides and the congregation he gathered is a power for good in its side of the city.

"In Minneapolis, St. John's and its organizer, the father of English Lutheranism in the Northwest, were not yet in our synod. But we had the valued counsel of Dr. Trabert, who came in later with his church and has been a power for good not only in the Mississippi Valley but in the whole church.

"The Rev. R. L. Leatherman was the gatherer and organizer of Salem Church. A southern man, also fresh from the seminary, he found it somewhat hard to fit himself into the teeming life of the mixed population of the ambitious young city.

"South of Minneapolis, at Red Wing, Pastor Trabert had gathered a little flock of English Lutherans. Here the Rev. A. Steimle, a New Yorker by birth and breeding, also just out of the seminary, was doing primitive pioneer work. He was our musical genius; with his magic touch of the keys of piano or pipe organ he would oft charm away the clouds and the blues. A combination of philosopher and hard worker, he was in danger of becoming impatient because of the meager results of his persistent push. He loved to meet the brethren, and after we had exchanged experiences and encouraged one another he would go back with new heart and new hope to his hard work.

"On the north, among the cliff-dwellers of the Zenith City of the Unsalted Seas, lived and loved and labored our genial, smiling, great heart, our Irish brother, the Rev. H. L. McMurray, whom we all loved. After doing successful work in the Pittsburgh Synod and in the District Synod of Ohio he had followed a call to the young, stirring, stormy city of Duluth, to raise among its money-mad and amusement-crasy denizens, the banner of the old faith in its new tongue. His voice was as big as his heart. His Swedish neighbor, while the faithful 'Mac' was gathering money for a new church, said to the writer: 'Brother McMurray doesn't need to build a church; he can stand on the top of the hill and preach to the whole city.' His companionship was like the incoming of the blessed springtime. His counsels were wise and valued. His faith and hope were a tonic. Like some of the rest of us, he is aging in years, but not in heart. God bless him and his.

"In the heart of the Red River Valley, whose chief products were number one spring wheat and young Lutherans, in the wind-swept, boom-bursted prairie city of Fargo, in the then Territory of Dakotah, lived *the first president of this synod*, which the Wisconsin Synod *Gemeindeblatt* once sarcastically designated as 'This little body (*Koerperschaft*) filled with the overweening conceit of its own importance.'

"In view of the fact that so many people know so much more about this first president than he knows himself, we need say nothing further about him here."

In the new prairie country among a new people we naturally had many new experiences.

Here is a strange one. In the Norwegian Free Church Body—then called "The Conference," there rose up a layman who was called the "Trance Preacher." Some of his sarcastic critics said: "He could take inspiration-fits by appointment." He would lie down on a couch, close his eyes and then begin an incoherent series of reflections and exhortations. He would quote Scripture profusely and correctly, all in the Norwegian tongue. One strange feature was that he would make an appointment, like a regular preacher, so that people might come in and hear him. The novel performance attracted growing attention. The rumor spread. Before long every house where he spoke was crowded. He was persuaded to go to church, lie on a lounge and speak there. He drew crowded houses. Ere long he claimed that the Holy Spirit had told him that he should now begin to preach from the church pulpit. So he began a series of revival meetings. By this time I knew enough Norwegian to be able to follow the trend of a sermon. So I went several times to hear Brekhus. His preachments were not sermons. They were incoherent and jumbled words, Scripture quotations without aptness or fitness. It was mostly exhortation seemingly earnest, sometimes violent. He claimed a sort of immediate inspiration. He made some strange demonstrations. On one occasion he stopped suddenly, fixed his eyes on a good woman of the church, pointed his finger at her and said that she was doing great good for the Lord and was a chosen vessel to do much more good! I knew her as a modest, earnest Christian woman. I did not notice that the personal prophecy made any change in her life. She was still the same quiet, devout Christian mother and church worker that she had always been. Many another woman might have had her head turned.

At another time Brekhus pointed to a young man, an easy going, worldly fellow and said: "There sits a young man who is in great danger. Unless he speedily repents he will go straight to the devil and drag others down with him." As I did not know the young man except from hearsay I do not know what became of him. Brekhus had an appointment to preach in the Lutheran church in Hillsboro. The pastor of the congregation conducted the opening service. Then Brekhus took his place in the pulpit. With closed eyes he stood silent. He opened his eyes, looked over the congregation, moved his lips but was silent. This suspense lasted for several minutes. Then with a deeply troubled look he stammered out something like this: "This church is too dead. The Holy Spirit does not want me to speak here!" He walked down from the pulpit and left the church.

I invited the pastor with whom Brekhus was staying to bring him over to see me. He did. I took them into my study. The young man seemed dull and dazed. I drew from him that he had been a poor farmer boy in Norway and had only had a country school education, that God had made it possible for him to come to America and had called him to preach. I tried to show him from Scripture that when God wants a man in the ministry He makes it possible for that man to get a proper preparation. I advised him to go to a practical seminary if he could not possibly go to college. My words were wasted. He heard me with indifference. He said he would do what God wanted him to do. We can do nothing with people who claim an immediate inspiration. Luther had to leave the Wartburg and hasten back to his Wittenberg Church where a group of such men had arisen and were raising serious disturbance in the congregation. When Luther tried to show that their way was not the Lord's way to do the Lord's work, they said: "Yes, you have the letter, but we have the spirit." Luther answered: "I'll slap your spirit on the snout." Then Luther for six days preached daily in the church. He preached the Zwickau prophets out of town and went back to his Bible translation. I don't know what became of Brekhus. He certainly left no mark on the church.

Here is a different experience: I was attending a Norwegian *kredsmøte* or circuit conference. One of the attractions of that particular conference was to be a wedding in the church. The bride and groom were both well connected with ministers' families, were well known and stood high in church circles. The wedding was set for four o'clock, and the great country church was crowded to capacity. The bridal couple marched in while the whole congregation was singing a suitable hymn. Two chairs had been placed for them at the end of the aisle immediately before the chancel. Here the couple were seated. Then began a most remarkable ceremony. I don't recall how many preachers took part. It was quite a group. There were at least three hymns, three Scriptural lessons, three prayers and three sermons. The couple sat it thru. Then they stood up and took the solemn life-vows. Then they kneeled and were blest. It was six o'clock. The service had lasted exactly two hours. The two fair young people were still living! How would our young brides of today like a ceremony like that?

The big bell now rang out a glad peal. The couple had to stand thru another long ordeal of crowded congratulations. The conference supper, participated in by several hundreds under the sun-set glow of a summer evening, was the wedding feast. The newly-weds sat in the center of a group of preachers. They were radiant. They had not even lost their appetite. I sincerely hope that they lived happy ever after. They certainly deserved it. God bless them.

Here's an opposite experience. In Fargo we buried a well-known minister's wife. The service was even more long drawn-out than the aforesaid wedding ceremony. There were even more sermons and hymns. A long procession of carriages, vehicles of every sort and marchers on foot followed the plumed hearse from the house to the church. In advance, on both sides and behind the hearse marched the becreped ministerial pall bearers. Broadway had been cleared for the procession and the business houses were closed. What seemed to me a strange and impressive sight was that when all was over and the coffin was about to be closed the widowed preacher arose, stood at the foot of the coffin, faced the beautiful body of his long time faithful and helpful companion and delivered a touching tribute and a tender farewell until he would meet her in the never-to-be-broken-home on the other side. So spontaneous, so natural, so unaffected are these Lutheran Christians.

My time in Fargo was drawing to a close. What rich and varied experiences! What needed lessons I had learned! What new visions had opened before me. How my view of the Lutheran Church, her people and her mission, had broadened. I had had six more years in God's school. Six years of training. Six years of learning that the mission of the Church is missions.

And again I must refer to the valued privilege of

learning to know the Scandinavian Lutherans. Except from the reports of Doctor Passavant I knew nothing of the great, growing Western Scandinavian Lutheran Church. I can now see how my Lutheran life and work and vision would have been narrowed without my contacts with these people and their work. They did me much good. I do feel that it is a serious loss that so many of our Eastern Lutherans know little or nothing about the great Lutheran bodies and their work in the West. The East and the West need each other. They don't know it as they should. I do feel that the first vacation that an Eastern young minister can take ought to be spent in the Northwest. If possible take in a convention of the Augustana and the Norwegian Lutheran Church. There is now English enough at both to make it profitable for the outsider. Visit their publication houses. Interview all their presidents and executive secretaries. They are genial, congenial and hospitable. If possible visit a woman's missionary convention. They had wonderful women as well as we. Visit their institutions of charity and mercy. Get acquainted with their home finding work. Spend a while during term-time in their splendid colleges and seminaries. We can learn much in all these lines. Their beautiful spirit of piety and consecration is refreshing. I call it sound pietism in distinction from unsound pietism. We need much of the former. We cannot have too much. There is serious danger in having too little or none. The Laodecean spirit is our Church's greatest danger. It grieves me, it cuts me to the quick to hear Lutheran ministers belittle, ridicule and warn against pietism and never make a distinction between the sound and the unsound. I have discovered, admired and I hope profited by the sound pietism of the Scandinavian

Lutherans. This is one of my great Fargo blessings.

Changes had taken place in our family. Esther, our oldest, was finishing her second year in high school. Her Fargo credits were accepted without question in Chicago. Emma, our missionary, was rapidly working toward the upper grade in grammar school. I have already noted that we had one sad funeral. Annie Comfort had died of malignant scarlet fever. There is a lonely grave in the wind-swept cemetery south of town. Ruth had been carried to Fargo in arms. She was now in the primary department of the grammar school. Best of all, while we had no boys when we came to Fargo, now we had two! Richard Henry and William Passavant. Everybody knows the busy field missionary of Minnesota, as also my long distance successor in Fargo. After Fargo we neither added to nor lost from our living flock of five. It has been probably my greatest, lasting, earthly joy that all five are in parsonages today. Esther is the wife of the well-known Dr. J. R. E. Hunt, of Chicago. She has been president of the Lutheran Woman's League and is a leader in Lutheran circles. Emma, as already noted, is Mrs. C. K. Lippard. They have spent twenty-seven years in Japan, are going back from their present furlough and have their daughter, Faith, an officially constituted missionary directing the Kindergarten work in the Saga district, where she was born. Ruth is the wife of Rev. W. C. Stump, field missionary of Wisconsin. He has, at this writing, planted thirteen missions in his district. Ruth has been secretary of the Milwaukee Inner Mission Society and president of the Milwaukee Lutheran Woman's League. She is now president of the Wisconsin Conference Woman's Missionary Society and has just been appointed to help on the

Synod's Seven-Year Program. I have mentioned the
work of Rev. Dick and Rev. Bill, our Fargo babies.
Their work is well known. It speaks for itself. Truly
God has blessed me and mine in a rich heritage.

And now I had a call to a professorship in the young
Lutheran Theological Seminary in Chicago. This was
the most important call I had ever had. It is a great
thing to be called into the holy ministry—the highest
office in the world. But to be called to become a human
maker of ministers, this is the highest ministry. My
call weighed heavily on me. True, both Drs. Passavant
and Weidner had intimated to me that they wanted me
in the seminary. Outside of that I had never dreamed
of ever assuming so heavy a responsibility. I felt myself utterly unfit. I was unfit. I had neither reputation nor the scholarship that I believed one should have
before entering a work so great, so manifold and with
such unlimited responsibility. I hesitated. I prayed. I
consulted Dr. Weidner. I told him my misgivings. He
encouraged me. He assured me that he would help me.
I recall one of his chidings: "Faint heart never won
fair maid," he quoted to me. I did not want to be a
faintheart. In the Lord's name I had undertaken other
heavy tasks. He had always helped me bear them. I
had never yet been crushed. Why should I fear now?

I resigned St. Mark's. As with every former resignation I made it clear that this was final. I did not
bid for a complimentary refusal to accept the resignation. Emphatically I requested that they accept. They
did. I accepted the call to Chicago. We prepared for
the big move. We sold off much of our furniture. I
did not preach one of those farewell sermons that bid
for sob-stuff. I encouraged my little flock to remain
true to their Lord, their church and its precious faith.

I tried again to give them a prophet's vision of St. Mark's mission. I believe the vision has come true. The sad farewells were soon said and we were off for Chicago.

CHAPTER XV

BEGINNING MY PROFESSORSHIP

WE arrived safely in the big city. We were seven,
three girls, two boys, Mother and dad. At
first we were housed in Eliza Hall, which was, besides Dr. Weidner's house, the only building the seminary had. I had been to Chicago a number of times.
I liked it the first time I set foot in it. With every
visit I had become more fascinated with the great big
town. Even then, in 1894, when we arrived the city
boasted of a street twenty-four miles long. The seminary was located in Lake View, about five miles north
of the post office. To reach it from the city we took
a cable street car to the city limits. There we trans-
ferred to a horse-car. We always liked the ride as it
took us along the edge of beautiful Lincoln Park.
The North side had as yet no elevated railroad. How
happy we all were to get into a horse-car and then
into the rapid cable car and go down town for a lark!
How happy the children were when we took a court
house elevator up to the roof and looked out over the
winding, murky Chicago river, the railroads with their
countless trains running north, south and west, the
crowded streets and cars threading the tracks in all
directions and the black, moving and jostling masses of
people on the sidewalks that from our height looked
like ants running in and out of their hill. To the east
lay the ever interesting, great, blue Lake Michigan.
In every direction we could see vessels of all shapes and

sizes making their foamy furrows in the yielding waters. For us country Jakes the novelty of it all was better than a show.

From the court house we would go to Montgomery Wards, then on Michigan Avenue. There we would enter another free elevator that would take us higher than the courthouse. Here we had a different and if possible even more interesting outlook. Montgomery Wards later had one of those then rare luxuries, an automobile. In this they gave free rides up and down Michigan Ave., to their customers. Think of it, we greenies had never been in one. What a thrill we all had and how proud we were riding in a real auto! We wandered up and down Michigan Ave. and State Street doing curiosity window-shopping. I recall how curly-headed Emma excitedly pulled my coat and said, "Papa, what time is it? Sodas in the Boston Store for two cents from ten to eleven o'clock." Then we'd all have a soda. We soon found out where the best and cheapest lunch counters were. How the kiddies did enjoy those lunches. Chicago was and is probably the most democratic city in the world. There one person is just as good as another and a good deal better. There a governor or senator is jostled aside the same as a man in overalls. In the Boston or Hillmans and at their lunch counters one is likely to rub elbows with a merchant, a banker or a professor—especially this professor. Some of these counters and fountains were known for certain specialties, e. g., fried chicken sandwich or butter milk fresh from the visible churn and all at lunch counter prices. All sorts of people would enjoy them together. We did. I always was an independent kid myself. I am yet. Chicago suited me. I never did tire of Chicago city or life. I like it today.

Doctor Passavant had purchased ten acres of ground in Lake View township. He was holding the plot for a future hospital. Of this he offered two or three acres free to Chicago Seminary. When the seminary was opened in '91 the whole sand-hill was covered with scrub-oak and underbrush. We often saw cotton-tail rabbits, ground squirrels and other small field game playing in the brush. Birds nested and sang their spring songs in the trees. We built benches on the seminary end of the lot. In those early seminary years we had a delightful sylvan site.

It was not long until a sad change came over the scene. Doctor Passavant died a few months after he had proposed me and had me elected as a seminary professor by its board of directors. I had lost my best earthly friend. W. A. Passavant, Junior, took his father's place on all the boards of all the Passavant institutions, our seminary included. He was younger than I. From Thiel Hall days we had been bosom friends. In His inscrutable Providence God called him home in early life. I have often thought that if the Passavants had lived, the future history of Chicago Seminary might have been different.

The Passavant Hospital on our site was never realized. Its end of the square was sold. The trees were cut down, sand and gravel pits were planted down. The branch passenger rail road was turned into a freight switching track. A huge coal yard was built just west of our grounds. The place became more and more unsuitable for a theological seminary. These conditions finally made the seminary sell out and move. I am anticipating—of this more hereafter. I return to our settling in Chicago.

On the south front of his proposed hospital square

Dr. Passavant had built a chapel for a German Lutheran church. The building had a small pastor's residence in the rear, under the same roof. The German congregation had not been able to make it go. The pastor had resigned and moved out.

This chapel was proffered to the seminary for the starting of its classes. It was so used until Eliza Hall was built.*

The residence part of the chapel was vacant when we arrived. It was offered to us for a home. As my salary was to be a thousand dollars, I knew that with a family of seven I could hardly live in Chicago. So we accepted the cramped quarters in the chapel and moved in. I do not recall whether we paid rent, or if so, how much. We made ourselves as comfortable as possible. During the rest of the summer we were quite comfortable. I was young, below fifty, and enjoyed the novelty with the other kids. There was still plenty of shade outside and there were benches overlooking Clark Street. We spent an uncomfortable winter. Our water pipes froze. They could not be thawed out. We had to carry all our water for several months from our neighbors. I was working in my class-room. My! My! but I did work! I really found out what I would not have believed before, that I had never known how to do persistent, steady work. Before I became a professor I thought I did work. And I really was not idle. I did not loll and lounge away idle hours every day. I did not loaf away time at the store or shop. I objected to spending half a day, much less a day with a country member. With the exception of the trip to New Orleans I had never had a vacation. I could not

_____

*See *Life and Letters of Passavant,* pages 560 ff.

bear pure idleness. When sitting at home I was not comfortable unless I had a book or a magazine or a church paper or a daily in my hand. So I thought I was busy. But, oh, the time I wasted, sadly wasted, sinfully wasted! What countless precious hours I dawdled and droned away over papers and periodicals. Most of it waste of time. The daily ought to be skimmed. The headlines are generally enough. To read the ugly stories of vice and crime debases the mind and defiles the heart. Some articles and editorials ought to be read. The preacher ought to know what's going on in and among nations. He ought to have an intelligent view of great movements of thought, of public opinion, of the trend of the times, of the *Zeitgeist*. He ought to cultivate a keen discrimination. He ought to know what not to read. He ought to be intelligent on important current events and current thought. I had been stupid enough to imagine that I needed to read my papers practically thru. The sinful waste of time! And to think of ministers of the Gospel, under-shepherds, fishers of men, watchers for souls, idling away precious hours every day! Some ministers have time to read the *Saturday Evening Post* and several sensational if not shady magazines! My family together with the church papers was brought up on the *Youth's Companion* and *The Century Magazine*. I never read a story in the *Youth's Companion* that left a bad taste, that made a hero of a deceiver or lawbreaker, that glorified success attained by trickery and crookedness. Its tone was pure, elevating, uplifting. Hope it is as good today. The present *Century Magazine*, I fear, is not what it was a generation ago. Neither is the *Atlantic*.

When I became a professor I soon found that I had

no time for current literature. The daily could only be skimmed. *The Youth's Companion* and *Century* had to be left to the rest of the family.

How I did have to everlastingly dig for every recitation and lecture! And we had many of them in Chicago. Eighteen to twenty-two hours a week was regular. I recall a term in Maywood when I had four solid hours every forenoon from chapel till noon lunch. I made it a rule from my first to my last hour never to go before my class unprepared. Even after I had gone over the ground often and had become familiar with the subject, even when I taught from books that I had written I always wanted to freshen up the matter for every hour.

At first I felt and felt keenly that I was utterly unfit. But Dr. Weidner was kind, patient and helpful. He worked hard himself. He gave himself very little waking time for relaxation. He wanted the students to work hard. The rest of us often thought that he was unreasonable. Most students burned midnight oil. It was not unusual for some to sit up till one and two o'clock preparing Weidner's assigned Dogmatics or Hebrew. He had neither time nor patience for a shirker. He would berate him without mercy. When out of patience he would frankly and forcibly tell him that he had better quit and go west and "raise prunes."

Another thing I want to put down. The doctor had as little use for a lazy preacher as for a lazy student. He impressed it, rubbed it in, drove it home and clinched it that every minister worthy of the name ought to be a regular, daily, diligent, hard working student all his life. For this he worked out a course of post graduate study; a course that some might take in residence in the seminary and that all might take by correspondence. He wanted to help every minister to be a student, a persistent, daily, steady student but above all a systematic student. In this Dr. Weidner was a pathbreaker. As far as I know the Chicago Seminary was the first to offer such a course in the Lutheran Church in America. The idea was good. The conception carried great possibilities for the Lutheran ministry. The plan was admirable and attractive. I have long felt that next to an ever deepening spiritual life our ministers need a habit of diligent, daily, systematic study. Had I known and followed a plan like Dr. Weidner's from the time I entered the ministry I might have been a growing minister, a better equipped and more efficient minister. I might have been far more than I was, a workman approved by God thoroly furnished for every good work. Oh, the sinful waste of time, the precious hours, the half days and days that I had frittered away; the desultory, scattering, profitless reading that I had done! Busy? Yes, busy to no profit. Reading? Yes, but to no profit. Study? Yes, without real, healthful, helpful growth in such wisdom and knowledge as my high calling deserved and demanded. Really much of the time spent in reading was little better than loafing. I was not conscious of my sin. Dr. Weidner's course was comprehensive. It covered every department of theology. It was systematically arranged. It was flexible. The ministerial student might examine it and then make up his mind what subject and course he wished to take up, then what next and so on thru life. He might decide to give a year or several years to Exegetical Studies, or to Historical Studies or to Systematic Theology and its wide range of subjects, or to selected and successive phases of the ever attractive and ever helpful topics of Practical Theology. The student could **make** his own selection and his own succession of topics. **He** also could decide when and how long he would study each day. After the morning devotions, chores and breakfast he should resolutely and regularly go to his study and spend two or three hours in real study. Even should he be able to give only one hour regularly every day, concentrating all his mental energy on the lesson before him he would be surprised to find what he would gain and how he would grow in a year. And then to keep up the habit for five, ten, twelve years and thru life. He would know the joy of a growing scholarship. It's worth the price. It goes without saying that a minister is subject to interruptions. He should let his people know that his morning hours are for study, but that when needed he is always ready to go. Read again the chapter: "The Pastor In His Study" in *The Lutheran Pastor*.

Dr. Weidner's course was too heavy. It demanded too much. He recommended too many books. They were not always well selected. Many of them should not have been recommended at all. The younger Northwestern Lutheran Theological Seminary in **Minneapolis** has improved on Dr. Weidner's Correspondence Courses. I believe it has the best, the most practical and most helpful course now offered. I have given so much space to this matter because I have the growing conviction that the mass of ministers do not study as they should. They do not know the value of regular, continuous, systematic study. They are not growing. They deteriorate. They reach the so called dead line. Then they complain that the Church does not want them. It is their own fault. They have not been willing to pay the price.

Dr. Weidner was a path-breaker in other lines. The Chicago Seminary really was a new departure in Theological Education. The doctor had been twelve years a teacher in Augustana Seminary at Rock Island. He had also worked with D. L. Moody in his Bible Institutes and at Northfield. He had also assisted the wonderful Wm. R. Harper, the founder of Chicago University. All this I have written up in the "Character Sketch of Doctor Weidner." He was ever alert to learn new and improved methods of teaching. From the two great men just mentioned he had learned much. When he organized the Chicago Seminary he worked out new and original lines. He instituted new methods of teaching. From Harper he had learned to love the inductive method. Possibly he overestimated it. From Moody he had learned that ministers need a training in a number of subjects not heretofore given in our seminaries. He introduced new courses in Exegetical Theology, e. g., regular courses in Old and New Testament Theology, in learning the contents of the Books of the Bible and on other biblical lines. We had courses in Psychology and Sociology, in Moral Science and other lines not strictly theological but of untold value to a minister. We were the first seminary that gave full twenty-five hour courses in each of the three divisions of Missions. Our boys had to study the history, the theory and the methods of Inner, Home and Foreign Missions. In every department of Practical Theology there were advances. Our boys not only learned the history and theory of Catechizing but they had to learn how to Catechize. We had History and Theory and Practice in Preaching. We tried to have Inner Mission Clinics.

The professor of Practical Theology used to take

his classes down town to visit the Jail, the House of Correction, the Juvenile Court, the Hull-House and Chicago Commons, the County Hospital, the Municipal Lodging House and sundry welfare institutions. I encouraged my boys to go to hear renowned preachers and lecturers. I encouraged them to hear critically and if any doubts or perplexities were raised in their mind they should bring them up in the class room where we would examine and try to settle them. The Augustana Synod had a zealous and active city missionary working in the city. His name has escaped me. He did street-preaching, visited populous saloons, distributed tracts and dropped a word in season where he could. He visited prisons, hospitals and other public institutions. He went into the redlight district and distributed tracts and talked to the inmates of bad houses. He frequently assisted the Christian Midnight Mission in the heart of this Sodom. He was always glad to take the practical professor and any of his students with him. I would often speak in "Lucky Baldwin's" House of Hope Mission, in the Municipal Lodging House and kindred places where the flotsam and jetsam of the great city would huddle together to get warm, a cup of coffee and a bed. I would take some boys with me and encourage them to say a few words, to pray or to sing. And this reminds me again, how often have I felt that every theological student ought to spend at least a summer vacation working under and assisting a good, consecrated and active pastor. It is experience and practice that our prospective under-shepherds and fishers of men need.

Reverting again to courses of study in a seminary: Haven't our Lutheran seminaries been too one-sidedly theoretical? Our students have been given a good scholastic training. We have turned out exegetes and historians and dogmaticians and men who knew the History and Theory of every branch of Practical Theology. But have we turned out such exegetical preachers as could make Bible-truth so clear and plain that the wayfaring man, tho a fool, might understand and know how to put it into practice? Have our students learned that every text they must learn and be able to show clearly, first, what does it mean in itself, and second, what does it mean for me, for my heart and life and for each one who hears me? Have we turned out such historical preachers as know how to draw examples of inspiration and consecration from history's pages? Do our young preachers know how to so present the true doctrine that it will warm the heart, become an experience and incite to a consecrated life? Have they learned so to preach and teach as to grip the attention and the conscience of the hearer that he will be compelled to say to himself, "That means and fits me. I wish I were a better man or woman. I must repent. I will arise and go to my father and confess all?" Does every sermon win and build up souls?

I have often thought of the old, stereotyped method of teaching Symbolics and Apologetics. The former was taken up almost entirely with the confessional teachings of the old historic churches. What long chapters and many pages on the Roman Catholic Church the students were supposed to master. This is good. Every intelligent minister ought to know the history and the false teaching of this powerful organization. But the student ought to be particularly informed on the aims, the plans and the schemes, the crafty cunning and the Jesuitical methods employed to get control of our city, state and national politics, our public schools and social influence. The student ought to understand clearly that America is in danger. He ought to know that as a watchman he is to know the danger, to sound the alarm and to use all his influence to awaken a lazy, drowsy and careless Protestantism. And then the mass of dry stuff the student had to go thru on the old fossilized Greek Catholic Church. The intelligent minister ought to have a clear understanding of the history and teaching of this body and its workings and fruits in Russia and other Oriental lands. But that somnolescent body is not — in our day, at any rate—a menace to American life and government. It will be a rare case in which that body will trouble a Lutheran preacher in his parish.

It is important that the Lutheran pastor should know the teachings, the spirit, the work and the aims of the strong American Protestant bodies. We have much to learn from them in method and work. There is much that our people need to be informed on and warned against. It is not the people, many of whom are better Christians than many of our members, but their errors that are to be shown up and warned against. Our people everywhere ought to be made intelligently conscious of the superiority of our faith, our distinctive life and our message.

There are great, terrible and soul-poisoning movements abroad in our land. The emissaries of these dangerous organizations, systems, persuasive and kindly women are sneaking into houses leading captive silly women and weak men. They are a menace, a peril to American Christianity.

What do our seminary graduates know about Spiritualism, Russellism, Adventism, Mormonism, Christian Science, false revivalism, holiness propaganda, proselyting immersionist sects? What do they know of the hurtful falsities that lurk in the otherwise good Moody and other Bible schools? Ought not our ministers to be intelligent about all these cults and movements, know how to instruct and warn their people, by showing them how to give an answer to every man that asks them? Ought not a course in Symbolics in an American Lutheran seminary to so stress these ubiquitous dangers that our ministers will be able to safeguard their own and to win back many?

And in Apologetics, do we really fortify our students against the scourging inroads of Modernism? Are we equipping them so that they are able to convincingly fortify their people? And along all these lines are we directing them to the best apologetic literature? Ought not every student, in his vacation, and every minister, to mention only one powerful book, to read, mark and inwardly digest Earnest Gordon's *The Leaven of The Sadducees?*

Before I leave off these spontaneous and frank reflections on seminary curricula and training I do want to give voice to what I consider a confusing method in teaching Dogmatics. I refer to the arrangement, the systematizing, the order and sequence of the topics that come under Dogmatics. I am not criticizing content but system. We have inherited our awkward and difficult system. As I have, very briefly, stated my objections in Chapter Eleven in *Lutheran Fundamentals*, I need not say any more here. In the whole arrangement of Fundamentals I have hewn out a sequence and order of my own. If the old, traditional system is unnatural, confusing and awkward, why should not our American theologians in our American theological seminaries break away and show us a more excellent way? I give this as my own reflection. Take it for what it is worth.

As I revert to the early days of Chicago Seminary, I can see where we made some mistakes: Doctor Weidner wanted students. The seminary had no college to which it could look as a feeder. In later years students came from many colleges. Thiel College became a feeder. Wittenberg furnished a number. Now and then a few came from Muhlenberg. Southern colleges furnished men. More and more came from the Scandinavian colleges. Ordained ministers from the Western and Southern bodies came to spend a winter; some from curiosity, others for review and a few for post graduate work. The first few years were naturally meager. It was then that Doctor Weidner was tempted to admit too may students with inadequate preparation. He tried to persuade himself and his colleagues that many such students make very useful ministers. I felt that it was unsafe to let down the bars and lower the standard. Exceptions there will always be. All seminaries recognize this. And I know full well that some men who entered the seminary with preparation all too meager have done excellent work. They are worthy exceptions. But it is dangerous to build a practice on exceptions and so lower the time tried and recognized standards. Chicago Seminary hurt itself in the early years by admitting too many immature and unprepared men. These could not measure up in class with college men. As I try to look back on the ministry of some of these men I can recall how a number of them were unpractical and unsuccessful. Some became high church cranks and so hurt themselves and hindered their work. I can think

of three or four who left the Lutheran Church. Several
laid down the ministry. Others are weaklings or blun-
derers who are often unemployed. They are not bad
men. They were not sufficiently trained! Their minds
were not disciplined, their judgment had not been developed. They knew not how to discriminate, distinguish and discern. They are often inclined to get a one
track mind. They had missed not only the broad,
general knowledge, but also the invaluable mental
drill and discipline that a good college education gives
to every faithful student. They cannot measure up.

There was one discipline and experience that the
Chicago Seminary professors got that was peculiar.
As far as I know no other seminary had a rule such
as we had. At first we had no endowment and no
stated income. Our board made the rule that every
professor should spend three of the five vacation
months soliciting money for the support of the seminary. Altho this had not been stipulated or even mentioned in my call, I bowed to the board's resolution.
I took hold "with both hands earnestly." I went where
I was sent. It was expected of me and my colleagues
that we preach on the seminary, its great work and its
needs and its transcendent importance for the welfare
of the future church. Then, during the week we were
to solicit from house to house. My work was largely
in country parishes. I was by no means always welcome. The tales of woe I had to hear! The calamity
chatters were often appalling. The meals did not always suit my weak digestion. The beds were *not* what
I was used to at home. Sometimes there were vermin
bedfellows! But I kept resolutely on, counting the
weeks still left. Cold and storm often overtook me.
Sometimes a kind pastor or deacon would drive me

around. At other times I walked all day. Twice I was sent to New York City. I had a kind and sympathetic friend in the sainted Rev. Dr. C. Armand Miller. He encouraged and helped me. His kindness shall never be forgotten. I was always intent on saving the seminary expenses. Only on long trips, such as to New York, would I allow myself to patronize a Pullman or diner. While in New York I slept in the sainted Father Berkemeier's Emigrant House. I tried several times to eat with him at the table where the immigrants ate. But really this was too much for me. I could not stomach this! I excused myself and breakfasted for fifteen or twenty cents at a lunch-counter. At noon and evening I ate where I happened to be and where I could find a restaurant. I often worked till ten at night. When I could have an evening free with the saintly immigrant father it was a treat for me. I profited much and was greatly refreshed in spirit in his kindly and consecrated company. He did me much good.

I was usually away for three months. One summer I did not see my family for four months. This was a hardship at both ends. Bitter tears were shed when I would leave in the spring. I tried to write home every day. Perhaps it was my own fault, but the work became more and more obnoxious to me. I had to take so many rebuffs, if not insults. So often I had to hear: "Here comes that seminary beggar again, so you're out begging again." Probably I was not meek enough, not sufficiently consecrated. I did often feel hurt and offended. Possibly it was the enemy who whispered: "Is this becoming to a theological professor? Are you not lowering the dignity of your office and of your school?"

And so I came to dread the summers more and more, especially so when I knew I should go among the farmers. In my growing rebellion of spirit I did often reproach myself as being unwilling to bear this cross cheerfully. When I began the work I told the board that I would collect for ten years. I did full work for twelve years and partial work for several years more. I was not a brilliant success. While during these heavy years, when a pall of dread was hanging over me all year, fearing the coming of summer vacation, I did stick it out so long. I did raise more than my own salary. When the board after my repeated request did reluctantly let me off they passed a resolution that any professor who would preach during the three collecting months should turn all moneys received for such services into the seminary treasury! I felt that this law was for my benefit. I obeyed it, but not graciously. On this whole unpleasant subject I would still remark: Some men are fitted and gifted for this work. They have a special aptitude for it. They do not dread it. It is not obnoxious to them. Some like it. I've heard men say that they would rather go out and ask a man for money than eat! I was the opposite. Many a time I felt that I'd rather spend three months ditch-digging. Then my colleagues and I felt that our board did not understand nor properly appreciate the calling and work of a theological professor. They did not realize the range and the reach of what we ought to know. They could not understand how we felt our need of time for study along our respective lines. How eager we were for research work in our departments. I did spend some of my free months in the Chicago University. Once I took a six-week term in residence.

Well, I lived thru it. I did learn some important lessons. Some of my experiences were rich. I got some new insight into human nature. I got a deeper insight and a clearer grasp of Paul's sweeping saying that " the love of money is a root of all evil." I am glad that professors are no longer legalistically driven to such obnoxious tasks. I am hoping that our seminaries will soon be able to grant to all their full professors the Sabbatic year, or seventh year furlo for travel and study abroad. Other denominations have done this for years. We have been so used to pleading the poverty of our people that we have made them feel perpetually poor. In fact we are rapidly becoming the richest Protestant Church in the land!

While in the seminary at Lake View I had one diversion that comparatively few professors enjoy: I had two lively boys coming on. Their mother and I came to realize more and more that Chicago streets were a dangerous place for a growing boy. During their ten weeks of grammar vacation the street-school became more dangerous with each successive summer. We saw no way of relief. A twenty-year Tontine Life Insurance policy was coming to maturity. It had often been a real hardship to keep up the quarterly payments. But they simply had to be met. How we did have to pinch and save! We never would have saved the more than two thousand dollars in twenty years but for that Tontine Policy. I advise every young man to take out a safe policy. Then he will learn to save.

I got on the track of a fruit farm of twenty acres that was for sale at a sacrifice. With my insurance premium I bought the farm, with its old house, its well of the best water I had ever lived on, its dilapidated stable and its splendid young peach orchard within two years of bearing. The farm was within two miles of the little village of Grand Junction in Van Buren County, Michigan. What joyous excitement! What eager anticipations! What planning and prospecting! What counting of days till vacation. We were going to live on a farm for ten weeks. We were to have all the strawberries, grapes and other small fruits we wanted. There were three beautiful lakes full of fine fish within ten minutes' walk. The splendid pump water, the shade, the sun-set scenes, the fruit, the fishing, bathing and boating, the garden vegetables that we were to raise. It was to be a new Garden of Eden with untalking rattlesnakes a plenty. We secured a meager, primitive equipment and moved out. Joy did reign unconfined. The ride across Lake Michigan to South Haven, the eleven miles' ride on a train thru a new land, the three miles in a neighbor's farm wagon, all furnished tense excitement for our lively family. We were soon settled. And soon I had to leave my loved ones and resume my summer collecting. My joy was the anticipation of two free months in our own country home!

We spent ten summers there. During those summers I wrote *Life and Letters of Passavant*, *The Lutheran Pastor* and *The Lutheran Catechist*. I was trying to be a gentleman farmer. Farm work, real field work I did not like. I liked books. But the care of this life, the deceitfulness of riches and the lust of other things were stealing in on my unconscious heart. I was gradually, unconsciously, becoming entangled and enmeshed. I had not enough land to farm. Part of what I had was lake and wood-lot. I had too much to lie idle. My wily neighbor showed me that I needed his next twenty acres, with an apple orchard in bearing.

I was now getting some income from *The Way of
Salvation*, so I bought the next twenty. Now I needed a man, a team, a barn and what not. I was getting
roped in. My peach orchard came into bearing. I had
one fine full crop, then on a tenth of October came a
killing freeze. Late peaches and apples were still on
the trees. The freeze killed not only the fruit but the
trees in the whole peach-orchard! My fruit-farm was
ruined. Ruined when I was just on the point of real-
izing a profit. Probably I deserved it. I had tenants.
I tried to realize on poultry and other things. I had
all sorts of trouble with my men. I was working hard
in the seminary or out collecting. They were having
a good time. I realized that the cares of this life were
heavy and not conducive to spiritual growth. I trad-
ed my farm for city property. We have often talked
of those ten summers of experimenting. Financially it
did not pay. But we had other benefits and treasures.
My children were not robust. For several years Richard and Ruth had not been strong. The summers in
the country greatly improved them. We entertained
city friends lavishly. Our house was full most of the
time. Our growing boys and girls had city schoolmates and friends out for a good time. We had ministers and other friends. The children gained an experience that they otherwise never could have had.
They learned lessons in field and forest, in orchard
and garden that have been of great value ever since.
They learned to row and swim and fish and climb. The
boys even hived a swarm of wild bees. They killed
rattlers and black snakes. They caught and cleaned
and cooked and fried all sorts of fish and frogs and
eels and mud turtles. And how they could handle
horses and plow and harrow and cultivate and dig out

peach-borers and spray and pick and pack fruit. And
they did bronze and harden muscles and gain appetite and strength. And what fun they had studying
crude farmers and their ways! And what freaks *we*
all were among those farmers. And what tricks and
pranks the boys played with neighbors. It was great.
It was good. A heritage that we still live on when we
get together. In fact I think I can safely say that the
happiest memories and stories of childhood and youth
in my family are tied up with old Grand Junction
farm and its "Cottage Rest."

I might make mention also that I spent few idle
Sundays in Cottage Rest. I preached in school houses,
in groves, in the village Congregational church. I
know that in my grove preaching and also elsewhere
a number of rustics heard the Gospel for the first time
in their life. And also know that my labor was not
all in vain in the Lord. I hope that much of the seed
thus sown did sprout and spring and grow tho I know
not how. My family usually furnished the choir. Yes,
my gentleman farming experience had its value for
us all. God is good.

CHAPTER XVI

FURTHER SEMINARY EXPERIENCES

THE first move of our board for the physical comfort of the professors and secretary was to build homes for them on the seminary grounds. W. A. Passavant, Jr., was still living and was a leader in the board. Two commodious and comfortable double houses were built for the professors and the secretary. It was certainly a joy for our family to look forward to a permanent roomy and convenient home. We had three movings before we moved into the Professors' Row. All three of our rented homes had been cramped and inconvenient. A strike of the union laborers delayed the buildings. The workmen had no grievance. But the leaders of their union ordered them to quit. There were weary weeks of waiting. But all things come to him who waits if he waits long enough. So uncomfortable were we in our quarters and so eager to get into a real home that I fear we moved in too soon. How happy we were and how we rejoiced in our new comforts and conveniences. I can still recall how we sang in joy. The labor of moving and fixing up was a picnic. But, alas for the uncertainty of earthly joys, we were just about comfortably and happily settled when serious sickness sneaked in. Mrs. Gerberding, who was frail at best and prone to overwork, was taken down with typhoid fever. During the long, lingering weeks we gave her the best of care. We had a trained nurse and the best of physicians. With God's help they brought her thru. But she had received a serious shock. It left her weak. She never recovered her former strength. In her weakened condition her system was susceptible to new diseases. And the worst crept in. By early autumn she was failing, and it was found that tuberculosis had settled in. I arranged to have her taken to Melrose, Florida, where we had friends. She found a home with the Rev. J. A. Boord. I shall never forget the kindness of the Boords during that winter. Mrs. Gerberding improved and we were all hopeful. My daily grind had to go on. Spring came all too slowly. My wife insisted that she was able to come home. She should have remained a year. We had bought the Cottage Rest farm a short time before she left. She wanted to move with us as soon as the children's school would be over. So she came. She enjoyed one summer in Cottage Rest. The deceiving disease was still at work. Reluctantly we had to yield to the idea of sending her to Florida again. We had conceived the idea that Saint Augustine might be better. This time I took her down and saw her safely quartered in the quaint old town by the sea. With a heavy heart I went back to my home and my work. We soon discovered that the seashore was not as good as inland Melrose. My poor, weak wife went back to Melrose. When my Christmas vacation came I hurried down to Melrose. I was shocked when I saw my poor, failing wife. Kind neighbors told me that if I did not take her home with me she would soon follow in a coffin! The facing of the reality crushed me. On Sunday we walked to the little Lutheran Church which the Rev. Asa Waters had builded and was serving without money and without price. Monday my dear, brave little wife started with me. With the aid of stimulants she stood the long journey as well as could be expected. In the old Union Station, Chicago, we changed cars to a local train for Lake View. I carried her from the train to the house. She was glad to get home. She was brave and cheerful, tho she knew that she had come home to die! She received the Holy Communion, and after holding on bravely for about two weeks she slept away in Christ and in peace. We laid her away in beautiful Graceland Cemetery, where she awaits the Resurrection morn. Our long-time, intimate friend and coworker, the Rev. Dr. W. K. Frick, preached the funeral sermon.

The work of the Kingdom must go on. With a broken spirit I had to go back to my dear, motherless children, my books, my class-room and my soliciting. Then came about four years of widowed loneliness. No father ever had kinder and more affectionate children than I had—Esther, the oldest, postponed her wedding for two years for her father's sake. The children had most excellent schools and teachers. Horace Greeley School, a few blocks from home, had a young woman teacher whose name I cannot recall. But I can never forget what she did for my children. She knows that I appreciated it. We had her in our home at different times. She was an able teacher, a woman of exceptionally fine Christian spirit, a real character builder. Lake View High had a very strong and good faculty. The course was as good as that of many small colleges. Every teacher was a specialist. I became acquainted with most of them. Esther and Ruth and Richard graduated there. The Lake View years were happy and profitable years. Life long friendships were formed there. The pupils, as a class,

were a hightoned group. Many of them were quite
at home in our house. William afterwards graduated
from Maywood High, which, on the whole, was not so
good. Emma went to Lima College, where her grand-
mother lived. She also fell into good hands in that
school. The Christian atmosphere, the influence, the
teachers and the teaching were all of a high order.
Emma got great help there for her future work.
Esther, after graduating from Lake View, wanted to
prepare herself for a kinder-garten teacher. She took
a Normal Course first in Valparaiso, Ind., then graduated from Froebel Kindergarten College, Chicago.
She taught in the Hull House and in public kinder-
gartens in Chicago. I have always regretted that I
was not able to make college graduates of my three
bright girls. Emma got a partial college course at
Lima, Ohio, Esther a Normal Kindergarten Course
and Ruth some special courses in music. That was
the best that I felt that I could do for the girls.
They've done great, good work. God bless them.

The two boys graduated at Thiel College. The
character builder there was Dr. Franklin Sawvel. I feel
that he did the boys more good than any one else. I
owe him much. Some of the other influences at Thiel
were not so good. More's the pity! Thiel did not
always conserve the spirit of its founder, Dr. Passavant. It did not always perpetuate the beautiful
Christian life of old Thiel Hall.

Our family was thinning out. Esther had married
the Rev. J. R. E. Hunt. Emma had married the Rev.
C. K. Lippard, and they had gone to Japan. I could
not help thinking of my future. I was not sixty. What
would become of me when Ruth should marry and the

two boys would enter the ministry? Should I go thru life alone? I was not built for that. So I seriously considered the seeking of a life companion. I resolved not to act hastily, impulsively or without calling in my reason and judgment. I would not marry one too young. I wanted a companion, one nearly my own age, one who would live in the same world in which a three score old dwells. I had sense enough to know that one in the twenties lives in a different world from one in the sixties. Such two could not be congenial. The disparity in age would make a disparity in thinking, in judging, in desires and aims and hopes. Their mental worlds would be different. For years I had positively disliked to see an aging man marry a young girl. I believe still that it is against nature and ought never to be. My mind ran scrutinizingly over the list of good women that I knew. I thought long, carefully and hesitatingly. Finally my thoughts would repeatedly go to the mountains of Pennsylvania. I knew a good, matronly woman there who had been doing good Samaritan work for a generation, Dorothy Welty, of Jumonville, Pa. We started a correspondence. It took a year's hard wooing. I won. For over a score of years she has been a true helpmeet to me. She has been a real companion. For years it has been our custom that, in the evening when I am tired and smoke my cigar, she reads aloud. We both love the old English Classics. We find the best selections from them in the older school readers. I have had a penchant for these old readers for some years and have a good sized shelf full. We have also read many fine fiction books and some that are more solid together. This evening reading and my reading in bed has been about all that I have done in that line for years. I once asked my eye specialist whether this habit of bed reading is advisable. He said if my eyes were shaded and if I could fix myself into a sitting posture there could be no harm in it. To come back to my faithful helpmeet, she has taken such good care of me that I often think that, but for her, I might not have been here to write this today. I might also add that she is always most heartily welcomed into all the homes of her step-children. "He that findeth a wife findeth a good thing and hath obtained favor from the Lord."

As noted above, our seminary site in Lake View was becoming more and more undesirable. But it was valuable for other purposes. Our board resolved to put it on the market. Dr. Weidner consented reluctantly. When a buyer had been found a committee of the board and the faculty viewed a number of possible sites. Our then secretary, the Rev. Frank E Jensen, secured an option on what he considered a very desirable site in Maywood, eleven miles west of the loop. Practically all the faculty, as well as the city pastors, were opposed to going so far out of town. But the site was cheap. In fact it was practically a gift. It contained fifteen acres of ground. The village of Maywood also offered concessions, so the board decided to buy. I withdrew my objections and tried to believe the glowing commendations of our secretary. I lived to regret the choice. A competent architect was employed. He laid out a fine and attractive rectangular plat. He also designed an impressive group of ten buildings. All was harmonious and attractive to the eye. This was in the early summer. Our secretary was authorized to secure bids and let contracts for getting the grounds in readiness and putting up all the buildings. All was to be completed and ready for occupancy before October first. The secretary was to see the contracts carried out. It meant unusually rapid work. Chicago is noted for its ability in that line. Many predicted that it could not be done. Secretary Jensen who had grown up in Chicago said that he would see that it should be done. It was done. The row of fine, roomy, commodious and comfortable houses for the professors and the secretary were ready for occupancy in September. The seminary buildings were all ready for the opening day early in October. Mr. Jensen certainly showed himself a masterful executive. He deserves great credit for what he accomplished in four months' time. Our quadrangular plant of ten buildings elicited favorable comment and admiration on every hand.

Dr. Weidner's strength was rapidly waning. It seemed inexpressibly sad to see that erstwhile fine specimen of manhood wearily drag himself to his classroom. It was nearly ten years since he had had his first stroke of paralysis. Two years later while in Europe he had a second more severe stroke. After that he was a broken man. With wonderful will power he held on. God in His mercy kept his mind clear to the last. That marvelous intellect was working to the end. He leaned heavily on his Lord, whom he knew so well and loved so ardently. Day by day he girded himself anew. In Maywood he never lost a class hour. To the last he was writing and dictating at his desk when we felt that he ought to be in a hospital. All this as well as the coming of his end in Florida on Epiphany morning, 1915, I have written up in the character sketch of Dr. Weidner. In spite of his indomitable energy and will power, he had been weary during the last few years. He became remiss in his former exacting detail. In former years nothing ever escaped him. He had his eyes on everything and on everybody. He saw to it that every student had his bed made and his room swept and put in order before the first recitation hour. We had a matron for whom the doctor had written out a book of rules. She was to change every bed and give every room a thoro cleaning once a week. The doctor frequently and vigorously reminded the boys that they were to have a bath at least once a week. He practiced and recommended a daily plunge in ice cold water. He was ever urgent that his coming preachers learn to keep themselves neat and tidy. They were to keep their shoes shined. They were never to appear in chapel or in class-room with soiled collars, cuffs, handkerchiefs or other apparel. They were not to come to class in study gown, sweater or slippers. He wanted the building, the halls, the lecture-rooms, rooms and students always to be spotless, immaculate as befits a school for training gentlemanly Christian ministers. All this, I believe, is to be set down to the credit of our great teacher and administrator. Too many young men have not learned how to be exemplary, refined, cultured, high-toned Christian gentlemen before they enter the highest office in the world. And too many pastors' homes, that ought always to be models for cleanliness, neatness and order, are a disgrace to the profession. Against all these debasing things Dr. Weidner constantly cautioned and warned in no uncertain tones the incipient ministers before him. These lessons are needed in every school and especially in every seminary. In his failing years Dr. Weidner gradually ceased to notice lapses along these lines and a general deterioration soon became noticeable. Eternal vigilance is the price of a high-toned, esthetic Christian manhood.

Of the death and funeral of our dear doctor I have given a detailed account in my Character Sketch. The doctor had selected and purchased his burial lot in Concordia Lutheran Cemetery not far from the seminary. Mrs. Weidner brought me a letter from the doctor requesting that I select a proper tomb-stone and have it erected on the lot. In consultation with the doctor's cousin, Miss Weidner, and Mrs. Weidner, we selected the stone and the inscription. The stone can be seen and the inscription read from Madison Street on the north side of the cemetery.

As I said, my two boys went to school. They largely worked their way. Richard got work in the college building. He also found work in Greenville during the first summer vacation. There he also found that wonderful, that exceptionally fine wife of his, Mildred Hamilton, a Thiel classmate. One of the arguments for coeducation! The boys, when at home, ever since they were able worked Saturdays and during both Christmas and summer vacations. They gained much valuable experience. They had quite a variety of employment. They always pleased their employers. They were never dismissed. They earned more than their own clothes. They could have earned more at college if Thiel had been located in a city. A goodly proportion of Wittenberg and Muhlenberg students pay their whole way thru college because both Springfield and Allentown cities are friendly to their schools and citizens make special efforts to furnish earning opportunities for the college boys. True, such earning boys cannot have all the so-called good times that richer boys can have. But they are saved from countless bad influences and temptations. They learn countless useful lessons in the hard school of life. The summer training in the University of Hard Knocks is incalculable in value. These lessons in economy are also a by-product of no mean value. I am not sorry for the hardships of my boys. "It is a good thing for a young man to bear the yoke in his youth." "A man is rich in proportion to the things he can do without."

All thru their seminary course our boys also worked and earned. They found no trouble in getting Saturday and vacation positions. They also had their daily tasks of manual labor in the seminary. They never asked for or received beneficiary aid. All this was also good for them. But with all this self-help there was a constant drain of dollars from their father's pocket. We noticed the difference when they were thru the seminary. We began to feel that we were on Easy Street. We found that we could begin to lay up and invest for old age. I had always taught my children that I was going to give them the best education I possibly could. That when they had a Christian character and a good education they had a fortune. That, barring accidents and disease, if they did not get along after that it would be their own fault. I also informed them that after they had received this goodly heritage Mother and I would feel free to take life more easily and save up for a home for retired old age. That came when I was almost four score. Yes, God is good. For many years I have watched the careers of the sons of rich men. Now and then one makes good. But among those whose life I followed there have been few exceptions. In Chicago I have noted sons and daughters of the Pullmans, the Fields, the Armours, Leopold and Loeb. Doubtless there are scores of others. I think

of the notorious Harry Thaw of Pittsburgh. I think
of a rich farmer in Ohio from whom I tried to get a
subscription for Chicago Seminary. He had one child,
a fast young man who inherited all. After his father's
death, in less than a year that boy had gone thru
it all and was a ruined profligate. I can think of other
petted and pampered boys who never learned to work
and became dismal failures as men. If we could have
a record of the sons and daughters of all the million-
aires it would doubtless be a tragic story. A list of
rich students in the great universities and even in our
own colleges, together with a record of their achieve-
ments would also make interesting reading. Better let
us make our boys bear the yoke in their youth.

Chapter XVII

A CHAPTER OF TRAGEDY

I SINCERELY wish that this startling story would not need to be written. What happened in Chicago Seminary in 1920 was the tragedy of my life. I feel that I owe it to the Church, in which I had gained a wide and good reputation; I owe it to my colleagues and to myself, not to pass by this sad and strange event in these reminiscences. I have prayed for a long time that the good Lord help me to lay aside all personal bitterness.

I can say without hesitation that I had loved Chicago Seminary as I loved my life. I had given to it and for it twenty-six years of my life. I wanted it to be a model seminary in our church. Because of my intimate connection with Doctor Passavant and his worthy son, and because these men of God wanted me to give my life to this young school of the prophets, I did want to help to make it a school of the Passavant spirit. And in this aim and purpose I felt that Dr. Weidner and I agreed.

After Dr. Weidner's death the guiding hand was gone. The loss soon made itself felt. Disagreement arose in the faculty. Dissatisfaction sprang up and spread among the students. Our carefully drawn constitution provided that in the selection and calling of professors the board should consult the faculty and if possible get its approval. On several occasions the board disregarded the desires, the arguments and the votes of four-fifths of the faculty.

After a succession of disagreements and unpleasant-nesses the faculty was asked to resign. Four of us refused. We demanded charges and a hearing. We maintained that we each had a divine, official call to do a divine work.

The board called a special meeting in Fort Wayne. We were summoned on short notice. We had to travel in a coach from midnight till morning. One by one we were summoned before a full board. I was called in first and asked to resign. I said something like this: Twenty years I had been in the ministry. I had helped to organize one synod and became its first president. Helped to organize the Chicago Synod and became its second president. Had been a delegate to most of the conventions of the General Council and of the U. L. C., and for twenty-six years I had served the seminary. A year ago this board had given me a banquet. I have a large loving cup and a big book of testimonials and tributes from that banquet, and now I am asked to resign? Why? What am I charged with? Has there been a complaint of my conduct or my teaching? I didn't know. I challenged the board to call the roll of the alumni. Ask *them* of my teaching and my influence. Concluding I said: Gentlemen of the Board, I appeal to you. More than one-fifth of you were my students. I appeal to you, what was the tone and character of my teaching? What was the atmosphere of my class room? I appeal to you, did I not always hold before you the highest Christian ideals? Didn't I always urge and insist on the deepest consecration by every one who would enter the holy office? And now you ask me to resign, without a given cause, without a charge, without a trial! No, I cannot resign! Some of the board members hung their heads. I walked out. One by one my three colleagues also refused to resign. After the meeting adjourned we were informed that our chairs had been declared vacant! When this action had been taken, four members of the board, two ministers and two laymen, arose and declared that they could no longer belong to a board that could take such action. And so they walked out. We wondered what next.

We did not have to wonder long. Another strange thing happened. From the board's view-point we were out. We knew that constitutionally we were not out. My morning mail brought me the following letter from the board:

July 29, 1920.

The Rev. Prof. G. H. Gerberding, D. D., LL. D.,
1626 S. 11th Ave.,
Maywood, Ill.

Dear Doctor and Brother:

At a regular meeting of the Board of Directors of the Theological Seminary of the Evangelical Lutheran Church at Chicago, Ill., held at Ft. Wayne, Ind., on the 27th inst.; pursuant to a decision to reorganize the faculty, you were reelected to the chair of Practical Theology.

It is understood that your duties as well as your salary and house rent are the same as heretofore. Our Board trusts that the great Head of the Church will lead you to accept the renewed call and that you may be spared for yet many useful years in a capacity in which you have so well served the church. For the Board of directors,

Fraternally,

Samuel Wagenhals, Pres.,
J. Allen Leas, Sec'y.

This "call" was signed by the president and secretary of the board. Now, as the boys say, "What do you know about that?" or "Can you beat it?" The board that had declared my chair vacant, now in a signed communication assured me that I had served well in the past. "Nuff sed." I answered briefly that I did not consider myself constitutionally out, and that until the board would reconsider its illegal action I could not consider any new proposal. Two of my colleagues received similar "calls" and returned similar answers.

The next communication that we received was a notice of eviction. Our houses were to be vacated by a certain date! We had to begin to pack! Can you imagine our feelings? Many bitter, bitter tears were shed in our home. I had served over a quarter of a century. I had been publicly banqueted and eulogized. Now I was evicted!

But let it go. God lives. God knows. God is good. Mistakes I doubtless made. Sins I committed. God's pardon is mine.

The impossible had happened. Three synods, the District Synod of Ohio, the Chicago Synod and the Synod of the Northwest had passed resolutions requesting our seminary not to take the step and dismiss four of its faculty. The secretary was soon avalanched by protests from alumni and others. But the blow fell. We were dismissed, in the eyes of some who did not understand, disgraced and evicted!

All this aroused a deep indignation among the students. With the exception of fewer than a dozen, they determined not to remain in the Chicago Seminary. We had as competent and as good a body of students as the seminary had ever had. A serious question confronted the discharged professors and their sympathizers: What would become of this fine body of students? If not taken care of they would scatter and some might, at least for the present, drop the ministry. The executive committee of the Synod of the Northwest called a special convention. That convention, after hearing and discussing the report of what had been done, resolved that in the name of the Lord, the Northwest Synod would establish a seminary to take care of the stranded student body of Maywood and to carry forward the work under church control instead of under an independent, self-perpetuating, irresponsible board.

A committee on opening the proposed seminary and on ways and means was selected. This committee had a heavy responsibility and a difficult task. They were men of faith and of courage. Time was short. The four former Maywood professors were called by the synod to be the faculty of the new seminary. The synod was acting strictly within the rights guaranteed to all synods by the constitution of the United Lutheran Church.

Where should the new seminary open? In order to bridge over the emergency and take care of the student body, it was decided to open in Chicago. I was conscientiously and outspokenly against this. I did not want the Passavant Seminary to die. I could not be a party to establishing a second *permanent* U. L. C. Seminary in Chicago. It was not until I was assured that this was to be an *ad interim* or temporary seminary, opened with the hope that the Maywood wrong would soon be righted and that in the interim we must take care of the waiting student body that I consented to be a part of the faculty of the ad interim seminary in Chicago. We located on the South side. We had a good year. For local reasons a few of the Maywood emigrants went to near home seminaries. All the rest came to the ad interim. A fine body of new men came. We graduated as fine a class as ever.

The officials of the U. L. C. advised the Synod of the Northwest not to open a second year in Chicago. They advised that we locate "not east of Fargo." Against our better judgment we submitted. I knew Fargo, the country north and west of there and the kind of people who lived there. I was fully convinced that a seminary of the Northwest Synod could not prosper there. I laid my misgivings before the president of the U. L. C. He advised us to try it, and if we found that we really could not prosper there, it would be all right for us to move. With that understanding I again consented to go. Barring our unsuitable and uncomfortable quarters, we had a good year. However, we felt more and more that this was no place for our seminary. We had one church, St. Mark's English Lutheran. It was a good church and congregation, whose pastor and people were exceeding kind to us all. We shall never forget this. The other nearest church of our synod was eighty miles away. The students had no supply work. The dissatisfaction grew. We saw that if we did not move, our seminary would die in Fargo. The U. L. C. had previously sent a commission of three prominent men out to survey the church and school situation from the Twin Cities to the Pacific Coast. They rendered a voluminous report. They offered some strange recommendations. As stated above, the constitution of the U. L. C. grants its synods home rule as to starting and managing its own institutions. The Pacific Synod for good and valid reasons had established its seminary in Seattle. The U. L. C. commission recommended that it move to California. The Pacific Synod men who were on the ground and understood the whole situation knew that to follow this recommendation would be fatal to the future. They exercised their constitutional right and resolved not to move.

When we of the Northwest Synod were convinced that for our seminary to remain in Fargo would be fatal to its future, tho the commission recommended that we do not move, we exercised our constitutional rights and moved. The cases of the Pacific and Northwest Synods were similar. Both acted within their constitutional rights. Without intended disrespect, both were convinced that they could not follow the advice of an outside commission that could not appreciate the situation.

We had gone thru the laborious and expensive task of moving from Maywood to the South Side, Chicago. We had gone thru the more laborious and most costly task of moving over seven hundred miles from Chicago to Fargo. And now we had to move eastward again from Fargo to Minneapolis. Three moves in less than three years. According to the old saying, three moves are as bad as a fire. We had our share of wreck and ruin in our three moves. But we lived thru it.

The great majority of the synod approved our

necessary move. Our committee on location found a
large temperance Y. M. C. A. building on the North-
east side of the city for sale. By the Bloomington-
Columbia Heights street car line it was less than fifteen minutes' ride from the city post office. The building is of solid brick, large, commodious and well suited
for our purpose. There is ample room for the president's family on the first floor. There are also a
students' reception room, four lecture or class rooms,
a library room and a large chapel room. On the second floor there are cheerful and comfortable student
rooms in which thirty students can be comfortably
housed. There is also a reading room. Here in a steam
heated suite of three rooms and bath, Mrs. Gerberding and I took up our abode. We enjoyed our
student neighbors on the same floor.

CHAPTER XVIII

SOME BACKWARD GLANCES

LOOKING back on the migratory life, after the Maywood tragedy, I can see how God made the wrath of man to praise Him and restrained the remainder of wrath. The great Lutheran land of promise now has a debt free, prosperous English Lutheran Seminary with a strong, sound, orthodox faculty and a future bright with promise.

As for my own personal advantage I have nothing to regret. As noted above, I did all I possibly could to avert the saddest tragedy in the history of the educational work of the Lutheran Church in America, From the banquet that the board gave me, one year before my eviction, I carried away my loving cup, my large book of testimonials and tributes. Tho our living quarters were cramped and uncomfortable on the South Side, I got much personal joy out of that year. We had a large back yard on the shore overlooking beautiful Lake Michigan. Thither we carried our chairs on many a beautiful summer night, formed a large circle, watched the brightly lighted pleasure boats and spent happy hours in social converse. I always did enjoy exploring new scenes, watching and studying new people. I had never lived on the South Side. To me it was a new world in Chicago. Our neighbors were different. They never showed us any neighborly hospitality. Rooming and boarding houses abounded.

Where an ancestral home was left, its inhabitants as a rule were aristocratic, isolated aged people, the relics of former family groups. I have never seen so many seeming spinsters leading about pet poodles as in our neighborhood. The spinsters were to me a greater natural curiosity than were their hopeless dogs. Our nearest Lutheran pastor told me that he had never before found a neighborhood so dead socially and spiritually. The one crowded congregation was the one that ostensibly worshiped in a large Christian Science temple. I attended once. I carried away enough contempt and disgust to last for my remaining days. Not much better was a service in the largest, most exclusive and most wealthy synagog in the city. Rabbi Hirsh, a radically liberal Reformed Jew, rated by many as the greatest orator in Chicago, orated when I was there. Not the remotest reference to religion or to the Jews' Bible was heard. Professing themselves to be wise, this crowd of hero worshipers had become fools!

Once I went into a large, beautiful, costly Gothic green limestone church. It was an old Congregational church. It was a sight to see the few scattered, listless people there. A few relics of former, better days. I heard a well dressed, starchy looking preacher harang on the Evolution of the Race. As I was leaving he greeted me at the door and invited me to come again. I told him that I didn't expect to because I did not hear any Gospel of Christ and His Salvation.

On a Sunday afternoon I went to a high church Episcopal vesper service. All the colors, all the genuflections, all the intonations, the processions with acolytes, cross-bearers and swinging incense; all the galloping thru the long service was there, and then a good, Evangelical twelve or fifteen minute sermonette. The barretted priest met me at the door, wanted to know who I was, where I lived and whether he might call. I told him that I had dropped in casually, that I was a Lutheran and his church had gotten all the best it had from the Lutheran Church. And so I was learning and teaching. My boys got the benefit of it in class-rooms.

For years I had been a pedestrian. From two to four miles a day was my life and my joy. As I said, I loved to explore and observe. Several blocks west of us we had a large section of dark Africa. During the war, when labor was so scarce, the great packing houses had imported thousands of negroes from the South to work in their plants. It was claimed that at that time there were one hundred and fifty thousand in Chicago. They had taken possession of a large section of the South Side. The whites had been crowded out. Property had greatly deteriorated in many places.

Many whites had lost heavily. The darkies were, as is usual, happy. Many had already become prosperous. They bought up rows of once fine homes. There were all grades among these. From those living on the boulevards in brown stone mansions to those crowded in rickety tenements five and six stories high entered only by shaky outside stairs. I loved to walk among them and study sociology. It was always interesting to walk up and down the crowded, black business section of South State St. Chickens, live and dressed, sweet potatoes and fish of all kinds were openly displayed, fingered over and smelled over on the side-walk. Husky dames jostled one another, gossiped, turned up the whites of their eyes and ha-hawed loudly and unrestrained. Street fakirs abounded and always had a grinning audience even when they had no customers. Doors were open into close, noisy dens that I believe were boot-leg shops, gamblers' resorts and entrances to vice dens in the rear. All seemed to be care-free, unrestrained, taking no thought for the morrow. It was all new to me. So near home and so different. I had my own thoughts as I walked, observed, mused and pondered. And again I asked: What is our great Church doing for these untutored sons and daughters of Africa? I proposed to our student missionary society and the faculty that we start street preaching when weather permitted. I was overruled. Nothing was done. Our nearest English Lutheran Church was on the edge of the black belt. The congregation felt that they must sell out and move. An appeal was sent to the home mission board that it purchase the property and start a Lutheran Mission among the negroes. Nothing came of it. The Methodist Board did what we declined to do. We missed another golden opportunity.

In my exploring walks I also would often go to Jackson Park far to the South. I came to know that interesting region with its World's Fair relics, its university campus and its numerous interesting spots and institutions and the aristocratic Hyde Park region. So I learned to know the South Side.

Then there was the Illinois Central R. R. with its superb, frequent, rapid and cheap suburban service. For six cents we could run down to the heart of the Loop in a few minutes. The beautiful lake was in full view most of the way. We never tired of that romantic ride. Since then the whole suburban service has been electrified and frequent trains carry the passengers at the rate of a mile a minute as far as Blue Island and South Chicago. I have often said that if I should now choose a home in Chicago or its suburbs I should make my home on the South Side.

A year in the ad interim seminary has left to me many happy memories. The thus pictured year has many bright spots for me. God is good.

And now I cast a backward glance over the year in Fargo. Should I let myself go it would be one long, lingering look! But my book it getting too long. To go back to Fargo, to live again in the town where my two boys were born and where I had all the experiences delineated above was more or less of a thrill to me. I was all alert and keyed up with interest. How the town had changed! Fine paved and brilliantly lighted streets. Big banks and business blocks on Broadway. Fine new post office, fine, large Lutheran hospital and, fronting on the same beautiful Broadway, the large, massive First Lutheran Church whose shiny cross overtops the Catholic Church across the street. For solid and imposing massiveness, I have often said that this church surpasses any other Lutheran Church building that I know. There are a number of metropolitan hotels and two handsome new rail road stations. I never wearied in walking the more than a mile long stretch of bright, beautiful, lively Broadway. And then the wide, well shaded residence streets with their large, beautiful homes, the new court-house, the stately new high schools, the attractive, thickly wooded Island Park on the bank of the Red River of the North. On the Northwest side is the State Agricultural College with its impressive buildings, its broad experimental fields, gardens, groves and orchards, its flocks of sheep and poultry, its hordes of hogs and its herds of cattle, and, best of all, its more than a thousand students from the fields and farms of North Dakota, mostly Scandinavians. Surely this is not the Fargo that I once knew so intimately!

There was my St. Mark's Church, the first purely English Lutheran Church in the Dakotas, the church that had been an ocular demonstration that it is possible to be a sound Lutheran in English and had shown how to do it. Surely I was interested in St. Mark's, that I had left thirty years ago. It was a new, a strong, a greater St. Mark's. Its spacious, churchly building is a monument to Dr. Ulrich. It had recently become too small, and a large, roomy gallery has been built in. I rejoice in the growing numbers and the growing influence of St. Mark's. It was a joy to me to worship in St. Mark's and sometimes to preach there. And then the joy of meeting and greeting again the dear, former members of mine, grown older now! The joy of meeting men and women here and there who would introduce themselves and inform me that they used to go to my Sunday School or that I had baptized or confirmed them. They had not all remained faithful. For this I was sorry. I still hope for their return.

Everything in this world has its drawbacks and disappointments. It was a sorrow to me that some on whom I had set bright hopes had fallen from the faith. One of the saddest cases of apostasy was a young man grown prosperous as a merchant. I had known his parents as devout members of a Norwegian Lutheran church. This boy had wanted to come to St. Mark's Sunday School because it was English. His good but mistaken father, who was a good friend of mine, said, "No, my William must be in the Norwegian

Sunday School and confirmation class." The boy went unwillingly and was glad when he could no longer be compelled to go. He was now soured on the Lutheran Church. After I left he became a Russellite! He was now a leader among these dangerous people. I was told that he gives one hundred dollars a month for the spread of Russellite literature. It might have been different if he had been allowed to learn his father's faith in the language in which he was to learn the practical things of this life. This is one case of thousands all over our land.

When our seminary moved to Fargo it was difficult to find and rent a place to live. We did find a suite with a few rooms and bath that were furnished for light housekeeping. We gladly moved in. It was not long till we found that our down-stairs landlord and his wife were rabid Russellites. While they were otherwise kind they soon began to try to enlighten us on how to be true "Bible Students." We had many interesting conversations. How they were wedded to their heresy. How they did study the big five Bible Volumes of Pastor Russell. They put hours on it every day. Would that our Lutherans would all study their Bible and Catechism as eagerly and diligently as these people study and follow their false prophet. That false prophet was more than once in court and was not decent enough for his wife to live with him. A wolf in sheep's clothing!

Our neighbors kept on extolling their Bible study and wished that we might join them. I offered them that tho I was quite busy I would give them an hour every Monday evening for Bible study. They said they would appreciate that. I proposed that we study St. Mark's Gospel. We started in. It soon became evi-

dent that on every point they wanted to find Russell's
opinion. I insisted that we wanted to study Mark and
not Russell. We had only two or three lessons. What
can one do with people who have a closed mind? Once
or more a year one of the well-paid, well advertised
and well camouflaged lecturers would come to Fargo.
How our neighbors did try to get us to go and sit on
the platform with the other "Protestant Ministers."
I declined. I told them that many jail birds and boot
leggers and thugs, thieves and gamblers and harlots
would be there to applaud the teaching that there is
no hell and would be confirmed and encouraged in their
wicked ways. (Read Dr. Joseph Stump's Tract on
"Russellism.")

Another of my joys in getting back to Fargo was
in getting in touch again with Concordia. As noted
above, I had labored for Concordia College and been
vice-president of its first board of directors. On my
first opportunity I visited the school. It made my
heart rejoice and thank God for what He had wrought.
The enlarged campus, the group of fine, big buildings,
the large faculty, the half a thousand students—all
this was an inspiration. The wonderful young president, Dr. Aasgaard, now president of the Norwegian
Lutheran Church of America, was always cordial and
friendly. So was Pastor Sorenson of the large new
Lutheran "Church of The Shining Cross." So were
all our Scandinavian neighbors. One of them informed
me that a Norwegian professor in St. Paul had advised him that the Norwegian pastors of Fargo ought
to have nothing to do officially with the men of the
Northwestern Seminary. He was one of the few who
believed that the Northwest Synod and its seminary
had no business out here and ought not to be recog-

nized. My neighbor had answered the gratuitous adviser that he and his Scandinavian brethren had found us Northwestern men to be Christian gentlemen, and so long as we showed ourselves to be such they would freely fellowship with us. And they did. And we appreciated it and helped them all we could.

President Aasgaard had each one of our faculty deliver a week of chapel talks in Concordia. In addition to this we were often called on for special occasions. Fargo and Moorhead were all kind to us. Had it been possible for our seminary to do the full work needed by our synod and remain in Fargo, we should have been happy to remain.

For me, personally, my second residence in Fargo has left many bright and happy memories. God bless Fargo and Moorhead and the good Lutherans there and in the great Red River Valley.

Chapter XIX

NEW BEGINNINGS

O UR school on wheels now moved to Minneapolis.
Ever since I first came to Minneapolis I liked the
city. There is something attractive, winsome and fascinating about this water city:—that's what its pretty
name means. It stretches its length along the banks
of the majestic Mississippi. Within its corporate
limits it comprises ten beautiful lakes. Steam and electric pleasure boats ply the waters of these romantic
lakes. Boating, bathing, fishing are enjoyed all summer long. In the winter the city lakes furnish sports
in ice-boats driven by the wind and in skating. The
wonderful wooded driveways and boulevards that skirt
the urban lakes are a never failing source of delight.
Every lake has one or more parks on its shady shores.
A number of these parks have pavilions for free band
and orchestra concerts and community singing. Again,
for winter sports, some of the heights overlooking the
parks, boulevards and lakes have long, steep toboggan
slides, coasting places and inclined planes for skiing.
In the summer time the many large conservatories and
open flower gardens are a constant wonder and delight. St. Paul has many of the same natural attractions. It has its Summit Avenue, often claimed to
be the most beautiful avenue in the World. But St.
Paul does not have within its limits ten beautiful large
lakes. In fact, no other city can boast of an attraction

like this. In this, Minneapolis is ahead of all other American cities. It is the largest city in a state that counts within its borders ten thousand lakes. "Can you beat it?" Minneapolitans used to boast of its Minnehaha Falls, immortalized by Longfellow in his picturesque poem, with its moving, skipping, stirring rhythm and meter. Yes—barring its bitter, biting, long winters—who wouldn't live in Minneapolis?

I also always loved Minneapolis and St. Paul for the strength of their Lutheranism. True, it is divided. It is variegated. It is lively with rivalries. There are five Lutheran theological seminaries in the Twin Cities. Norwegians and Swedes abound. The former have two seminaries and two publishing houses. The latter have a branch of the Augustana Book Concern. Every Lutheran body has its own ministers' association. There is also a general association to which all Lutheran ministers are invited. I like all Lutherans and like to meet with men of all Lutheran bodies—so long as they will act like Christian gentlemen. I believe that Twin City Lutherans have a mission to perform in the line of future Lutheran unity. I like the peppy English Mission work of the N. W. Synod in the Twin Cities. I did not like the retreat of our oldest English Lutheran Church. There surely was enough down town work to be done. They had a fine property, well suited for aggressive down-town work. An opportunity was lost.

I like the Central Lutheran Church. It is vigorously, courageously attacking the down-town problem. It is all English. It is soundly Lutheran. Its able and aggressive pastor has put English Lutheranism on the map all over the Northwest. Central Church is an abiding encouragement to every English Lutheran minister in the great Northwest. I glory in Central Church. I rejoice in and thank God for its rising, half-million dollar cathedral that will seat over three thousand worshippers. I believe that this grand Lutheran landmark is also a prophecy of a great, harmonious and cooperating English Lutheranism in that strongest Lutheran section in America.

I like the Northwestern Lutheran Theological Seminary. It is the only purely English Lutheran Seminary between the Great Lakes and the Pacific Coast. Its nearest all-English neighbor is four hundred and fifty miles to the east. There is a place and a work for it where it is. Tho misrepresented and misunderstood, in the few years since its opening it has justified its existence. It has shown itself worthy. It has won confidence all over the Church. Its graduates and their work are its credentials. Its beginnings were hard. We had two lean years. After that, up to this writing, we have not fallen below thirty resident students, nearly all college men. The seminary is a pleasant place to work in. There is a most cordial and friendly spirit between teachers and students. There is a fine fellowship between the members of the faculty. During my six years in the seminary I do not recall that I missed a single faculty meeting, unless I was out of the city, and during those years we never had one unpleasant word. We often differed from each other. Especially I! But we differed as Christian brethren. After the business was transacted and when time permitted we had a social chat and good fellowship. We looked forward to these meetings as periods of recreation and refreshment. I miss them now.

In spite of my determination and effort to remain young the years kept piling up. Nature's powers wane as age creeps on and creeps up. I was working full time in the seminary during the year preceding the year when I would be four-score. The rigorous climate was telling on me. I had had four painful operations in the last five years. I wanted to do some more writing. I felt that I might live longer in a milder clime. I was also rounding out fifty years in the ministry. Here, it seemed to me, was a propitious stopping place. I wrote out and handed in my resignation to take effect at the end of the school year. I wanted to give my board time to seek out a successor. As the faculty has a voice in selecting a professor we talked it over, after the board had accepted my resignation. To our own surprise we all agreed on a young man whom I suggested as my successor. So the Rev. Jonas Dressler, who had proven himself to be a good minister of Jesus Christ, a good student and a good teacher, was recommended to the board and was unanimously elected.

When the school year was drawing to a close the board and faculty were busy with preparations to give me a farewell reception. The synod also was busy. So I was to have a two-fold reception. The seminary arranged for one in connection with the board meeting and commencement. Arrangements were made for a brilliant banquet with an elaborate program. The students fitted out and decorated and beautifully illuminated a large basement room. Over two hundred people sat down to a sumptuous feast. There were representatives there from New York to the Pacific Coast. Every Lutheran body was represented. Even the Synodical Conference was there with a personal tribute in verse. I shall not here report the festal program of the evening. Neither can I begin to mention the countless telegrams and letters of congratulations and felicitation. It was hard for the guests to get away. Words can never express my appreciation. Perhaps the dear students whom I should meet as a group no more moved me most.

In a few weeks came the convention of the synod of the Northwest at Marinette, Wisconsin, of which my son William was then pastor. The program committee had set apart an evening for my farewell reception. It was held in the beautiful new St James' Church. There was a fine musical program. The addresses were all too fulsome for me. Then the treasurer of the synod arose and made one of his short, terse, straight to the mark addresses. He informed the synod and the congregation before him that he had been commissioned to apprise my former students and also a few special friends of the festal celebration, the golden jubilee as he called it, and had suggested a purse. He informed his hearers that gifts had poured in so freely that I had been made a Patron of Andhra College, and that in addition one and a half times as much more was given to me and my wife as a personal gift! A beautiful basket of fifty American Beauty Roses was handed to Mrs. Gerberding.

My dear old classmate of Muhlenberg and Philadelphia Seminary who had been ordained with me fifty years ago, the Rev. Doctor D. Luther Roth, was present as an applicant for membership in our synod. He received due recognition, a well merited tribute and a basket of fifty American Beauty Roses.

I must also mention that I have a beautiful morocco bound and inscribed book of autograph tributes from life-long friends, leaders and former students. There are some things that gold can never buy. Yes, God is good.

For some years back we had faced the fact that if the good Lord would spare us, the time would come when we ought to retire. I had seen too many men hang on when their powers were failing and when younger, capable men, might have been doing better work in their places. It should not be so in my case. It was a pleasant diversion to let imagination loose and see ourselves settling down in a new clime. One thing was settled: We must seek a milder clime. Another we settled: We did not want to go to California. It seemed so far away that it would be impossible to ever get back. Besides, it had earthquakes. Neither did we want to go to Florida. For the larger part of the year that land of flowers is too hot to live in. We wanted a year around climate. I had been to Hickory, N. C., several times. I liked it better with every succeeding visit. It lies in the beautiful and salubrious Piedmont region. It is in the foot-hills of the Blue Ridge Mountains. It is twelve hundred feet above sea level. It is claimed that there is no better year around climate than in this Piedmont region. It is not winterless. There are enough cold days and weeks to kill germs, purify the air and brace the system. Roses and other flowers bloom till Christmas. Daffodils, golden bells, violets and other flowers bloom in February. Cherry, peach and plum blossoms were out also in this short month. But this does not mean that summer is now nigh at hand. March can bluster here also. On its first day we had a sixteen-inch snow fall. It was not cold. The town went wild with the snow coming down. By police order several hill streets were closed to all traffic and were reserved for young and old coasters. It was a winter picnic. There is scarcely a winter week when park seats and porch swings are not used. So we have variety enough to keep us from going into tropical, lazy, sluggish lassitude. It is rare to have a distressingly hot summer night. The evening breezes come playing down from the mountains with refreshing coolness. We chose wisely when we chose Hickory. From the front porch of our cozy little bungalow we have a fine view of the Smoky Mountains of the Blue Ridge. And we are only thirty-six hours from Chicago. We never had more kind, more friendly and more sociable neighbors than these warm-hearted Southerners. They welcomed us with a generous donation on our arrival and had our porch decorated with fern and flowers! We like the friendly, homey little Dixie town. Strangers bow and lift their hats to my winsome Mrs. They say "Good Mawnin', Sir," to me. Some say, "How ah you all this mawnin'?" or "How ah you all feelin' today?" Well, we like it.

And then it is a strongly Lutheran town. In Hickory and the environs there are six Lutheran churches. Lenoir Rhyne College, with its more than three hundred students, is here. We chose our home site near the college. The large, shady campus with its inviting seats lures us to bide a wee. The ten thousand volume library and reading room is open to us to use and enjoy. The faculty, with their Southern suavity and hospitality, afford a group of friendly, cultured companions. The attractive and aggressive young president, Brent Shaefer, and his interesting family make a host in themselves. We have more invitations to automobile rides than we can accept. And this is cheaper than owning a car!

And so I am happily retired. But not to be tired. Not to be idle. Not to rust out. I average more than once a week speaking or preaching. During the rougher, winter months I turn down many requests, but more than make up in the good old summer time. This book is the first fruit of my retirement. For nearly six months I have given to it five forenoons a week. I have not missed half a dozen forenoons. Tired? Yes, tired in the work. But if it helps to serve my Lord, my fellow men and my dear Church never tire of the work. Tired? Yes, after the toil of a forenoon's grind I am invariably too tired to eat. Before I lunch I must walk a mile or two. Before nightfall another, longer walk. These walks, these deep breaths of this Piedmont air have been my life. At times I did fear that my strength would not hold out. But God is good. Here I am closing my task just as the blessed spring time is ready to burst upon us with all its beauty, its bird song and its mundane prophecy of that land where everlasting spring abides. Have heard the blue-bird and the mocking-bird. Thank God. A dozen books are laid back, waiting to be read. No, I'll not be unhappily idle.

SOME CLOSING REFLECTIONS

Once more I cast a backward glance over my long, eventful and varied life. I glimpse again the strange, striving, streaming, surging story of humanity. I ask again: Why these restless movings back and forth and up and down? There is evidently an inner driving urge, an outreaching and upreaching after something not yet attained! Is it not the age-old quest: "Who will show us any good?" I look again into the *Zeitgeist*, the spirit of humanity as it surges and swells around me. It seems to be more restless, more reckless, more daring, more defiant than ever. It recognizes no bounds, no bars. There are outflashings of a heaven-defying materialistic, mechanistic, deterministic movement to give loose rein to the animal instincts of violence, crime and the lowest lusts. These baser burstings of humanity are fed and fanned and stimulated by a suggestive and ever more outspoken press and movie, and our children and youth are drinking in the soul poison! What shall we say? What can we do! I look again into the one old Book whose spirit and wisdom come from another world. It knows. It opens. It explains the heart of humanity. It makes clear that human nature, unrenewed and unchanged, is low, lawless, base, shameless, wicked, desperately wicked. For a summary read again Romans 1:18-32. The old Book gives me the one remedy, the one hope, the One, the only One who can save even to the uttermost. The old Book, God's Book, answers what the wisdom of the wise, their schoolmen and their schools can never answer. Back to the Bible and thru the Bible to the Christ of the Bible.

There is still left a consciousness or a sub-consciousness among the more respectable leaders of thought that we dare not throw away the Bible. But the unrenewed among the wise do not like the humiliations of the Bible. These must be eliminated or explained away. The old Bible must be made modern, made to suit the modern old Adam. Such a changed bible, a bible from which sin has been expunged, which neither needs nor knows a divine-human Savior, cannot help humanity. It cannot arrest its rush to destruction.

The only hope is the Bible of the Prophets and Apostles and Martyrs and the Churches that still preach, teach and confess its whole, unadulterated Old-Time Religion.

Even the recognized Evangelical Churches have and hold and teach and confess what they accept as the teachings of the Bible in varying degrees of purity and fullness. Some are less pure and some more pure than others in the body of their beliefs and teachings. It is the duty of every earnest Christian to endeavor, with an open mind, to satisfy himself as to which church comes the nearest to teaching all things that Christ has commanded—not here and there, one thing or *some* things—yes, *all* things that Jesus commanded.

For my part, as this book shows, I came to my convictions thru much confusion and doubt and struggle. I am neither a tradition nor an authority Lutheran. Am glad that I am not. I had to search and sift and dig before I found satisfaction and peace of mind and heart.

As is apparent from the past pages, I love all Christians of whom I am persuaded that they are sincere and in earnest. I have no use for the shallow, flippant and oft irreverent, unclean and unholy church member, whether he bears the name of my church or the name of some other church.

For the reasons given above I have found my spiritual home and my work shop in The Lutheran Church. The better I know her, the more I love her. I know and sadly lament her sad and largely sinful divisions. I deeply lament her colossal losses. They have largely been her own fault. I lament the narrow, ignorant, inexcusable and fatal fighting for a foreign tongue. I fear the indifference to doctrine that still prevails here and there. Just as much do I deprecate that bitter polemic still heard in some pulpits and in some classes and conventions. The spiritual life cannot be nourished by polemics. Oh, that all might learn to preach the truth in love! Still more do I fear that dead orthodoxism that is satisfied with and glories in possessing the true doctrine. As my books and my teaching show, no one can prize and love true, sound, Scriptural doctrine more than I do. But to my sorrow I know and have too often noted that it is possible to have the true doctrine in the head and to have, at the same time, a heart as cold as a hail-stone. The heart is deceitful. I fear the influence of those among us who are so deeply in love with our liturgical forms and ceremonies that they so stress and press them that they seem to make them a badge and mark of true Lutheranism. Of all these things I have spoken more fully in preceding pages. I fear those ministers among us who seem to be terribly afraid of Pietism. They do not explain the distinction between a false and a true Pietism. To have ever a greater and deeper measure of the latter is surely one of our greatest needs. It fits so beautifully into our Lutheran system that it ought to be a part of its warp and woof. Indeed it is the very essence, the heart and life of true Lutheranism. God give us more of it! Then too I fear those who are so wonderfully jealous of what they call their Christian liberty. It does not seem to occur to them that their liberty may become a stumbling block to some for whom Christ died. Real Christian love abdicates even rightful liberty when its exercises might cause offense. The insistence on and practice of a claimed liberty has discredited and brought much reproach on the name of our poor Church.

To sum up again: The greatest needs of our dear Church are:

First and foremost, always a deeper spiritual life in pulpit and in pew. The spiritual heart and life that real Lutheranism contemplates in our ministers, in every home and in every heart, would make our Church the greatest spiritual power in America.

Second: Given this real, inner experience of spiritual life, how our beautiful doctrine of the Priesthood of Believers would fruit into and function in Christian activity. How our Evangelistic campaigns would reach out and win outsiders on every hand. In thousands of communities, if every neighbor would personally try to reach the soul of his neighbor, what soul-winning there would be. How busy every pastor would be in training and directing personal work. How busy he would be in following up reported prospects. What adult Catechetical classes he would have, and what private instruction he would give to those who can not come to class! And how the seven-year programs and all financial programs would prosper! How the voluntary tithes would roll in! And, it ought to go without saying that every such activity constrained from within, from the love of Christ in the heart, would be seasoned with prayer. The spiritual life is always a prayer life.

This would be a true Lutheran revival. It would be life from the dead. We need it everywhere and everywhen.

A third great need of our Church is a coming together of our divided sections. I believe this can be done. I believe it is coming. What we need is what has been mentioned above. Then friendly, private contacts and frank discussion. Then larger conferences in the same spirit of friendliness and love. Pulpit and press polemics ought to be taboo. They are not from above. Practices and associations that hinder harmony ought to be gladly given up. And so unity will come. Then Union will come.

In proportion as these concluding reflections, these pious desires are carried out, in that proportion will that old Church that once saved Europe save America.

O America! Dear America! The land chosen of God to give humanity a new opportunity! The land the springs of whose liberties lie back in The Reformation. The greatest, grandest, best land under the sun! America needs the old, sound, Bible Church of the Reformation. If we could everywhere from the right heart, in the right spirit, in the right, simple, earnest, touching, moving, winning language bring our full Gospel to the attention of America, I believe America would accept it. The other Protestant Churches are on the rocks. They are in danger of going to pieces. We are on the impregnable Rock of the Word. If America knew what we stand for and what we offer, better America would flock to us as doves to their windows. Yes, then would our Church go forth "bright as the sun, clear as the moon and terrible as an army with banners."

And again, in the words of Tiny Tim: God bless us every one!